CRACKED

CRACKED

HOW TELEPHONE OPERATORS TOOK ON CANADA'S LARGEST CORPORATION ... AND WON!

JOAN M. ROBERTS

DUNDURN
TORONTO

Project Editor: Dominic Farrell
Copy Editor: Paul Taunton
Design: Laura Boyle
Cover Design: Sarah Beaudin
Printer: Webcom

Library and Archives Canada Cataloguing in Publication

Roberts, Joan M., author
    Cracked : how telephone operators took on Canada's largest
corporation...and won / Joan M. Roberts.

Includes bibliographical references and index.
Issued in print and electronic formats.
ISBN 978-1-4597-3172-1 (paperback).--ISBN 978-1-4597-3173-8 (pdf).--
ISBN 978-1-4597-3174-5 (epub)

1. Bell Canada--History. 2. Telephone operators--Labor unions-- Canada--History.
3. Telephone companies--Employees--Labor unions-- Canada--History. 4. Women labor union
members--Canada--History. I. Title.

HD6073.T32C3 2015   331.4'81384650971   C2015-906016-8
                                               C2015-906017-6

1   2   3   4   5   19   18   17   16   15

We acknowledge the support of the **Canada Council for the Arts** and the **Ontario Arts Council** for our publishing program. We also acknowledge the financial support of the **Government of Canada** through the **Canada Book Fund** and **Livres Canada Books**, and the **Government of Ontario** through the **Ontario Book Publishing Tax Credit** and the **Ontario Media Development Corporation**.

VISIT US AT
Dundurn.com | @dundurnpress | Facebook.com/dundurnpress | Pinterest.com/dundurnpress

Dundurn
3 Church Street, Suite 500
Toronto, Ontario, Canada
M5E 1M2

In memory of Walter and Daisy Roberts,
who gave me the courage to stand up for my beliefs.

Table of Contents

Acknowledgements

Thanks so much to all my family and friends who supported me through the writing of this book. I wrote much of the book while I was experiencing a serious health challenge, and by keeping me feeling well-loved and supported, they enabled me to keep working on the manuscript. I was able to feel that I was still part of the working world and that I was contributing to society. Writing this book became a key part of my healing journey.

Specific thanks go to my son Neil Mentuch, not only for his unwavering support during my illness, but also for his ongoing technical support in keeping my computer and Internet going despite various viruses and glitches.

I owe a huge debt of gratitude to my friend Michelle Dooley, who got me my job at Bell Canada in 1973. Michelle continues to be a great friend and she supported me throughout my illness and the writing of this book.

Ed Seymour and Bill Howes, former Communications Workers of Canada (CWC) staffers, provided invaluable assistance reviewing the early manuscript and providing feedback to ensure that the content was readable and factually correct. Once I finished the manuscript, they initiated a fundraising campaign for publication of the book. Bill even took me to medical appointments. They did whatever it took to make the book a success, I will be eternally grateful.

Ed Seymour deserves particular mention because he supported me through the writing of the book and editing. But, more importantly, because he had the foresight and determination to retain a large number of files and documents from the organizing campaigns of the CWC. I was able to use hundreds of original documents. The Ed Seymour Archives at McMaster University became an invaluable resource throughout the writing of this book.

A special thanks goes to Janice McClelland for allowing me access to the many files she diligently kept from her entire tenure at Bell Canada. She also spent hours reviewing the manuscript and supported me throughout my illness, keeping track of my medical appointments so she knew when to check in on me, and taking me to concerts to keep my spirits up.

Thanks to Ann Newman, who reviewed the manuscript and provided me with photos and articles from the campaign, as well as moral support.

Without your help, dear family and friends, I might not have finished this book.

Thanks to my editor, Lorna Simons, my publisher, Dundurn Press, and project editor Dominic Farrell.

I would like to give special thanks to my sisters and brothers in the labour movement, particularly those from IBEW 353, the York University Staff Association, UNIFOR 6004, UNIFOR 6006, UNIFOR Local 35-0, UNIFOR Ontario Communications Council, UNIFOR National Office, and the Canadian Labour Congress. Your interest in this project and the support you have provided me are greatly appreciated.

Special thanks goes to Sean Howes, a national representative with UNIFOR, who organized a presentation on the book project to the Ontario Communications Council.

Finally, I want to thank my daughter Erin Cooper, not only for all her support, but also for making me a grandmother during this time and bringing immeasurable joy into my life.

Introduction

This book tells the tale of how a group of women working as telephone operators — women living otherwise ordinary lives as wives, mothers, and girlfriends — stood up to the largest private-sector company in Canada to claim their rights as workers and a share of the economic pie.

I felt this was a story that needed to be recorded and told to a broader audience while most of those courageous activists were still alive. It is a historical account of working-class women taking control of their destiny while confronting a telecommunications monopoly and institution in twentieth-century Canadian daily life — Bell Canada.

The story occurred in the late 1970s and 1980s in Toronto, a time when change that had been percolating since the 1960s led to sweeping demands for more democratic, less authoritarian structures in government, corporations, and the family; as well as grassroots struggles for civil rights, workers' rights, and equality for women.

I was there. I lived this story as a minor player and always knew how privileged I was to witness and take part in a major event in Canadian labour history. After thirty years of waiting for someone else to tell the story, I have decided to step forward and tell it with as much objectivity as is possible for someone who was part of it. I will share my own story, too.

Key Themes

First and foremost, this book provides a comprehensive written record of a union organizing campaign and a first contract strike in the late 1970s, the beginning of a historical period when technology changed the nature of work itself. It was also the period that saw the beginning of the drive toward globalization and the gutting of the branch-plant manufacturing economy in central Canada. The story of workers fighting back is an important and noteworthy one in Canadian labour history.

Second, the book gives a historical account of a group of high-profile female workers. As almost everyone engaged with a telephone operator at some point in daily life during the twentieth century, the job was a familiar one, and one that many women passed through — a pink-collar ghetto. (The bargaining unit also included the staff of the company's cafeterias [Dining Service] — a small percentage of the overall membership — also primarily women.)

The telephone operator campaign parallels other pink-collar organizing campaigns of the time, including those by nurses, teachers, and public sector workers. While middle-class women were advocating for reproductive choice and trying to break through the glass ceiling of the corporate hierarchy, working-class women were fighting to better their lives, too.

Last, the book chronicles and explores company unionism in the context of this occupational group, as well as the system of labour relations in the early telecommunications industry in the middle and late twentieth century.

The Reason I Wrote This Book

Obituaries for operators with whom I had worked started to appear in the local papers. Time was marching by, and as a student of working-class and social history, I did not want this story forgotten as has happened to so much of "herstory."

I sometimes feel great despair as a result of the backlash against the gains women have made in society, the workplace, and the home. Many young women now express reluctance to do the difficult organizing work needed for social and political change. I want to show them the value of face-to-face organizing and of building relationships, and how major social change comes about from all the groundwork undertaken by grassroots organizers, primarily through the relationship-building that occurs in one-on-one conversations and group meetings.

Although I am sometimes disappointed with the pace of social change, as I reach middle age I find myself grateful for the wonderful life I have had, despite being a woman from a working-class background. The successes I have had in my life were made possible by supportive government policies that helped me get a university education, and societal changes that permitted me to work at meaningful employment and create a successful life for myself and my children. I could not have had this life without a great public school education, an inexpensive university education, affordable child care, and the opportunity to work in non-traditional occupations.

When I look back, I realize that I developed many of my leadership skills in the union campaign and strike that are the subject of this book. I discovered a voice that could be harnessed to advocate for change, that I had nothing to be ashamed of for having working-class parents, and that by assuming a leadership position in the campaign, I could contribute to making real financial gains for myself and others.

I now earn my living as a trainer and consultant and have the privilege of teaching young people and newcomers to Canada. Through many conversations and a lot of research with both groups, I have come to believe that both could benefit from learning about union struggles and how we gained gender, human, and workers' rights through engaging in collective action. Without education about how existing rights were won, new generations will fail to discover that it was people just like them who engaged in the struggle for them. My hope is that new generations will continue the struggle for equality and better working conditions that has stalled with the economic restructuring and globalization of the last twenty years. I hope the stories in this book will inspire readers to organize with others and confront the growing poverty and inequality in Canadian society.

Research and Structure of the Book

Although the union organizing campaign and strike involved the employees of Bell Canada in the provinces of Quebec and Ontario, this book focuses on the activities in Toronto. Sometimes I mention events or organizers from Quebec or other areas in Ontario, but I have focused on Toronto because of the richness of the historical documents and the accessibility of key organizers. I do not intend to downplay the contributions of anyone not mentioned in this book, and hope that projects will be undertaken to capture the activities outside Toronto.

* * *

My starting point for this book was a forty-four-page paper I wrote in 1981 for an undergraduate Women's Studies course at the University of Toronto. In addition to that paper, I did a literature review of journal articles about women and union organizing. Additionally, I had the wonderful opportunity while working on this book to research primary sources related to the Bell Canada organizing campaign due to the amazing diligence of Ed Seymour, formerly a national representative with the Communications Workers of Canada. Ed had the foresight to collect and catalogue all the original documents used in the campaign and strike, and he deposited those documents with the William Ready Division of Archives and Research Collections at McMaster University in Hamilton, Ontario. Furthermore, Janice McClelland, the first president of the telephone operator local (CWC Local 50), provided me with the personal files that she had kept from the campaign and strike.

During 2011 and 2012, I interviewed many of the original organizers, both telephone operators and staff with the Communications Workers of Canada. The recordings of these oral interviews will be deposited with the Ed Seymour Archives at McMaster University. The interviews bring to life the chronology of events, and I thank the following people for sharing their memories and recollections with me:

Irene Anderson
Laurie Cumming
Bill Howes

George Larter
Janice McClelland
Helen Middlebrooks
Ann Newman
Fred Pomeroy
Ed Seymour
Cynthia Tenute
Linda Young

Except for this introduction and part of the conclusion, I have written the book using the third person and used endnotes to identify information sources. However, I was there and played a role, and I can sometimes provide a unique perspective. So, when needed, I have added a personal explanation, speaking in my own voice about my experiences. This material is boxed and italicized.

Description of the Chapters

The book begins with a chapter describing the employer, Bell Canada (Bell Canada Enterprises). Bell — originally incorporated as the Bell Telephone Company of Canada, its name was changed by federal legislation to Bell Canada on March 7, 1968 — has been the largest private-sector company in Canada for over a century, and after the federal and provincial governments, is one of the country's largest employers. Management runs the company with a private-sector sensibility, but it functions like any large bureaucracy, with occasional accusations of being out of touch and insensitive to customers and employees.

The second chapter explores the historical occupation of telephone operator and the unique characteristics of company unionism at Bell Canada.

Subsequent chapters describe the conditions that led to a desire for change among employees, the pre-campaign activities, the organizing campaigns, the reaction of the CUC, the vote campaign, the wait for the decision, the second campaign, and the eventual strike.

The concluding chapters identify what happened to the major organizers after the strike and the impact of the campaign and strike by CWC Local 50.

Some readers may question why I use the term "campaign" rather than "raid" to describe the card-signing campaign by the Communications Workers of Canada (CWC) directed toward the membership of the Communications Union of Canada (CUC). While it is true that Bell Canada telephone operators and its few dining service employees were technically members of a union, the CUC was a not a member of the mainstream union movement, which was best represented by the Canadian Labour Congress. The CUC evolved out of an internal management-employee consultative process, and proudly asserted a no-strike policy. Many CUC members and other unions considered it a company union. According to the grassroots organizers, "It didn't act as a union so it could not be raided like one."

My Background and Role

I started at Bell Canada in Dining Service in Toronto in 1973 at the age of seventeen, working part-time in the winter and replacing full-time staff in the summer while I attended high school.

At that time, Bell Canada provided freshly prepared food in cafeterias for its staff (although many operators might disagree with the "fresh" label), and most of the company buildings that housed telephone operators and other office staff had cafeterias. I first worked at 76 Adelaide Street, looking after the short-order grill and vending machines on the tenth floor near the Traffic Department (switchboard operators) offices. I later learned to prepare meals and desserts in the larger cafeterias during summer vacations.

It was hard work, but I was young, and as the eldest child in a working-class family, I was already used to cooking and cleaning. The money was better than what I had made at a Zellers department store in a local shopping plaza.

From the tenth floor at 76 Adelaide Street, I watched the CN Tower go up, floor by floor, until the crowning moment when the giant Sikorsky Skycrane helicopter, nicknamed "Olga," put the

102-metre communications mast on the tower, making it the tallest tower in the world for the next thirty-four years.

In Dining Service, I worked with other students on the weekends. During summer vacations, I got to work in the big kitchens preparing food for the cafeterias. The regular staff was made up predominantly of older women, almost all first-generation immigrants. The chef would usually be male and, again, from an immigrant background. The staff was from many ethnic and racial backgrounds; the workplace was very diverse, without a main ethnic identity, as was then common in the factory workforce in Toronto. I remember that the chef at 76 Adelaide was Bulgarian, the dishwasher was a lovely Jamaican woman, the baker was Polish, and the pudding maker was Scottish. On a daily basis, they shared their lives' lessons with me and fondly forgave my mistakes.

Working with them was comfortable and pleasant, as I had grown up in a multicultural, working-class community in downtown Toronto. My parents were from Newfoundland, and at that time Torontonians labelled Newfoundlanders as "stupid Newfies" and mildly discriminated against them. I could easily have passed as a native Torontonian with my Anglo name and local accent, but I identified more with the newcomers, who suffered much more intense discrimination and racism than my parents or I ever experienced. I had grown up in an immigrant neighbourhood, watching the ongoing exclusion of newcomers on the playground and in the classroom; I had decided discrimination was unjust and that I wanted to confront and stand up against it.

So, when I saw that in the midst of this multicultural cafeteria workplace, the Communications Union of Canada union rep was an English woman, who, although an immigrant herself, was privileged in this WASPish corporate setting and sat up on her high horse, spewing judgmental and racist pronouncements on any topic that came up in conversation, I quickly began to see she was part of the problem, not the solution.

High school went to Grade 13 in those days, and I was nurtured by extraordinary teachers who exposed me to feminist and working-class history in my last year. I did a major project on the Great Depression; I learned how the financial follies of the rich and government policies designed to serve the interests of private corporations left the poor to suffer with a small share of the economic pie. It was not much of an intellectual and emotional leap to apply the same political analysis gleaned from the lessons of the Great Depression to what I was experiencing in my job.

Sometime later, I was making pudding in a steam kettle and listening to my co-workers complain about being mistreated. Not thinking about any repercussions, I joined in and said that they needed a union — a real union — to resolve their problems with the company. They replied that they had a union already but it never helped. "What good would a new one be?" they asked.

I told them about the benefits of unions (knowledge absorbed at the kitchen table from my father's experience as a member of the United Electrical Workers and from what I had learned in school). The conversation went on and I continued making my pudding. All of a sudden, in walked the supervisor, a young woman maybe five years older than I. She hurriedly approached me and asked what I was talking about. She went on to say there should be no talk of unions here. I nodded and kept my mouth shut, wondering who had squealed on me. I guessed quite quickly that it was the sandwich maker, the only non-immigrant working there. (The sandwich maker acknowledged later that she had reported me to management.) I decided not to confront her, but vowed to do something when the time was right. I think this was my first experience of the maxim: "Don't get mad, get even."

I learned a few valuable lessons that day. First, my workplace was not much different from the non-organized workplaces of the thirties. Management was still deathly afraid of unionization, but didn't consider the CUC union that represented the workers a threat. That left me questioning just what kind of union it was. Second, I became aware there were potential scabs in the very cafeteria where I worked, and I could get in trouble just for talking about and advocating for workers' rights. Wow! I also learned that the historical conditions that led to the workers' actions that I had read about were playing out right then and there. I realized that superhuman beings aren't the ones who make history; it could be anybody who reacts against what is happening right in front of them. This gave me much to ponder.

After Grade 13, I went to the University of Toronto and tried to learn more about working-class history. I took sociology and a lot of history and political science. By that time, a number of historians had emerged who were devoting themselves to the history of Canadian workers, so I immersed myself in that subject. I began to develop a solid class consciousness and started campaigning for the New Democratic Party (NDP) in elections.

I moved out of my parents' home right after Grade 13 and was paying my living expenses and tuition with my earnings from Bell, so I decided to see if I could get a higher-paying position as a telephone operator. The company always needed operators, and it was not long before I got a transfer to the toll (long-distance) unit at Dufferin Street. I received training as an operator on the old cord switchboard. The first day at work, I took my seat in a chair that had a back that provided no support. Chairs with good back support were something all operators desired, but few got. If there were any decent chairs, the full-time operators had already grabbed them. I did not blame them, but seven and a half hours sitting and working in a chair without proper back support was the beginning of lifelong back problems. The message I got from the company through these broken-down chairs was that my welfare was not important. It was not the last message of this ilk.

Soon after I arrived at Dufferin Street, I heard that the Traffic Operator Position System (TOPS), a term used to describe computerized switchboards, would be coming soon. With the changeover to TOPS, there would not be enough operator positions at Dufferin Street, so I would be transferred elsewhere. I can't recall the options I was given, but I transferred to the SOST office at Asquith Street. "SOS" stood for Special Operator Services; the "T" maybe stood for "traffic" (traffic meaning the routing of telephone calls). The special services included mobile and marine calls. Operators considered these the most interesting telephone operating functions.

I really enjoyed my time at this office. The calls were more complex. In fact, you could spend many minutes on a call with a customer who was trying to reach a particular person on board a ship. Most of the people who owned mobile telephones were salesman carrying big phone apparatuses in the trunks of their cars. They were very friendly and flirted with all of us. I thought this was what it must have been like in the early days of the telephone.

It was at SOST in the summer of 1978 I learned about the CWC organizing campaign and became convinced I should join. It didn't take much to win me over — I was getting so few hours of work that I was afraid I wouldn't have enough money to return to university for my fourth year.

I requested full-time work as an operator, knowing that I would end up in Directory Assistance, which was more boring than long-distance operating but would put me at the centre of the company union territory. During the following two years, I organized for the CWC while taking one university course a year. I knew I was in the midst of something special, and to capture history as it was happening, I wrote a paper about the campaign and strike. This paper recorded the events in real time and became the backbone of this book.

The Context: Working-Class Women's Work and Union Struggles

I was a young woman in the 1970s. My generation grew up watching *Leave It to Beaver* on TV. Although filmed in the 1950s, the show played incessantly in reruns during the sixties and seventies. It depicted middle-class family life, but a version where the dad worked and the mother stayed home. Much of the culture of the fifties and sixties duplicated this idealized picture of the family and sent the message that the nuclear family and a stay-at-home mother were the norm. Betty Friedan[1] and other second-wave feminists countered this widespread cultural belief with the assertion that many women suffered from being locked into this stereotype and needed meaningful work outside the home for creative expression and a sense of purpose. Maybe this was the case with middle-class women, but most of the women I knew were already working. They worked, as my mother had, as soon as their children started school or they could get a good babysitter. They went to work because they needed the money.

This was no different from earlier generations of women. Working-class women had *always* worked because they needed the money — and many working-class women needed the money because they were the principal breadwinners for their families or themselves.

Women also belonged to unions. The largest employer of working-class women in Toronto was the garment trade, and many of my friends had mothers who were seamstresses working in the rag-trade businesses around the intersection of Spadina and Queen. And many of these garment workers were members of the International Ladies' Garment Workers Union, whose precursor union, the Cloakmakers' Union, had launched a strike for the forty-four-hour work week in 1919.[2]

Women worked in manufacturing plants as well, especially during the Second World War, when the corporate sector recruited women for the workforce in Toronto's wartime manufacturing plants, since much of the male workforce had joined the armed forces. In 1943, only one plant had a majority female workforce that was unionized — Inglis Home Appliances (formerly John Inglis and Company). Its workers had signed up with the United Steelworkers of America.[3] Although popular history depicts women returning to the home during the 1950s, there were still plenty of women working outside the home. Women were driven out of the manufacturing plants to make room for the men who returned after the war, but they were still in demand in pink-collar ghettos like retail stores and hospitals.

Between 1948 and 1952, the United Steelworkers launched a drive to unionize the female workforce at Eaton's department store, headquartered in Toronto. The drive, led by strong woman organizers, was not successful. Although the campaign ultimately failed to win a union, the employer was forced to spend millions to increase women's salaries and offer them pensions — all this just to stop them from organizing.[4] The desire to unionize Eaton's continued after the period covered by this book with a campaign by the Retail, Wholesale and Department Store Union, Local 1000.

Between 1965 and 1975, the number of employed women in Canada increased by 79 percent. High inflation rates prompted many women to seek employment to offset the decline in their family's standard of living. In 1965, only 16.6 percent of all union members were women; ten years later the figure had jumped to 26.3 percent.[5]

This increase was largely due to the rapid unionization of the public sector, where nearly half of all workers (not including management) were women. By 1975, the Canadian Union of Public Employees had become the largest single union in Canada, representing the largest number of women.

Women needed the strength and power that came through unionization, as they faced many barriers and challenges in the workplace. Women's pay rates were locked in at about half the pay rates of men. Often there were clearly discriminatory clauses that compensated women less or penalized them for maternity leave. Most traditionally male occupations were closed to them. Childcare was solely the woman's problem, and if she needed to take time off, she could get fired.

The amazing thing is that women did fight back. Despite having to go home and fix dinner, do housework, and make sure their kids did their homework — while overcoming their own fatigue and demoralization — they fought back. And sometimes they even won.

Chapter 1

Bell Canada: The Company

Bell expects that the public will use his instrument without the aid of trained operators. Any telegraph engineer will at once see the fallacy of this plan. The public simply cannot be trusted to handle technical communications equipment. Bell's instrument uses nothing but the voice, which cannot be captured in concrete form ... we leave it to you to judge whether any sensible man would transact his affairs by such a means of communications. In conclusion the committee feels that it must advise against any investment whatever in Bell's scheme.

— Minutes of a Western Union meeting, circa 1880 [1]

Alexander Graham Bell invented the first practical telephone in 1874. With his new invention, he transmitted speech in 1875 and received the Canadian patent in March 1876. He received the master patent for the telephone in the United States in the same year. Although many others laid claim to the invention, Canada's thirty-seventh Parliament passed a Canadian Parliamentary Motion on June 21, 2002, affirming that Alexander Graham Bell was indeed the inventor of the telephone.[2]

Bell on the telephone in New York
(calling Chicago) in 1892.

The word *telephone* is derived from two Greek words: *tele* (far-off) and *phone* (voice or sound). The earliest examples were no more than pairs of wooden hand telephones that operated between two locations, such as from a store to a nearby warehouse, or from a business to an executive's residence, similar to what we know today as walkie-talkie systems.

Bell Canada, formerly known as Bell Telephone Company of Canada (BTCC), was developed over 130 years ago in Ontario and Quebec to provide everything associated with telephone systems: not only the telephone apparatus, but also the physical infrastructure, including the phone lines and switching stations to facilitate phone calls.

Bell Telephone Company of Canada and then its renamed version, Bell Canada, has always been one of Canada's most important corporations. In 1975, the government listed it as the fifth-largest company in the country. It has played a pivotal role in changing business, social, and family life in central Canada and has always employed a large workforce, hiring many members of every community and neighbourhood. This book will explore the history and role of the telephone operator in providing telephone calling assistance to the customers of Bell Canada, in the broader context of these workers' struggle with the company.

Canadians became early adopters of the first telephones, as they did with mobile phones in the late twentieth century. The new invention helped to overcome the geographical distances of this vast country. Because the monopoly corporation had a captive market, and its financial interests were protected through federal regulation, it became a blue chip stock attractive to the middle class. From early on, the firm used the slogan "A telephone business run by Canadians for Canadians."

This new communication technology changed the culture in ways that are still emerging. In the twenty-first century, the modern version of the telephone — the mobile phone — is now used for business and personal communication on a global scale. At the same time, we are also witnessing its use as a tool of protest and for regime change in far-off dictatorships. Originally conceived of by its inventors and initial investors as a tool for business, the telephone, as with other life-changing technology, has had applications developed for easier family and social communication.

The large corporation that developed to support making a telephone call was nicknamed Ma Bell, because of its monopoly status, and it became known for its seemingly remote attitude toward customers and workers, and arbitrary business decisions. Monopoly status gave the company a position similar to the government in its influence in day-to-day life. The nickname "Ma" shows that Canadians in central Canada considered the company close enough to be family. Throughout the life of the company, the benefits of monopoly status, including a captive market and service rates approved by a government body, did not result in a public perception of good customer service or rates that favoured the ordinary customer.

Corporate Growth

Bell Telephone Company of Canada was incorporated on April 29, 1880, by an Act of the Dominion Parliament, to develop a telephone system in Canada based on Bell's patents. This was just four years after the telephone's invention, a very fast timeline for any startup company to attract investors, create a corporate infrastructure, and get the national government on its side. The company's charter from the government granted it the right, but not a monopoly, to offer services to all provinces except British Columbia (Alberta, Saskatchewan, and

Newfoundland and Labrador had not yet entered confederation). The company would later focus its service delivery on heavily populated areas of the provinces of Ontario and Quebec.

In 1881, one year after incorporating, the company had exchanges in forty cities and had a long-distance line from Toronto to Hamilton. By 1890, the firm was offering long-distance service over 3,670 miles.[3] In 1880, Bell had only one hundred subscribers, but through slow but steady growth and cutthroat tactics against the competition, the number of subscribers went up to 1,500 in 1886.[4]

In the pre-monopoly period, dozens of entrepreneurs seized upon the opportunities presented by this new invention and many telephone companies were incorporated at the same time as Bell Telephone. Charles Fleetford Sise, the company's first general manager, called the competitive environment that Bell Telephone operated in "guerrilla war."[5]

Sise directed Bell to match the tactics of the competition and compete ruthlessly. This included giving exclusive privileges, including free installation and cheap rates, to railway stations and doctors, as well as stopping competitors through injunctions, cutting rates and even tampering with their phone lines.[6] Bell's incessant lobbying of provincial legislatures and municipal councils enhanced the cutthroat competitive behaviour. Monopoly status was the goal and to achieve it, Bell sales agents were not above lying or even installing telephones for free until the competition was dead. Of course, once the competition was gone, the cost of telephone service reverted back to full rates.[7]

When telephones were first in use, marketing them as an aid to family life was not part of the company's sales efforts, as middle- and working-class families could not even afford the rates for a telephone until early in the twentieth century. To encourage the exclusive use of phones by the business class, the company kept its rates high and even tried to increase the cost of public telephone calls.

Bell Telephone was a major corporate player right from the beginning, but growth did not come overnight or easily because the company was the subject of continuing government interest. Government regulation of phone service developed concurrently with the company's growth. An 1892 amendment to the Charter of Bell Telephone

1902

The logo used by Bell Telephone Company of Canada from 1902 until 1922. Interestingly, the logo uses American flag–like stars. A later version incorporated maple leaves instead.

Company of Canada read, "The existing rates shall not be increased without the consent of the Governor in Council."[8]

After the turn of the century, government regulation of Bell Telephone increased. In 1902, the government amended the company's charter to include a regulation requiring Bell to provide service to whomever applied for it, with the allowance that the instrument would not have to be placed far from a road.[9]

The turn of the century was a time when the public was clamouring for government intervention in the delivery of what were coming to be seen as basic necessities of life, including water and electricity. These demands were due to the failure of the free market to deliver the commodities at a fair price and with adequate concern for public safety. Various organizational structures delivered these services, including monopolies run by the government, public utilities run by arm's-length government bodies called commissions, and regulated monopoly corporations like the railways. The telephone company became the focus of ongoing public debate about public versus private control. Despite much competition by small municipal telephone companies, regulatory decisions by the Canadian Board of Railway Commissioners between 1912 and 1916 gave Bell Telephone exclusive control over the infrastructure for long-distance calling and led to the gradual disappearance of most of the competition and virtual monopoly status for the company. Some small telephone companies remained operating until the 1980s.

This debate emerged again in the 1970s with the new drive toward government deregulation. But in the late twentieth century only very large competitors could compete with Bell.

Bell's triumph over most of its competitors and the related public scrutiny led to a special investigation by a parliamentary committee in 1905. The committee produced two thousand pages of testimony and exhibits, but concluded the investigation without any recommendations for change. Bell Telephone put its own spin on the inquiry by claiming total vindication with the following statement: "Although the records of the Company have been searched from its organization twenty-four years ago, not a single fact has been adduced which reflects discreditably on the integrity or the justice of the management."[10] Despite the lack of conclusions by the parliamentary committee, in 1906 the government decided that Bell Canada should be included in the Railway Act of 1903, meaning rates would be regulated by the Canadian Board of Railway Commissioners.[11]

From then on, this arm's-length, quasi-governmental body would decide the rates Bell could charge its customers. This changed the nature of the business. Offering telephone service had now become a social obligation and the public could have a great deal of influence over the rates charged for phone service. With the mandate of providing service to whomever requested it and a government-determined rate structure, Bell Telephone was now closer to operating as a public utility than an unrestrained private corporation that could determine the best use of its resources to meet the needs of the marketplace. After just twenty-five years, Bell Telephone was officially a regulated monopoly corporation.

Bell Telephone Company was serving 237,000 subscribers by 1914. The First World War created overwhelming demand, but with shortages of supplies, the backlog for phone installations lasted well into the 1920s. However, innovation from new technology kept the company growing. For example, the company introduced the vacuum tube repeater in 1915 and enabled the development of a transcontinental network for long-distance calling.[12]

The capital costs of building a long-distance network prompted Bell to apply for a rate increase in 1918. By this time, the public understood its power vis-à-vis the company and a well-organized protest movement countered the request. No one believed that the company was going to give a 75 percent wage hike to its operators, as it suggested in its submission as a reason for the rate hike.[13]

The company's interaction with the federal government was also mirrored at the local level, with local municipal councils having regulatory jurisdiction over the placement and rights of way of phone-line poles and wires. Local Bell management had to become involved in community and local politics to push its case for access to public space and special land uses.

* * *

It took a large workforce with staff assuming many roles and responsibilities to build a telecommunications network. Nonetheless, the first point of access was the voice at the end of the line.

> At least for the public, the true voice of the networks was the operator. Across Bell's territory, from the big cities of the Dominion down to the small towns, the operator was the "human switch through which passed the first traffic of the telephone age."
>
> Eventually, Bell operators became a mainly female force not only connecting subscribers, but also offering breaking news, the time, and the latest hockey scores; tracking down doctors and firefighters when needed; and even offering advice on how to keep the telephone in good working order. Operators soon came to occupy a unique status in the public imagination as a remarkable channel of all kinds of information and advice.[14]

By 1909, political pressures in the western provinces, especially against large eastern corporations, led the company to sell its western assets to provincial and municipal governments. These jurisdictions set up government-run telephone companies, but the loss of these geographically dispersed markets in the West had only positive repercussions for

Telephone operator in 1910.

Bell Telephone, as it allowed the company to concentrate on more profitable urban markets in Ontario and Quebec.[15]

In the 1910s, telephoning from one city to another required an average of five operators to facilitate the connection.[16] By the mid-1920s, the connection time for a long-distance call had gone from seven minutes to just over two and a half minutes. Installation of automatic exchanges had the greatest impact on operators, as it made customer self-service possible. The first automatic exchange opened in Toronto's "Grover" central office in July 1924. (Early on, telephone companies named the telephone exchange or the central office for about one thousand subscribers "Grover." The first three letters of the phone number corresponded to the first three numbers of the telephone number — so GRO represented 476. The Grover exchange building was located on Main Street just north of Kingston Road.) Underground cables, which had many times the transmission capacity of above-ground lines, also improved regular phone service a great deal. The first long-distance call from Montreal to Vancouver via an all-Canadian route occurred in 1926. By the late 1920s, Bell had linked Canada to Britain via the phone system in the United States. Long-distance calls to many countries around the world became possible soon after.

Toronto's 1928 telephone directory contained 576 pages of listings. The number of Bell subscribers increased from 95,145 in 1906 to 761,456 in 1929. Toronto alone had 4,200 Bell workers in 1929, while the entire workforce of the company was 18,067 employees.[17] All this innovation and growth provided good reason to call this period the Golden Age of Telephony.

The Golden Age was not to last. The Great Depression dramatically slowed down the industry's growth. In the first three years of the Depression, Bell lost 15 percent of its customers. In 1930, telephones were in 87 percent of all homes in Bell Telephone territory, but by 1935 the number of households with a phone had dropped to 68.2 percent. In 1932, the Bell stock dividend fell for the first time in four decades.[18]

The company was reluctant to offset the loss in revenues by cutting its workforce. Employees were highly trained and loyal to the company, so to counter the decline in revenue, Bell instituted "short timing" in 1931. This consisted of cutting employee hours and wages while keeping all of its employees on its payroll. Yet management kept the same level of spending on constructing telephone infrastructure (such as exchanges and long-distance cable) to position it for the growth that would occur when the Depression ended.[19] Despite the doom and gloom, the seven major telephone companies in Canada even joined together to develop a coast-to-coast system of telecommunications called the Trans-Canada Telephone System.

Canadians had little time to recover from the Great Depression before they followed Great Britain into the Second World War. The war brought new challenges to Bell Telephone Company of Canada. Out of a total population of 11.5 million, a million men and women were mobilized into the Canadian Armed Forces. The economy now suffered from a new issue: a shortage of workers. Bell faced similar labour issues, yet the Bell network, now considered a strategic national asset, had to dramatically expand its services for war purposes. Bell granted the Canadian government exclusive use of the transatlantic Montreal–London telephone cable. Simultaneously, telephone companies had to restrict their service to the general population, and Bell telephone acquired a huge backlog of seventy-two thousand phone orders by war's end.[20]

As with other industries, the telephone companies made up the shortage of male workers with women, who took over traditionally male jobs and assumed positions on the craft side of the company. Bell Canada, imbued with a spirit of public service, supported the government's war effort and met every expectation.

At the close of the Second World War, the company was managing 1.2 million telephones and handled 127,000 toll calls per day. When the Montreal–London circuit reverted to civilian use, it handled four times as many calls as before the onset of the war.[21]

The CBC online radio archives contain a broadcast made on April 29, 1945, a few months before Victory in Europe Day. It was entitled, "Telephones Become a Necessity, Not a Luxury." The following is a portion of the broadcast:

> Couples court, businessmen deal, and firefighters help — all by telephone. Nearly all aspects of Canadian life have changed since the telephone took hold. Even before the start of the Second World War, Canadians made more phone calls per capita than citizens of any other country. Now, as the war draws to a close in 1945, CBC Radio host John Fisher predicts "the very words of victory shall be spread by telephone."
>
> Fisher is saluting the sixty-fifth anniversary of Bell Canada, the largest of the country's four thousand telephone companies. In 1914, he notes, the telephone had been a luxury in Canadian homes. But now there's one phone for every five people, and Canada supplies phone equipment to many other countries. Because of its speed of communication and the way it has shaped users' lives, the telephone is a necessity for everyday life.[22]

The radio broadcast also notes that 1945 was the year that saw installation of the millionth telephone by Bell Canada.

The end of the war ushered in a second golden age for telephony. Rapid corporate growth to meet the needs of a growing population required a corresponding increase in the workforce. Bell's twenty-one thousand employees in 1946 grew to forty thousand in 1966. The slogan developed in the 1940s, "The Bell is a Good Place to Work!", reflected a systematic approach to the attraction and retention of employees. The company's need to retain its employees, in whom they invested a great deal of training time, led to workplace improvements, including the introduction of a five-day work week in September 1946.[23]

The war had also catalyzed large union-organizing campaigns in the manufacturing sector, whose workers wanted a share of the economic gains made by their employers in wartime. The labour movement developed a new model for worker-management relations through collective bargaining for large workforces. Large international unions like the United Steelworkers and United Automobile Workers (UAW) had recently organized steel and automobile plants in Canada. With a workforce of forty thousand, Bell Telephone was ripe for organizing. To prevent this from happening, Bell presented its employees with the Canadian Telephone Employees Association (CTEA) and the Traffic Employees Association (TEA), two employee associations that undermined the drive to organize into a legitimate union but presented an opportunity to engage in collective bargaining, which began in 1945 and 1946. Bell's approach to industrial relations was to give its employees just enough to keep them happy and stymie any organizing drives.

The company provided for its employees a well-rounded security program, comprising a plan for pensions and a plan for sickness, accident, and death benefits financed entirely by the company. A group of voluntary payroll deduction plans enabled employees to buy shares of the company's stock and to meet premiums on regular life insurance and group insurance policies, government annuity contracts, and hospital medical care contracts. In the larger centres, the company maintained well-equipped, professionally staffed medical departments where employees could obtain minor treatments, medical examinations, and health advice without charge.[24]

Paternalism infused the benefit program, as the company focused on security and benefits instead of wages. In Canada, generally, women were under extreme pressure to return to the home after working in munitions plants and many other jobs. They were told to free up jobs for men returning from the war, and communities frowned on women who were in jobs that men could do. Those lucky women who remained in the workforce, like Bell operators, were under extreme pressure to conform and accept lower wages in return for the security of having a job. Other female workers had to give up basic human rights, such as the women in the Canadian civil service who had to stop working upon marriage. In this climate, most working women would fear for their jobs.

Remember when?

This reminder of the way things used to be for women in the Public Service was found during a recent office clean-up by Nancy LePage of the Labour group's Federal Mediation and Conciliation Service.

OFFICE OF THE SECRETARY

CIVIL SERVICE COMMISSION

CANADA

OTTAWA, JULY 2, 1947

Circular Letter 1947-20

Deputy Heads, Government Departments, Ottawa.

It appears that Departments are still under the impression that female employees who marry and who wish to be continued in employment may be paid, after marriage, the same rate of pay they were receiving prior to marriage.

While authority for this was granted during the war years under the War Measures Act and was continued under the national Emergency Transitional Powers Act, the Commission now wishes to advise all Departments that, as authority under these Acts expired on March 31, 1947, female employees can be paid only the minimum salary of the class, after marriage.

Section 113 of the Civil Service Regulations provides that a female employee in the public service shall, upon the occasion of her marriage, be required to resign her position. Any employment, thereafter, even without break in service, is regarded as a new appointment, and must necessarily be made at the minimum rate.

[signed]
R. Morgan
Secretary

Editor's note: In 1955, the government removed restrictions on the employment of married women in the federal Public Service.

With a complacent workforce, Bell Canada was free to respond to market demands. After 1945, the company was installing a million telephones every three years or so, and had spent over $100 million to improve and expand telephone service in Ontario and Quebec by the end of 1947.[25]

In 1947 Bell introduced mobile radio telephone service to the public in Montreal and Toronto.[26] Taking up half the space in a car trunk, sixty-five mobile telephones went into service by the end of that year.

On December 23, 2007, Mike Filey wrote an article entitled "Toronto Was Experimenting With 'Cell' Phones 60 Years Ago" to draw attention to the fact that the cellphone was not really all that new.

> The cellphone phenomenon all started 60 years ago this year with a series of experiments with the goal of establishing wireless communication using what were initially called mobile radio-telephones. And some of those tests were conducted right here in our city by the Bell Telephone Company of Canada. Their experiments went like this.
>
> First, a radio transmitting station with a range of twenty miles was set up on the top floor of the Bell building at 76 Adelaide St. W.
>
> In addition, several of the company's green and black sedans were fitted out with low-power receiving and sending sets and were conspicuous with an eighteen-inch antenna on the roof.
>
> These vehicles would then wander the city to establish where signals between the car and the radio station worked best.
>
> It wasn't long before it became obvious that the twenty-mile range of the main station was insufficient to cover the sprawling (even back then) city. The numerous tall buildings in the downtown core also interfered with the signals. To get around these problems "repeater stations" would have to be established at various locations across the city where special equipment would capture the signals and send them on to the Bell building on Adelaide via the regular telephone lines.

Each of these locations would soon be known as a "cell." Thus it was that over time the original term "mobile radio-telephone" was replaced by the term "cellular phone" and eventually shortened once again to the modern-day "cellphone."[27]

Filey then went on to explain how, in those primitive days, a call on a cellphone was placed. First, the customer wishing to call the person with the cellphone had to call a special operator. The operator would then send a radio signal to the car with the phone, which would be set up with some kind of audio or visual signal to alert the driver. He would then pick up the phone's receiver, press the "Listen" button, and he would be connected.

In 1957, the company arranged the first one-way conference call for the Imperial Life Assurance Company, connecting twenty-six cities across Canada.[28] Bell operators provided these services. The introduction of direct distance dialling eliminated the need to have operator-connected long-distance calls. First introduced in Toronto in 1958, this innovation expanded throughout the company in the following years.

Continued growth created the need for more technological advancement. Bell was no longer just a telephone company; it was transforming into a telecommunications company by developing a transcontinental microwave system to support broadcasting. In early 1953, the company installed the world's first permanent international microwave television link between two countries, delivering programs from Buffalo, New York, to the CBC in Toronto.[29]

* * *

By 1966, an astonishing 95 percent of all households had a telephone. Because of this market saturation, the workforce was now at thirty-eight thousand; however, as was the pattern with technological change, the operator workforce had contracted, declining two thousand employees from its peak in the 1950s.[30] This theme of technical innovation leading to workforce decline is one of the drivers behind the eventual unionization of the company.

Bell Canada: The Company

On March 7, 1968, a new Canadian law renamed Bell Telephone Company of Canada, Ltd., as Bell Canada. The name change modernized the brand and clearly differentiated the Canadian company from American phone companies. It also signified that the company was now providing more than telephone service. A number of subsidiary companies developed shortly after that, and although Bell Canada still provided service to the public with voice communications, the focus of the company switched to investing in the emerging field of telecommunications, including defence communications and data transmission. Within Ontario and Quebec, some 670 independent telephone systems operated in cooperation with Bell Canada and serviced 290,000 additional telephones. The sixties and seventies became a period of consolidation, with Bell purchasing many smaller telephone companies.

In the seventies, however, the government developed a contrary vision for the company. Now the government decided to deregulate Bell Canada to position it to meet new demands, and to open the long-distance market to competition. Very high long-distance rates were subsidizing unlimited local calls, which were included in a cheap basic monthly package that all customers paid, regardless of how remote those customers were or how difficult the geography made it to serve those customers. The company was mandated to serve all equally. This situation led to the desire by the company to cut the costs of long-distance calls in order to meet the challenge of new competition who were not mandated to provide service to remote regions and pay for costly infrastructure that Bell had already built and paid for. To make up for the decline in revenue from long-distance calls, however, changes would need to be made in the company's other operations. As was the case throughout the company's history, change was to come and turn the work of the telephone operator upside down. Ma Bell, the formerly staid telephone company, found itself transitioning to an entrepreneurial culture and undergoing the modernization of its operations.

Chapter 2

The Occupation of Telephone Operator

Birth of an Occupation

In the 1880s, using the telephone was not simply a matter of picking up a receiver. First, one had to check that the carbon microphone contacts had recently been sanded and adjusted. Then one had carefully to attach the ammonia battery. Here, too, it was necessary to check whether the battery had to be refilled which was a delicate operation since one had to take care that no liquid spilled. Besides, it smelled terrible and could burn holes in the carpet. Then one had to turn the magneto crank to warn the operators at the exchange that one was on the line.

The weather was also important, since both the single wire that routed the communication and the insulators had to be dry. If there was an active telegraph or electrical wire nearby, all telephone conversations became inaudible. The receiver was the only relatively reliable element of the system. In short, the telephone required constant maintenance, which limited its use to offices, where employees could take care of it, and kept it out of the homes of all but a few innovative — and wealthy — handymen.[1]

In 1876 the first telephone operators were already working as telegraph operators. They were young and male, and acted as both couriers and operators in the telegraph office, often on a commission basis rather than for wages. As they were already working in communications and had some technical skill and knowledge of electricity, the new phone company hired them as operator-technicians to maintain the switchboards and equipment, as well as to connect calls. But supporting equipment installation quickly moved away from the operator function, and the need for operators to have technical skills diminished.

According to Jean-Guy Rens, a strike organized by the Knights of Labor in 1883 in the neighbouring telegraph industry may have been the main impetus behind feminization of the job of telephone operator. (Male boisterousness and playing while working was given as the official reason.) Young men could be rude and arrogant with customers, while women were considered better at handling customers in a pleasant manner and easier to discipline — and they could be paid less, receiving an hourly rate as opposed to the commission payment received by telegraph operators. C.F. Sise, the managing director of the fledging company, stated, "A woman would give better service and be a better agent."[2] Telephone operator was the primary occupation within the company's workforce; by 1912, two-thirds of Bell Telephone's employees were telephone operators and almost all were female.[3]

The main exchange in Montreal hired the first female operator in 1880, and the two Howell sisters were hired in Toronto in 1880.[4] The occupation of telephone operator was a new job opportunity for women, who had previously been restricted to teaching, factory work, and restaurant and domestic work. Although unskilled in the beginning, the operators received training on the job and the work became respectable, although not highly paid. The new operators had to master the skills of working on high switchboards while sitting on high stools and wearing the restricting fashions of the day. They had to plug in a cord with one hand and then plug in another with the other hand, while simultaneously writing down details of the call and carrying on a conversation with the customer — all under the pressure of an arbitrary time limit set by the company.

Mary Rosetta Warren, an operator in Montreal from 1880 to 1891, clearly summarizes the spirit of the operators of the period: "I doubt whether the modern operator [has] ever felt the thrill and glamour that we did in being part of the early telephone development.... It was a daily occurrence to be asked by a subscriber to say a few words to a gentleman who had never used a telephone before, which made me feel important."[5]

Bell also created the impression that working as an operator was a white-collar job in order to recruit middle-class women. In the beginning of the telephone industry, the customers were primarily middle-class businessmen, and Bell desired to attract woman workers who were more genteel than those in industrial work. Early recruitment attempts stressed the occupation's white-collar characteristics: a clean workplace, steadiness, possibility of advancement, shorter hours than factory work, and seclusion from the public.[6] These benefits continued to be stressed in the company's recruitment strategy throughout the history of the occupation.

The moulding of the perfect "Hello Girl" began during the recruitment process. The company screened out women with foreign accents, as it was generally believed that the public would be intolerant of accents. Even native English speakers were given elocution training, though the company relaxed this requirement somewhat due to the need for bilingual operators in Montreal. American sources report added recruitment criteria for height and weight. Because operators had to sit at the company's equipment for long periods, the company hired women whose height and weight fit within certain narrow boundaries. For example, in the early 1900s, the telephone companies considered most women under five feet tall too short to be operators.[7]

Although there was a class difference between operators and customers, a friendly working relationship developed, and customers expected to be able to catch up on the latest news on community goings-on as well as the weather and the correct time. While primarily serving the business sector in the company's early days, operators were deeply connected in the community, and residents relied upon both rural and urban operators to help access emergency services and deal with community crises.

One American anecdote illustrates the key role played in the community by telephone operators, and the role they played in process innovation. These first operators needed to have good memories, to know which people went with which plugs. In the 1880s, there was a measles epidemic in Lowell, Massachusetts. The doctors were worried that if all the operators got the measles, then nobody would be able to control the telephone operating system. A doctor suggested that rather than relying on operators' memories, each person should be assigned a number. This is how the telephone number came into play.[8]

The informality of the customer-operator relationship did not last long. Between 1884 and 1891, the company decided to formalize the job and institute rules and regulations and a supervisory hierarchy.[9] By this time, the principles of scientific management had permeated North American society[10] and Bell management began to look at segmenting the work process of telephone operating and attempting to reduce operator mistakes and errors to save time on customer interactions. After all, as a private corporation, the company's primary purpose was to make a profit, not to serve the community. This tension between the company's desire to provide good service to its customers and its desire to maximize profit is a recurring theme throughout the company's history and had an especially pronounced effect on the role of the telephone operator, right up to the end of the occupation within the company.

Along with dividing up the tasks of telephone operators, the company intervened in conversations with customers by composing and requiring standard phrases like "Number please." Bell created a management structure to oversee the work of operator staff. The company created the position of chief operator in 1884. She was responsible for the operator workforce and could make decisions on scheduling and operator requests. She was also held accountable for how telephone operators performed, and made sure that operators were following rules and standard procedures. She would pace continually behind them, listening in on conversations with customers or between operators.

Operators who broke the rules had to be reported to the company and could be penalized with a warning, denial of the rest period, stoppage of pay, a suspension for few days or weeks, or ultimately firing.[11]

The 1890s saw the continuation of this trend toward managing the work of telephone operating to find efficiencies and control the work process. Company management developed standardized operator training that focused on the quality of the operator's voice and the phrases used in customer interactions. In management's eyes, it was a waste of precious time when a customer had to ask the operator to repeat something she said. The time was better used to help another customer.

In 1892, to make sure operators delivered efficient service that satisfied the customers through standardized work processes, the company sent all operators a small booklet entitled "Rules and Instructions for Operators," which identified twenty-seven duties of regular operators and standard phrases for specific instances in a call. If an unusual situation arose, the operator would refer the call to the chief operator or her assistant.[12]

By the late 1890s, the chief operator (or the newly appointed supervising assistant chief operators) could listen in on operators' calls on a listening board that connected to all the lines on the switchboard if they suspected a breach of the rules. The new supervisor positions allowed Bell to standardize operator training throughout the company, as the supervisors could spend three to six weeks training new hires.[13]

Extensive job training taught not only the skills of answering calls on the switchboard and the expected words and phrases to use when dealing with customers, but also began to instill the desired social and feminine characteristics of the ideal telephone operator. Characteristics commonly associated with the working class, such as swearing, brashness, flying off the handle at customers, and giving as good as you got were programmed out of new hires.

Company training practices socialized new operators to be passive young ladies and to submit to discipline easily, and by the early 1930s, Bell Telephone opened schools in Montreal and Toronto to train new hires to become perfect operators.

"The operator must now be made as nearly as possible a paragon of perfection, a kind of human machine, the exponent of speed and courtesy; a creature spirited enough to move like chain lightning, and with perfect accuracy, docile enough to deny herself the sweet privilege of the last word."[14]

By the beginning of the twentieth century, the informal relationship between operators and customers that developed in the early days had dissipated, despite continued customer demand for information on such things as the weather or help with community resources. Standard answers to questions were developed by management and were stated by operators in a formal, detached tone.

Close monitoring of operator job performance continued throughout the early twentieth century, as this quote illustrates:

> The supervisors all wear telephone headsets with long cords, which are connected to an overhead instruction circuit, thus enabling any supervisor to communicate instantly with any other supervisor in the same office. A key and cord with a relay attachment enables each supervisor to communicate with any subscribers who may complain to the operator in that division, and also enables the supervisors to deal directly with all supervisors in any of the other offices.... It is thus made possible for subscribers to promptly get into communication with the supervisor and also enables the supervisor in any one office to refer a complaint either in reference to a subscriber's circuit number, or about any operator who is not handling her work in standard manner. With this system over 85 percent of operators are supervised as to inter-office regularities.[15]

Very early on, Bell management adhered to a maxim that developed in the late twentieth century: "What gets measured gets attention." By the 1890s, the company was measuring the average time for an operator to put through a call. The acronym for this measure was ACT, which stood for average call time. In the late 1890s, ACT was twenty-five seconds; in the first years of the twentieth century, it was only eight seconds.[16] This seventeen-second decrease represented a dramatic increase in operator productivity. In Toronto, an operator could now handle one thousand calls a day.

In 1894 the operators began implementing small forms of resistance. In the spirit of self-help, they created the Lady Operators Benefit Association, which allowed them to receive a portion of their wages after three days of illness.[17]

Despite the company's efforts to keep telephone operators submissive, widespread radicalization occurred. The speed and accuracy needed to answer calls, the high reach of the switchboards, the strict rules of behaviour, the risk of physical injury and even electrocution, the nervousness created by the fast pace of work, and low wages all contributed to operator dissatisfaction toward the job and the employer.

Operator productivity remained the subject of intense scrutiny. By 1903, attention turned to the hours of work. In 1903, the company tried an experiment in Toronto at the main exchange, decreasing the hours of work from eight to five. Some operators could pick up two five-hour shifts and earn enough money to make ends meet. Under this split-shift situation, operators got paid overtime for the second shift, yet they were suffering from this change. In December 1904, a group of four Toronto operators requested an increase in wages in a letter written to Mr. Maw, chief inspector of switchboard equipment. The letter stated that wages were insufficient to meet "the steadily increasing cost of the necessaries of life."[18]

The experiment of the five-hour shift did not last long, and the company reinstated the eight-hour workday on January 25 and 26 of 1907. With this new work schedule, operator wages went from twenty-one cents to sixteen cents per hour. This efficiency drive and wage reduction was not accepted meekly by the operators, who immediately held a meeting on January 27 and threatened to strike on February 1. While waiting for the strike deadline, the operators consulted a solicitor about their rights, developed a petition for operators to sign, and sent a deputation to the mayor saying that an eight-hour day was a physical impossibility; that they could not stand the strain of such long hours; and that the company refused to deal with them in any way. They made the case that the residents of the City of Toronto, with their business with the telephone company, had an interest in pressuring the company on the operators' behalf, and that a strike by the telephone operators would seriously affect the public interest.[19]

The mayor asked the federal minister of labour to get involved. While awaiting his response, four hundred employees in Toronto went on strike on January 31 for four and a half days. The strike partially crippled telephone service, so the company brought in operators from outside Toronto, including Peterborough, Kingston, Ottawa, and Montreal, to fill the places of strikers. The "Hello Girls" captured front-page headlines in the Toronto newspapers and garnered a great deal of public sympathy. As a result of public outrage over the strike, the federal government intervened. Under the British North America Act (at that time, the piece of legislation closest in nature to a constitution), the federal government was responsible for workers in the communications sector. Deputy Minister of Labour William Lyon Mackenzie King (later to become the tenth prime minister of Canada) offered to hold a Royal Commission to look into the operators' grievances and they agreed to return to work. The strike ended on February 4, 1907.

The Royal Commission held its first meeting on February 4, 1907. Co-chaired by John Winchester and Mackenzie King, its mandate was "to inquire into Bell Telephone Company Of Canada Limited and the operators employed in its offices in Toronto with respect to wages and hours of employment, and all matters affecting the merits of the said dispute and the right settlement thereof." The transcribed evidence of the *Report [of] The Royal Commission on a Dispute Respecting Hours of Employment Between The Bell Telephone Company Of Canada, Ltd. and Operators at Toronto, Ontario*[20] totals over 1,700 pages, exclusive of all exhibits.

The commission hearings occurred during the first two weeks of February. Many of the operators appeared as witnesses to give evidence on the five main issues:

1. Change in hours of work;
2. Causes of the strike;
3. Nature of the operators' work;
4. Medical opinion about the operators' workload;
5. The "listening board."

The listening board (used by supervisors to listen in on calls) was especially distasteful to the public, as they became aware of the lack of privacy during conversations with operators.

While Bell said they paid wages at market rates, the commissioners did not accept that the increase in wages would compensate for the increase in hours. When the commission hearings came to an end on February 18, Mackenzie King proposed a compromise to end the dispute. He proposed a seven-hour day for the wages paid for eight, which was still two hours more than the previous five-hour shift, with the option of an overtime shift.

The operators were clearly defeated. They could not continue to strike, as they were not unionized. The company was not affected enough by the adverse publicity, and strikebreakers continued to provide telephone service.

Once Bell agreed to the commission's proposed terms of work, the company called back only select workers (it is safe to assume they were the ones who had caused the least trouble) until forced to call back all the strikers a month later.

One can ask why the operators did not organize into a union, but went cap-in-hand to the government so quickly. Most likely operators did not look to unionization because a backlash toward female operators remained from the telegraph operator strike in the 1880s, and mainstream unions refused to organize them. The International Brotherhood of Electrical Workers gave advice to the telephone operators during their strike but did not attempt to organize them until 1918. We must also remember that trade unions were still organized on the craft model (occupations rather than workplaces) and that unions did not organize large industrial workplaces until the 1930s. However, by playing to their strength, which included both the prominent role operators played in the community and the fact that by this time telephone services had become essential to business, telephone operators wisely chose to fight in the arena of public opinion. By appealing to the government and emphasizing their place in the community, the operators could capitalize on their role as genteel women and pander to a sense of paternalism and public sympathy rather than directly confronting the power dynamic of employer and employee.

While the company gained the upper hand after the dispute, it faced the new situation with the knowledge that even a female workforce could be motivated enough to take direct action against the company. Employee labour action hurt the company's reputation and, indirectly, its growth and profit projections. The company agreed to the labour minister's proposal to set up a workplace management-employee consultation process. The employees elected representatives to joint management-labour conferences where working conditions could be discussed. The employee representatives had no bargaining power, but the company listened to employee perspective and complaints.

After the strike, for instance, the company decided that attempts would be made to foster better communication with its employees and keep them closely informed of the company's plans, and made some pretense of consultation and improved office surroundings. A few months later the company also decided to supply a free medical examination for every operator.[21]

So successful was this resolution that Mackenzie King wrote a book called *Industry and Humanity* in which he advocated for the establishment of company unions. While on political hiatus, King went on to set up company unions in the steel industry for the Carnegies and Rockefellers in the United States. These joint management-labour conferences at Bell Telephone Company of Canada formed the basis of its labour relations approach and the company managed to keep labour peace for over seventy years.

How the Occupation Evolved over the Following Fifty Years

By 1910, the industry had expanded rapidly and calls were coming in so fast that operators could not take their eyes off their switchboards, even for a second. Bell began providing telephone services for doctors by 1902, and telephones in hotels facilitating room service and information became available by 1915. Rapid corporate growth after the First World War led to increased work systemization in the telephone system.

Growth during this period forced the company to continue to hire large numbers of telephone operators despite automation of switching equipment. The same inadequate wage structure and working conditions drove Toronto telephone operators (at this point there were four thousand in Toronto alone) to organize themselves in August 1918. This time they affiliated with the International Brotherhood of Electrical Workers. Five hundred operators held a meeting on August 10 and decided to form a local of IBEW and demand a wage increase of $3 per week. A few days later Bell granted them the wage increase but refused to recognize their union. The union local did negotiate a first contract but it had no duration clause. A year later, the IBEW local disintegrated and the company instituted "Employee Representation Plans." This pseudo-company union structure had no fees; the company picked up its operating expenses, and monthly meetings were held to resolve issues between management and employees.[22]

During the 1920s, operators continued to perform hard manual work, working in a fast-paced environment without holidays and without paid sick days for $11.50 a week. The dial exchange arrived in 1924, which permitted telephone users to dial a party directly without waiting for an operator to come on the line. The new technology eliminated the need for telephone operators to facilitate phone calls — except for long-distance and collect calls. By the time of the start of the Great Depression, the need for telephone operators had dropped substantially, not only because of improvements in technology, but also due to reduced demand for phone service due to the economic downturn.

The dial exchange also brought technological improvements to switchboards; improved productivity and diminished demand led to telephone operators working only three days a week during the 1930s, about half the hours they had put in before. When the Second World War began, however, the wartime economy increased the need for telephone communications and the company called all operators back to work.

The rapid expansion of the consumer-based economy after the war led to a rise in wages and disposable income among Canadian consumers, and telephones became extremely desirable to Canadians. Just after the war, in 1945, Bell Canada installed its one-millionth phone.[23] The introduction of direct-distance dialling (DDD) eliminated the need to have operators connect most long-distance calls. Operators were still needed to connect person-to-person long-distance calls, calls from hotels and payphones, and to provide directory assistance. The DDD innovation was introduced first in Toronto in 1958, and implemented throughout the company in the following years.

Despite these innovations, the cord board remained basic equipment for operators until the 1970s. They continued to sit in front of the boards, answering and connecting calls. Directory assistance operators worked with large phone books organized for ease of access and quick retrieval of numbers. However, improvements in technology meant that fewer operators were required for these operations; once again, the operator workforce contracted because of technological change.

Beginnings of Resistance

The Bell Telephone Company moved from a small entrepreneurial business to a large private monopoly during the first half of the twentieth century. This period of growth and technological improvement led to the depersonalization of the operator's work. A job that once was the very heart of communities and neighbourhoods across much of eastern Canada became absorbed into an assembly line of connecting phone calls to and from nameless customers. Operators were forced to use standardized phrases that depended on automaton-like behaviour, not the creativity and warmth of a human service provider.

The company boasted to its staff that they were one big family, but in reality the operators functioned mainly as low-paid labour, whose duty it was to fulfill corporate goals and meet expected call-completion deadlines and customer service standards. Despite the pressures to conform to corporate expectations, operators found small ways to resist.

Operators could undermine company policy by opening the phone lines to talk to other operators in other towns or neighbourhoods. They mimicked the corporate hierarchy by exploiting new operators and getting them to do most of the work, or assigning them the more menial tasks. When pay phones didn't work, the operators could decide whether the customer would get a free call. Rude or angry customers who vented at the operator would likely be out of luck and have to deposit another dime. On regular lines, rude or angry customers might receive poor or slow service.

When you were exasperated by angry subscribers, you can for instance; switch three or four couples together … and then sit and hear them rage at each other. If you're feeling particularly wicked, you can open the listening key and the call circuit at the same time so the poor subscriber will have a Babel of talk deluging him from the order wire.[24]

Sometimes there were telephone operators who gave as much as they got — one of those discouraged "working-class" characteristics — and subscribers would submit complaints of rude, unladylike behaviour. But profanity on the telephone (primarily by customers) became so frequent that in 1915 the Ontario Railway and Municipal Board passed a regulation to prohibit swearing on the telephone, enforced with a fine of $25 or twenty days in jail.[25]

Even the "perfect operator" [is] human and apt to get hungry. After a while your nerves get frazzled — you begin by being absolutely impassive and impersonal, you work like a machine, but by twelve o'clock, after a bad forenoon of arrogance and egoism, you grow actually murderous. You take things pretty seriously.[26]

Resistance on a personal level was covert and unorganized. However, the postwar period brought new rights to workers, enabling them to unionize more easily, and telephone operators had to make some choices on how best to relate to their employer. In 1945, Prime Minister Mackenzie King, the same politician who had stifled operator resistance in 1907 as labour minister, presented an opportunity, through changes to the Labour Relations Act, for telephone company workers to have a real union and effective collective bargaining. In the next chapter, we will explore the company's reaction to these new developments and review the birth of company unionism at Bell Telephone.

Chapter 3

Co-opting Organized Resistance: Company Unionism in Action

While the twentieth century saw the birth of industrial unions in the manufacturing sector, telecommunications companies sought to co-opt their employees' attempts to organize into legitimate trade unions by creating employee associations, which had some of the usual powers of trade unions but took direction from the company. As discussed earlier, the term used to describe this type of employee organization is "company union." This chapter will explore the concept of company unionism and its application to the workplace at Bell Canada.

What Is a Company Union?

One of the primary characteristics of a company union is that it only represents the employees of one company. Such unions are often formed when a legitimate trade union is trying to organize a workplace; to counter this, the company will establish its own union and give it financial and in-kind support, as well as its tacit endorsement. Managers might whisper their endorsement to their staff, or it could be distributed through print materials. Whatever the method, the employees get the message about what the company wants to see happen.

If successful at overcoming a grassroots union drive by a legitimate trade union, the company union leaders align their interests with the company and put the interests of the company ahead of the workers in collective bargaining and on a day-to-day basis. The desire of workers for economic just desserts is undermined by misinformation, constant emphasis on the interests of the company, and fear of job loss. Furthermore, leaving department representatives untrained and exposed only to company propaganda means that any existing grievance procedure is left unused. When problems emerge in the workplace, departmental representatives turn to management for help and may even focus blame on employees for raising the issues. Finally, if the company association has the right to strike, it is rarely used.

> The telephone operators' strike of 1907 prompted Bell to start incorporating some elements of a company union into the Traffic workplace, although the company did not put a formalized structure in place until 1919. The company also saw the strike as an event of some significance. Bell later claimed that the strike "brought an important new step in our labour relations thinking." The operators' firm resistance to Bell's wage cutbacks and efficiency drive fostered the company's increasing awareness of the need for more refined management and stimulated the introduction of consultation and welfare measures designed to enhance employee loyalty and defuse unionization attempts.[1]

The sugar that coated the pill of reduced workers' rights took the form of paternalism as the company doled out some benefits to employees to keep them subdued. By 1912, the company had introduced a health benefit plan to aid its employees in time of illness. In 1917, they instituted a pension plan as well as disability and death benefits. These interventions, along with the fervour of patriotism that also was used to stifle industrial discontent, seemed to help quiet activities on the labour front during the war years.

The International Brotherhood of Electrical Workers (IBEW) made many attempts to organize telephone workers in the United States, and in 1912 the IBEW began accepting telephone operators as members. A joint organizing campaign by the IBEW and the Women's Trade Union League in the Boston area was very successful and won major concessions in 1914 and 1915.[2]

The end of the First World War brought a resurgence of union activity to Toronto and Canada. Telephone operators followed this trend, and the IBEW organized a local with seven hundred members (IBEW Local 83A) in Toronto in the summer of 1919. The "A" indicates that it belonged to the "telephone girls" section of the international union. The union applied to a board of arbitration — operated by Canadian Board of Railway Commissioners (which regulated telephone companies at that time) — which sided with the operators, ordered a wage increase, and ordered Bell to meet with the new union.

This activity, and an April 1919 strike by telephone operators of the Bell system in New England that threatened to go nationwide, prompted the Bell companies in the United States to aggressively promote company unions and fight all organizing drives.[3] Faced with similar union activity, Bell Telephone Company of Canada followed its American counterparts in setting up formalized employee associations. These company associations succeeded in destroying the IBEW telephone locals and went on to dominate the telephone industry.

This began to change in 1935. Union-friendly legislation such as the National Labor Relations Act was passed in the United States; and then in 1944, there were changes to the Wartime Labour Relations Regulations (Order in Council P.C. 1003) in Canada. Governments needed the cooperation of labour during the war, and made concessions in labour reforms to keep workers on the job.

In the first phase of labour co-optation, Bell developed joint conference committees involving elected employee representatives. The employee representatives discussed wages and working conditions, savings plans, benefits and medical supervision, toll equipment, and any other issues that impacted employee morale.

In the second phase, Bell doubled operator wages twice in 1919 and created a stock purchasing plan.[4] By 1920, the membership of IBEW local had decreased to twenty. Many operators believed that the company's welfare measures made the union unnecessary. For operators, it was wonderful to have a benevolent parental figure looking out for their interests so they would not need to exert their own personal or collective power. It was easier to trust that the company had their interests at heart. By 1921, the Telephone Operators Association had replaced the IBEW local.

Bell also set up social and recreational programs for employees in order to foster a feeling of corporate identity. The company even created a Distinguished Service Award, which allowed the operator to use the acronym DSA after her name. Many awards were given out each year to recognize acts of courage and devotion to fellow employees, the company, or the public.[5]

The position of telephone operator was one much in the public eye, and operators were often portrayed in the popular culture of the day. Radio dramas, films, and magazine fiction often represented the ghost in the machine — the disembodied voice. They celebrated the operator as ingenious, independent, and subversive — a maverick who flouts the rules and blithely transgresses social boundaries. The salient modes of this imagined operator culture include the disaster tale, the detective story, and the romantic comedy. All three genres allow the operator heroine to manipulate the tightly regulated system that seeks to control her, asserting that the operator's position afforded her opportunities of resistance, expression, and even pleasure. Telephone companies assumed that women's traditional domestic training (emulated in the Bell System's operator schools) would suit the industry's demand for automatic operator compliance. But the stories suggest that because women were also encouraged by society to be relationally oriented, they could become invested in the people they served — motivated by human interest and empathy — and therefore less amenable to company regulations. As brain stems of a communal nervous system, these heroines use the power of the switchboard to manifest their own vision of the social good.[6]

The telephone sector used this vision of the telephone operator as heroine and community servant to subvert any inclination for operators to improve their working conditions and wages and join a union. In the story *Along Came Mary* (1919), written by S. Crofoot, a union agitator,

Mary Schroder, tries to organize an operator strike during a flood but cannot overcome the women's consciences.[7]

Automated dial exchanges introduced in 1924 led to industry-wide wage cuts of 5 percent by 1926. Telephones were not yet cheap enough to be affordable for the average person, and growth was not fast enough for direct dialling on a mass scale. As the depression intensified after 1929, cancellations of service outran installations and business became dismal for phone companies.

In 1929, there were 8,367 female Traffic employees, whereas a mere five years later in 1933 there were only 4,187, just half as many. The number of telephones per switchboard operator in that time increased from 91 to 160. The number of manual telephones per operator increased from 64.2 to 77.5 and of automatic telephones per employee from 26.8 to 88.5.[8]

In 1929, telephone installers and repairmen established (no doubt with a lot of company support) the Plant Employees Association, a voluntary organization at Bell Canada.[9] It could not bargain collectively and provided few tangible benefits. After its formation, the company may have encouraged it to prevent organizing by legitimate unions, but no evidence exists of a union drive in 1929. Yet times were tough and keeping a job was more important to the company's employees than increasing wages or improving working conditions. The Depression threatened and employees tempered their demands with the need for any kind of job.

Operators who kept their jobs faced competition from other workers due to very high unemployment in the job market. Many operators were the breadwinners for their families and knew the company they worked for was not doing well. All these pressures would keep employee activism on the back burner for the decade and made keeping her job the telephone operator's top priority.

To combat loss of revenue, the phone companies engaged in an "Everybody Sell Campaign."[10] When customers did not complete their long-distance calls because there was no answer, operators would follow up with the customers the next day and ask them to try again. Now operators had to sell, as well as connect calls. Operator activism would have to wait for better days.

Any stirrings of resistance among telephone operators were quickly quelled by employee representatives. These representatives, often the natural leaders in an office, were co-opted with expense-paid trips to conferences and time off the switchboards when attending meetings with management. In a 1980 interview with Jean Roddy,[11] who was an employee representative during the years of the Second World War, the author asked whether her sympathies lay more with management or employees. She replied that her concerns were fifty-fifty; she was simply caught in the middle. As an employee representative, she had attempted to solve some of the problems faced by operators, although they could not discuss wages and benefits. She remembered achieving some improvements in cafeteria services as a result of her efforts. In 1943, the company promoted her to management, which was a typical career path for employee representatives.

Despite the job growth that followed the dismal years of the Depression and the Second World War, job security for telephone operators remained in danger. Automation of dial telephones became the dominant threat during the next phases of the occupation's history. Automation reduced the need for telephone operators and reduced the number of jobs. The possibility of job loss created enormous pressure on the operators to lie low, not take risks, and seek favoured status from managers and company officials.

Postwar Change

The Second World War brought upheaval to the Canadian labour scene. During the war, the federal government suspended provincial labour legislation. Yet increasing unionization and victories by the CCF (Co-operative Commonwealth Federation, the precursor to the New Democratic Party) during the war years led Prime Minister Mackenzie King to implement changes to the Federal Labour Code. The Wartime Labour Relations Regulations of 1944 introduced provisions for certification of unions. These regulations also included a requirement that both parties meet and bargain in good faith, instituted the prohibition of unfair labour practices, and established a labour relations board.

These new regulations prohibited companies from taking a direct interest in or any control over employee associations, including those at Bell Telephone. This was a tremendous opportunity for BTCC employees.

The success of major organizing drives in the manufacturing sector must have made Bell employees hopeful about the possibility of getting out from under the paternalism of the company.

Telephone industry employees now had the right to freely organize into collective bargaining associations. With the new labour legislation, employees at Bell could have adopted the industrial union model of the United Steelworkers and United Automobile Workers now in place in the big manufacturing plants.

Bell Canada employees had to choose whether to join established international unions, organize their own Canadian union, or change the existing joint management-employee conference format to comply with the legislation. However, Bell acted quickly to ensure that legitimate trade unions would never gain a foothold at the company. A form of company union that had collective bargaining power became the option favoured by Bell, which found employees who were willing to campaign on its behalf.

The government certified the Plant Employees Association in February 1945. The Ministry of Labour certified additional bargaining agents for Bell staff, including the Accounting Employees Association and Commercial Employees Association, in 1946.

These two clerical associations complicated bargaining relationships. They were eventually absorbed into the Plant Employees Association and the new Canadian Telephone Employees Association (CTEA) that was certified by the ministry in 1949 to represent the employees of the craft and clerical sections of the company.

Operators were not forgotten. The government certified the Traffic Employees Association (TEA), a newly configured company union, to represent telephone operators on December 5, 1945. The telephone operators wanted to keep their own organization, and Bell probably saw the benefit of a divided bargaining unit. The TEA was merely a modification of the previous system of labour relations and fostered the same sort of employee identity, company loyalty, and submission that the joint employee conferences achieved.

Every TEA member without exception has an obligation toward the future . . . an obligation toward the well-being of her co-workers, toward her employer to apply reason, efficiency, and application to her tasks — so that union strength across the bargaining table may remain untarnished.[12]

Regional differences threatened to pull apart the new organization soon after its formation. Eventually a leader emerged who was strong enough to manage regional differences and work within the company union structure.

Mary Lennox had a great deal of knowledge of unions — her father was of Scottish origin and a strong trade unionist. Her grandfather, the late Jimmy Lennox, was a boilermaker who had immigrated to Canada and served as the secretary treasurer of the Boilermakers Union in Toronto. Mary was not happy with the labour situation at Bell, and soon after being hired, angered by the lack of organization in the employee association, she decided to become involved. She was elected chairman of the western area of the TEA (Ontario).

In 1950, Mary Lennox was elected chairman of the entire TEA. She immediately ratified a new constitution and built the TEA into a viable organization. She worked within the framework of the association, despite massive company influence on the union, and she believed that by acquiescing to a no-strike agreement she could do more for telephone operators. She had a quite imperious personality and dominated the TEA until her retirement in 1978.

According to Jean Roddy,[13] for the first few years after certification, the company continued to pay expenses for association representatives to attend conferences. Membership in the association was voluntary until 1970, when the TEA won a contract with the right to a closed shop, which meant that union dues became mandatory for all operators and cafeteria staff.

Under the TEA, company management met regularly with regional union officers and representatives to update them on company plans and to answer questions. Union reps could ask questions but rarely attempted to change the course of company plans. Mostly, they helped disseminate the corporate communications plan and manage any grassroots dissent. Company plans were presented as *faits accomplis*, and union reps were conditioned to accept the proposals as inevitable. This worked to the company's advantage; TEA reps could manage resistance to change, as they were better placed than managers to hear grumbling and discontent. Grievances were rarely filed and were not encouraged by TEA reps. When problems arose, reps would try to resolve them in management-labour office meetings. The TEA and the company negotiated collective agreements easily, and labour peace continued until the 1970s.

The union claimed that its organizational structure was based on the structure of the Canadian government, i.e., representative democracy. Once elected, representatives were entitled to make any and all decisions, just like members of Parliament. There was nothing akin to party discipline, although, of course, the union leadership exerted pressure on union representatives to conform to their preferred course of action as would a prime minister administer party discipline.

For efficiency, the union's organizational structure paralleled the company structure; employee representatives reported to district chairmen, who were considered at the same level as district managers in the company. TEA staff dealt primarily with staff in the company's Labour Relations Department. Following this logic, the president of the TEA was considered to be at the same level as the president of the company. Of course, the two were enormously unequal in power, but this belief provided some comfort to union members.

Although the union structure mirrored that of the company, there was a huge difference between the two organizations in terms of bargaining power. Docile members and a no-strike agreement left the union with neither the power base nor the tools to take on the economic and political power of a monopoly corporation. Real confrontation between company and union was unlikely.

Under Lennox's leadership, the TEA occasionally won improvements in working conditions and wages. For the 1965 contract, the union negotiated the industry's first seven-and-a-half-hour day, and the TEA was the first Bell union in North America to get a special Saturday night wage differential. This contract also saw operators get triple time when working on Christmas or New Year's Day.

When pressed, the TEA would exert some of its bargaining power. During a stalemate over wages in the contract negotiations in 1963, the union requested the assistance of a conciliator for the first time. However, the company and the union resolved the issue before the union went any further and took the step of being in a legal position to strike.

Threats of raids by legitimate unions remained, and the IBEW attempted to organize the craft bargaining unit in 1964. The campaign failed when the Canada Labour Relations Board (CLRB) found that only 45 percent of craft unit members had signed membership cards. Company actions strongly contributed to the failure of the campaign. The company had to submit four different employee lists before the CLRB agreed to one. According to Menno Vorster's paper "A Study in Company Unionism, the Canadian Telephone Employees Association," the company hired twice the number of staff normally hired and pressured them to support the CTEA in the card-signing campaign. Within a year of the campaign, 1,500 CTEA members were laid off.[14]

For a few bargaining concessions, the TEA provided the company with a docile workforce that was content to be employed at Bell Telephone Company of Canada. But there are always free thinkers and the curious in any group or organization. Company unions needed to keep tabs on the questions, observations, and concerns that percolated throughout the workplace. The TEA used its channels of communication to counter any threats to the prevailing belief system.

One very interesting piece of company union propaganda was contained in a booklet entitled *Articles on the Function, Methods and Responsibilities of Unions*. The Traffic Employees Association published it on January 19, 1960, with the TEA logo, "The Voice with the Smile," prominently displayed.

In a question and answer format, the article posed and answered questions:

> **Question:** What is the forgotten truth about industrial relations?
> **Answer:** That industrial relations mean human relations.[15]

> **Question:** What is the consequence of forgetting this truth?
> **Answer** Industrial war that injures Management, Labour and the people of the nation.[16]

Question: What is the government's duty toward radical leaders?

Answer: The authority of the state should intervene to restrain these disturbers, to save the workers from their seditious acts, and to protect lawful owners from spoilation.[17]

Although propaganda like this was useful in cultivating a culture of loyalty, the primary benefit of having company unions in place for Bell was economic. Wages were kept low compared to similar jobs in other industries, and avoiding disruption to business operations from strikes saved millions of dollars and protected the reputation and brand of the company.

With the facade of a union in place, new employees, unless they came from a labour family, didn't know the difference between a real union and a company union. The company and its union together communicated certain norms: that employees should not rock the boat; that filing grievances was discouraged; and that employees should know better than to ask questions, but should do as they were told. This led to a culture of employee passivity and allowed the company to successfully co-opt any employee activism.

One of the characteristics of a company union is regular employee consultation. Meetings between labour and management can be used to communicate and manage upcoming change; at the same time, management can learn from employee representatives what key concessions or crumbs will satisfy their employees. Grievances can be aired and strategies developed to manage and defuse them, and to discredit and isolate the complainers. Bell's approach to bargaining for new collective agreements was to keep pace with industry and community wage rates but never lead. They just gave enough to maintain the social contract with employees.

The reader may ask why Bell employees put up with it so long. The answer is that almost all workers who live paycheque to paycheque are afraid of going on strike. Going on strike causes great pain and suffering to workers and their families. Workers at Bell feared it too, and company unions fostered that fear. However, the collective withdrawal of labour is the ultimate expression of the power workers have to back up their demands for improvements to wages and working conditions. And in negotiations when everything else has been tried, *real* unions back up their financial demands with strikes.

While wages at Bell kept up with those of unionized workers in contract negotiations, there was little pressure from members to take drastic action. Employees did not have to risk losing their jobs, being disciplined, or falling out of favour with company managers; and employee representatives in the TEA received various perks, such as attending conferences and getting time off. All of these factors bred complacency. But many of these factors would soon shift and create new conditions for change.

In 1970, through collective bargaining, the TEA achieved a union-shop clause that required all employees to pay dues and become members. Ensuring that all employees paid union dues was a measure designed to stabilize the TEA and stave off the threat of outside interference (outside threats always meant a raid by legitimate unions). So even though compulsory dues were vehemently opposed by management almost 100 percent of the time when there was a *real* union in place, a solvent and financially healthy TEA was in the company's best interest.

However, the times were changing in the 1970s. The service-providing industries had grown rapidly during the Second World War, and women had filled most of the jobs in them. This pattern continued in later decades: during the 1970s alone, 83 percent of labour force growth was in this sector. In 1941, a significant 40 percent of the labour force was in the service sector; by 1981 it was 65 percent. In 1982, women filled 49 percent of these jobs as compared with 23 percent of jobs in the goods-producing sector.[18]

More women were joining and remaining in the workforce than ever before. This new generation of women workers were organizing and making use of the right to strike. The seventies brought a lot of labour action, with nurses becoming more militant and strikes at manufacturing plants, including Irwin Toy Limited and Fleck Automotive. In the fifteen years between 1965 and 1980, the number of women unionists increased by 219 percent.[19]

As women stayed on the job longer, they began to take more of an interest in their work environment. The members of the TEA followed this trend; irked by mandatory membership in a weak company union, they began to demand better wages and working conditions.

Chapter 4

Setting the Stage

Beginnings of Discontent

During the 1971 contract negotiations, TEA membership showed new militancy, as the association sought wage parity with what was offered by the phone companies in the western provinces (whose wages had increased ahead of Bell employees), a better grievance process, and seniority rights. Contract negotiations began in June 1971. Rank-and-file agitation began with passing around unauthorized leaflets and initiating spontaneous work slowdowns. The union requested conciliation to resolve the impasse over wages with the company; the government appointed a conciliator but negotiations broke down on August 7. By August 13, operators had begun work slowdowns in Quebec City, Montreal and Sherbrooke.

The conciliation board failed to bring a resolution, so on October 22 operators walked out in Windsor, St. Catharines, London, Toronto, Hamilton, Ottawa, Pembroke, Sault Ste. Marie, Hawkesbury, Renfrew, Montreal, and Kingston. The next day, North Bay operators walked out, so 95 percent of the company's operators were off the job. A company-wide illegal walkout occurred over the weekend of October 23 and 24, and was more or less authorized by the union executive, as many union representatives walked out with the employees (some even using whistles to alert other employes to the start the event). But the walkout overwhelmed the resolve and resources of the union because, as it was illegal, there was no strike fund to sustain a strike of any length.

Linda Young remembers the strike:

> I started at Bell in Toronto in September 1971. I finished my three weeks of training and showed up for my 4:30 p.m. shift. There was a demonstration outside. I walked into the office and there were all these men sitting on the cord boards.
>
> The manager, Norma Guy, said, "Hang up your coat and come join us."
>
> I called my husband, and he said, "Didn't you listen to the radio? You are on strike."
>
> So I left the office and went back outside, where a policeman directed me to the union steward. We went to the Royal York Hotel for a meeting. There were all these women shouting that they were not going back to work. Mary Lennox got up to speak and the next thing we knew, we were calm and all going back to work. I think we were out for three days. In the mix-up, I still got paid for the three days.[1]

After that company-wide illegal walkout on the weekend of October 23 and 24, the union held a chaotic meeting with six hundred Toronto operators shouting "We won't go back. We won't go back." Union leaders told the striking operators that they had to return or Bell would interview every operator who had walked out. Although there was no contract or any gain, the union urged operators to go back to work by the end of the weekend, saying the conciliation report would be in their favour.

Echoing comments made by former labour minister Mackenzie King in 1907, Janice McClelland noted that Bryce Mackasey stood up in the in the House of Commons to call the strike completely illegal. He declared that it was in the best interest of industrial relations if operators returned to work.[2]

Toronto operators reluctantly returned to work, and by October 27 almost all operators were back on the job. Nevertheless, this was an important event in raising the consciousness of the union members. By walking off the job, despite not being in a legal position to do so, they had taken action instead of submitting and accepting whatever the company or union said. In today's vernacular, they became empowered. While the operators walked the picket lines, the press interviewed them, and the operators told the public exactly what their jobs were like and the pressure they felt.

In March of 1970, the labour reporter for the *Toronto Telegram* interviewed Bell operators at the Savarin Tavern on Bay Street. One of his unnamed respondents complained about her working conditions:

> You get four sick days without pay a year, and then you're through. After five years you get paid for one additional day. I was sick one day last year and he [a supervisor] called me three times to see if I was home and really sick.... You have to sit on those wicker stools all day. I go through three pairs of stockings a week. And the boards are filthy. I get dirty from here — pointing to a hand — to here pointing to an elbow.[3]

On November 9, union negotiators rejected conciliation board recommendations proposing a raise of only $19 a week over a twenty-six-month agreement. The union appointee to the conciliation board was Doug Fisher, a former New Democratic Party MP; he suggested $30 a week. The union held strike meetings all over the province and voted in favour of a strike. According to notes by Janice McClelland, the president of the TEA Mary Lennox said she was considering affiliation with the Canadian Labour Congress, "as it's going to be absolutely necessary to be in the mainstream of the labour movement to combat this company."[4]

There was a lot of pent-up anger and frustration in the ranks. For a sense of the workplace, we can look at Doug Fisher's dissenting comments in the main report issued about the conciliation board meeting, chaired by Thomas O'Connor, on November 1, 1971. Fisher describes how the union bargaining committee felt about the company:

It is clear to me that the bargaining committee of the union distrusts the company, its policies, and the officers with whom it negotiates and the "line" officials with whom it deals during the term of contracts. Indeed, "distrusts" is too mild a word; "detests" is better. Good will toward the company hardly exists. When a union spokesperson refers to Bell management as "smarmy two-faced lying bastards," it is more than windy rhetoric designed for the occasion.

The TEA and most of its members, if one takes the bargaining committee seriously, believe that Bell management is mean, rotten and self-deceiving. Such beliefs may be stupid, may reflect ignorance, may reflect a frustration of the inadequately endowed. They exist. They are real. They explain, I believe, the union determination to go to the ultimate test in order to win a contract which leaves them with a decent wage and some self-respect as trade unionists....

I took from the words and attitudes of the Bell committee that the company has little respect for the executive of the TEA[,] for its bargaining, [or] for the work TEA members do. In my opinion, some of the patronizing attitude is male chauvinism, in its most blinkered and fatuous state. But more of the patronization flows from past timidity of the union and its slow maturing to responsibility. It is rare for me to meet a management so certain of its own righteousness, so proud of its record of benevolence.[5]

By saying that the TEA was partly responsible for the paternalism of its employer, Fisher recognized that the association was trailing behind its membership's desire to shift the power relationship between employees and employer. The union spokesperson's words describing Bell management were much more militant than had ever been used before in TEA print material. Union grassroots leaders may have unknowingly sent a message to their membership that they could be militant and make demands like a real union.

Fisher sought explanations for the present difficulties, and found one in Bell's wage survey, a tool developed in 1945 and used by the company to decide operators' wages. Bell would survey scores of communities to get actual wage rates that other employers paid women workers in their communities. The company would determine the average wage paid to women in the community and then set the operator wage by selecting the amount in the middle of the scale.[6]

The wage survey sample relied on data collected from nonunionized law firms, insurance companies, and banks. In those settings, women workers did not deal with the challenges of a telecommunications environment, contact productivity measurements, supervision at your elbow and demands for increased productivity, and above all, pressure to be nice, to be ladylike, and to get their count up.[7]

"The ranking must not be at the top," Fisher stated. "Why not? A Bell district manager could not face his friends at the weekly Kiwanis meeting if he was hiring women operators at the top rate in town. You think I am exaggerating? Being silly? Not a bit. This is the justification as I got it."[8]

Once the conciliation board report failed to become the basis for a settlement, the federal government assigned two of its mediators on November 17, 1971. By November 24, the two parties reached a tentative settlement. Despite the settlement, however, twelve Sudbury operators walked out the next day. On November 26 and 27, operators at Dufferin Street in Toronto (the most militant office) walked out, but most returned the following day. On December 4, a full 90 percent of the membership who voted approved the contract. The operators got a raise of $20.25 a week over a twenty-six-month contract, a little more than what the conciliation report recommended.

On November 25, 1971, Wilfred List announced the new contract in the *Globe and Mail*:

$20 Weekly Pay Raise in New Bell Contract

The increase falls short of demands for a $30 weekly increase over a two year agreement. The operators goal had been to match rates in British Columbia which will reach $134.75 on January1 for the highest paid classification. The current rate for comparable groups at Bell is $104.75.[9]

The above article ends with the statement that although operators in Ontario and Quebec had staged a wildcat walkout three weeks earlier, there had never been a legal strike in the TEA's twenty-six-year history. The walkout precipitated a new decade of discontent within the membership of the Traffic Employees Association. However, immediately after the walkout, Bell came down hard to prevent further eruptions of militancy. The company forced everyone who had participated in the walkouts to sign a document promising that they would never go on strike again! This instilled such fear in operators and cafeteria staff that people only spoke of the strike in whispers, while those who hadn't participated would point to those who had and say, "See what happens if you try to fight back!" This action on the company's part was similar to what the union movement called a "yellow dog clause" in an employment agreement. It could even be a verbal oath taken upon hiring that the employee would not join a union; if they did, they agreed to forfeit their employment. This form of union busting was outlawed in the United States and Canada in the 1930s, but other versions still emerged from time to time.

Operators did not forget that they had stood their ground and fought back for once. In the strike of 1980, it became an important subject of conversation for those who had walked out in 1971. They looked back on the earlier walkout as a step in the right direction and preparation for more militancy, even though many of them feared that the paper they had signed would come back to haunt them.

* * *

The next few years after the walkout were relatively calm; the union made only token gestures of standing up to Ma Bell and easily fell back into submission. In 1974, on the one hundredth anniversary of the invention of the telephone, the association celebrated the occasion with an article in its magazine, *Belle Femme*, chronicling the love affair of Alexander Graham Bell and Mable Hubbard Bell:

Now, gentlemen of Bell Canada, we've told the Bell Centennial story our way. It is our wish that the great capacity for love and concern for people demonstrated in the lives of Mabel Hubbard and Alexander Graham Bell may flourish during the next century in the corporation his invention spawned.[10]

This pandering to women's attraction to romance novels was demeaning to the female membership. Begging for love and understanding never put food on anybody's plate, and operators received very little love and understanding in their day-to-day work. Indeed, tales of romance never prevented Bell managers from applying disciplinary measures in a very arbitrary manner.

Notices of discipline from 1973 to 1979 included the following cases:

- Operator received five weeks' suspension until she complied with a management directive;
- Operator received four months' probation for being absent eight days in one year;
- Operator placed on probation for three months for having an irresponsible attitude toward seeking medical attention.[11]

What is most peculiar is that all these operators worked in the same office in Toronto. The office manager should have garnered the attention of the union with a flood of grievances, but no record exists that the union filed any.

The president of the TEA was always up to the challenge of propagating the message that labour relations worked so well at Bell that it was worthy of a being designated a model for the entire world: "Now we believe we are entering into a new era of labour relations, one in which Canada, and Bell Canada in particular, has an opportunity to lead the world. I think a good name for this era would be integrated Labour/Technology/Management Relations."[12]

The association tried to keep up with the issues of the day. As a female-dominated association, you would think the women's movement was a natural fit for articles in TEA publications and union education material. And yet we find the union supporting perks like this: "We had matrons. Filomena was ours. She would press handkerchiefs or make tea. She was there until the eighties. Her position reinforced the mentality of operators being a lady, the image of us wearing white gloves."[13]

The most ridiculous example of pretending the union was a mouthpiece for women's rights — while at the same time keeping its members passive — is found in an article published in the Spring 1974 edition of *Belle Femme*. The article advocated for operators to file grievances when men were promoted over women. This might seem like an admirable comment, yet the number of men in the bargaining unit was less than one percent. In 1975, the union claimed only eleven men in the bargaining unit, and they were employed primarily as skilled cooks in the cafeterias. The column space would have been better used to urge operators to file grievances about their working conditions.

One issue that caught the union's attention in 1974 was the threat of losing free taxi transportation home after late-night shifts. The provincial government wanted to repeal legislation that made it mandatory for companies to send their female employees home in cabs if their shifts ended between the hours of midnight and 6 a.m. On March 25, 1974, the union sent out a letter to its membership exhorting them to protest the repeal with their members of Parliament. The issue received press coverage in an article in the *Toronto Star* on March 28.[14] It was rare for an operator to finish a shift before 6 a.m., but the TEA milked the issue at no cost to its relationship with the company. Just getting press coverage could be seen as positive by the membership as it would look like the union was an advocate for their interests even though the issue had little impact on their working conditions.

* * *

A November 6, 1974 newsletter began with the announcement that on December 5, the association's name would change from the Telephone Employees Association to the Communications Union of Canada. December 5 was the anniversary of the founding of the TEA in 1945. The newsletter also addressed administrative issues with the employer, such as paycheques, scheduling, instructions for buying company stock, and explanations for why there was no billing on local mobile calls. The only item that spoke to improving the well-being of the operators rather than the company was that bargaining for a cost-of-living increase would begin soon.

Despite the name change it was still a company union. Bell employees were beginning to see the company unions as impotent and working on behalf of the company. In 1974, dissatisfied craftsmen and clerical workers in Ontario represented by the Canadian Telephone Employees Association started a grassroots group that became known as Exodus. A similar group formed in Quebec called Bloc Action. Their mission was to find a real trade union for the CTEA membership. These Bell workers were starting to understand that the no-strike policy of the CTEA lacked the power necessary to offset Bell's new initiatives for worker productivity and financial belt-tightening. Wanting to make a move to a legitimate union, these groups shopped around to find the best option in terms of union representation for the CTEA membership.

Both groups chose the Communications Workers of Canada (CWC), which was a small union of approximately five thousand members that represented employees from Saskatchewan Telecommunications (also known as SaskTel) and Northern Telecom, because it was Canadian and had a democratic structure and a good track record. Also, they knew Bell workers would become the majority in the CWC.

Fred Pomeroy recalls the campaign:

> Bell Canada craft and clerical was one of the biggest card-signing campaigns ever. There were twenty-eight thousand craft and clerical employees to sign up. We were all over the province organizing. One of the biggest selling points we had was that we said to those Bell Canada employees that you are going to be the dominant force in our union. We had expertise in negotiating contracts as demonstrated by the collective agreements we had out west.[15]

The CWC had been the Canadian section of the Communications Workers of America (CWA) until 1972, when the Canadian membership decided to form its own autonomous union. During the second half of the twentieth century, many Canadian members of international unions, mirroring sentiment in the mainstream, became nationalistic and wanted to control local affairs, and began their own Canadian unions. This was the case for the Canadian membership of the United Automobile Workers (UAW), which seceded in 1985 to form the Canadian Auto Workers (CAW).

The split between the CWC and the CWA was quick and painless, as changes in Canadian pension legislation meant that the international union was going to have to change the way it funded pensions. The CWA was reluctant to accept these changes, so a split was an acceptable alternative.

The four-thousand-member Communications Workers of Canada held its founding convention in 1972 and elected Fred Pomeroy as president. At that time the membership was primarily based in the West at SaskTel.

Who Was Fred Pomeroy?

Fred Pomeroy was born in 1939 in Moose Jaw, Saskatchewan, at Old Wives on Old Wives Lake, formerly a First Nations camp that was just a dot on the landscape, with little more than a grain elevator and a very small grocery store. He grew up in a few locations around Saskatchewan and graduated from high school. Afterward he went to work for the telephone company, which was the government-owned SaskTel.

Fred remembers:

> Along the way, my father built a credit union. One day he had a meeting with Tommy Douglas, and I went along. We all went to the legislative cafeteria with Tommy Douglas for lunch. This was one of the highlights of my life and he was one of my heroes.
>
> The company [SaskTel] sent me to central Canada for training and Bell paid. We were fortunate. The industry was booming and was hiring lots of young employees. But we found employee compensation was always held back by the ceiling created by Bell Canada's CTEA contracts. I belonged to Local 1 of the Communications Workers of America.
>
> We [Canadian members of CWA] left the CWA in 1972. The issue we left about was a Canada Pension Plan issue. But the thought of leaving the CWA was brewing long before that. The CWA was a great union and still is today. But in the

hinterland, they tended to get ineffective characters as organizers. They had tried to organize Northern Telecom and spent lots of money but didn't get results. With a Canadian union we expected to have more influence over what happened in the Canadian telecom industry.

While working at SaskTel, I became the vice-president of the Regina Labour Council and Treasurer of the Saskatchewan Federation of Labour from 1967 to 1970. In 1967, I organized a Northern Telecom cable plant in Calgary. I knew very little and had to figure out how to organize. Being young and enthusiastic helped, but I probably made lots of mistakes.

I went on staff with the Communications Workers of America (CWA) on January 1, 1970. Soon after the Canadian section split from the CWA. I was going nowhere and thinking of moving on. One day I went out for lunch with Peter Klym. We started talking about the future, once the union left the International. We spent the afternoon talking, and by the end I had become a candidate for president of the new union. Ralph Wyatt and Peter Klym, although they were senior and I was the junior, didn't want the job, so they made me run for president. I was thirty-three.

Our goal when we went Canadian was to develop a pan-Canadian union for telephone workers. We thought it would take a few years. At that point we were a Canadian telecommunications union with locals at Northern Telecom and SaskTel in B.C. and Saskatchewan, and locals at Northern Telephone in northern Ontario and Quebec. British Columbia union members were the highest paid. Both western provinces wanted autonomy so they created a federation structure for the two provincial regions. While CWC president, I still serviced locals and while I did that, we spent time making contacts in Bell. I began servicing the Northern Telephone group in Northern Ontario and Quebec, and there was this English guy in a French area, Ted Levecque. I started working with him and gave him a heads-up that he was likely going to be pushed out. He later went to Toronto and never forgot my help. He later was working at Bell and phoned me after CTEA announced a new contract.[16] For some reason CTEA announced its new contract with Bell every Remembrance Day. Prior to the announcement, CTEA would have a meeting with local reps and squash any opposition or discontent. This fellow along with Bill Burns were somewhere in Ontario and were being ostracized from the CTEA. I started meeting with them and some others from the craft clerical group.[17]

* * *

By September 1975, a majority of plant workers had signed up. On April 28, 1976, the CWC won a certification vote and the right to bargain for Bell's plant workers — twelve thousand maintenance, repair, installation, and line workers. When the CWC left the CWA in 1972, the union had four thousand members. By 1975, when they started the craft campaign they were up to five thousand members. With the new craft and services bargaining unit of Bell Canada, the CWC had seventeen thousand members and had become a sizeable force for the company to reckon with.

Being a Canadian union gave the CWC an advantage in organizing. "Telephone workers are very nationalistic," explains Pomeroy, who became CEP president in 1995. "If you were shooting pool, it was like spotting you twenty-five points against IBEW or anybody that was an international union when you asked people to sign a card."[18]

This was a seismic event for the TEA. The association became quite apprehensive about the implications of having one of the other Bell bargaining units represented by a legitimate union affiliated with the Canadian Labour Congress. They rightly feared that operators would come in contact with the ideas and principles of trade unionism. The TEA decided to take proactive measures, and in 1975 it changed its name from the Telephone Employees Association to the Communications Union of Canada (CUC). The company union hoped that this change, and the right of members to ratify their collective agreement gained in 1971, would appease any demand for real change and confuse members about the real nature of the company association.

At the same time as it was organizing the craft bargaining unit, the CWC attempted to organize the clerical unit at Bell. This was very threatening to the CUC, and its leaders stated their opposition in an article in *Communiqué*, the new official organ of the CUC.

> We would like the Canadian Telephone Employees Association (CTEA) to have the time to take the steps to modernize its constitution, make its organization more democratic and its leadership more responsive to its members expressed needs. Then perhaps we, the CUC, could look forward to a close and mutually beneficial association with the CTEA in our negotiations.[19]

At some point during the campaign it was decided to drop the clerical campaign and concentrate on the craft. By 1976, the CUC was playing a different tune, as they began a card-signing campaign in the CTEA to form a clerical division in the CUC. Two card-signing campaigns, one after another, just served to confuse the clerical staff, and the CUC was unable to sign enough cards to make the Canadian Labour Relations Board call for a vote among CTEA members. Of course, this also served the company by defusing any real unionization of another of its bargaining units.

During the clerical organizing campaign the CUC openly confessed to its no-strike policy in an article in *Communiqué*:

> **Q.** How does the CUC feel about conciliation, conciliation boards, and strikes, etc.?
> **A.** CUC is a very responsible union and does not like the idea of strikes for several reasons:
>
> - Loss of income for our members;
> - Loss of income to the economy;
> - Causes great inconvenience to the public we are there to serve.[20]

Even though the CUC appealed to the clerical workers to join the CUC as a female-led union, most of the clerical workers saw there was little difference between the CUC and the CTEA.

CUC and CWC Merger

The vision of a pan-Canada union enticed the CWC to continue its efforts to reach out to the Bell bargaining units not yet within its fold. Hoping the CUC leadership would see the writing on the wall, the CWC arranged a number of informal discussions.

> For some time before any contact with CTEA members, I was meeting Mary Lennox and Shirley Nicholson. Both of them had come to the CWC convention in Regina, where Shirley and I had talked for hours. Merger talks weren't successful with clerical members in the CTEA, but I had two or three meetings with Mary Lennox and many talks with Shirley. Shirley always played the middle game. She hinted she would do more but Mary Lennox was holding her back. I went to observe the CUC convention. They realized that a raid was a good possibility. Unfortunately, the talks never led to anything and were probably just a stalling tactic.
>
> I had a lot of regard for Shirley Nicholson, but she was loyal to Mary Lennox. She later became a conciliation officer with the provincial government and got a good reputation for her work.
>
> Mary Lennox was another story. I knew John, her brother. He was a technician in Local 26. He was a solid guy, not looking for the spotlight, and was active in the union, whereas Mary had a huge ego. You can see this if you look up the profile of her in *Maclean's* where she claims she took on the suits at Bell. When she was alone with you, however, she could be fine.
>
> I also had talks with an advisor of sorts, Pierre Denault. During the merger talks. he tried to work out what Mary would do after. There was talk about her becoming a speaker for the Liberals.[21]

Operator Militancy Escalates

Little skirmishes erupted from time to time in Traffic offices. In 1976, there was a walkout at the Adelaide office (tenth floor) because it was infested with some sort of insect. A woman named Joan Perry also organized a right-to-pee campaign at some point. Fred Pomeroy remembers personally making contacts with operators:

> During the craft CWC campaign, while living in Kingston, Janice McClelland would show up and talk with CWC reps. The CUC was more of a union than the CTEA. The CTEA was totally run by the company. Their communications focused on congratulating the company for coming up with another wise decision. The president of CTEA was standing behind me in the bank lineup in Toronto once and never recognized me. He never showed his face during the craft and services campaign and seemed to operate as though he was above such things. So arrogant; he could not be bothered with knowing who his competition was; the CUC, on the other hand, was feisty, just like telephone operators. They made a racket. Bell had probably convinced him we couldn't win.
>
> Although Mary Lennox made lots of noise and got press portraying her as a tough broad, in reality she was a pushover. You could see this as Bell operators made the least compared to others.
>
> After organizing the craft and services I spent a lot of time in their bargaining process. From time to time I would run into Janice. Other operators kept in touch too, like the part-timer Sue [last name unknown] who would call me up asking me whether I remembered what it was like to live on a part-time wage.
>
> Janice McClelland and Ann Newman were talking to our office in Toronto. We always went a little slower in Ontario and were not as upfront. After the CUC convention the idea of joining the CWC spread almost like fire in Quebec whereas Ontario was more hesitant.[22]

Meanwhile workers across the country were under threat by anti-inflationary measures put in place by the federal government, led by Prime Minister Pierre Trudeau. Parliament passed an act in 1975 creating a new regulatory board whose mandate was to monitor and control wages and prices. Called the Anti-Inflation Board (AIB), it was composed of some two hundred members who had the power to roll back price and wage increases. Trudeau stated that the cause of inflation in Canada "is the attempt by too many people and too many groups to increase their incomes at rates faster than the increase in the nation's wealth."[23]

The AIB was to play a pivotal role in radicalizing telephone operators. Although not yet affected by an AIB ruling, some operators could see how they would be affected by the draconian legislation. In an article in *Communiqué* entitled "CUC President Speaks Out! 'I Don't Like What's Happening,'" Mary Lennox wrote of the union's newfound opposition to the anti-inflation legislation.[24] The article retracted the union's previous support of the anti-inflation program to express a new position of wholehearted opposition. She reported that she and Shirley Nicholson had spent the previous three months lobbying cabinet ministers and high-ranking civil servants in the Ministry of Labour, but had returned from these meetings frustrated and disillusioned.

Day of Protest

To organize grassroots opposition to the Anti-Inflation Board, the Canadian Labour Congress organized a day of protest to take place on October 14, 1976.

Despite vitriolic rhetoric against the AIB, the CUC had never taken part in labour movement activities. Fearing that many members would want to participate because of the threat to their wages and the mobilization of the labour movement, the union decided to take a poll among its members to see if they wanted to participate. Of course, the CUC knew full well that its members feared strikes, and suspected most would probably vote against participating in something that would lose them a day's pay and attract possible discipline from the company. Poll results showed that operators had voted 43 percent in favour of joining the day of protest and 57 percent against. Not such a passive result.

The union was off the hook and later explained its lack of support [in a report from its 1976 General Council Report]:

> Among other concerns was the fact the Communications Workers of Canada would be picketing Bell buildings and the District Leaders were concerned about the safety of their membership. The chairperson stated this possibility had been discussed with those responsible in Bell Labour Relations and it had been decided that if picket lines around Bell buildings were abusive, CUC representatives should telephone their local management officials, and those managers responsible should make arrangements for safe conduct across picket lines.[25]

It was ironic that the president of the CUC was already making arrangements to get members across picket lines when the results of the poll were announced at the same meeting. Company officials knew before senior union leaders that there would be no involvement.

The union decided not to take part, but some operators went anyway. A leaflet announced that workers in Kingston would be joining the National Day of Protest against Wage Controls. The leaflet informed readers that the CUC had voted by a small majority not to participate, and went on to say that union members had not been informed about what they were voting on. It urged people who were not working (as operators worked around the clock some might be available) to join the rally and stated that they needed to be informed about what they were voting on in the future. The leaflet ended with an invitation: "Join us in a stronger union and a more promising future," signed by concerned union members Janice McClelland and Linda South.[26]

1977 Bargaining Round Produces Little

The CUC collective agreement ended November 26, 1976. Bargaining progressed slowly during 1977. By May, there had been very little progress so the union took a strike vote to scare the company into action. There was no offer from the company for the membership to vote on, but 95.7 percent of the membership voted to strike if negotiations failed.

POINTS TO PONDER

UNION MEETING SUNDAY MARCH 13, 1977

Bell has offered us 8.4% over 2 years. That is an increase of approximately $11. - over 2 years - on the bottom rate of $135. / wk We've just come out of a three year contract, in times of high inflation, and Bell has offered us another 3 year contract. To add insult to injury, Bell has said, "NO back pay".

With an offer as unjust as this, we have no alternative, we have to show this Company that we are united and that we are seriously prepared to take action. As many of us say, we can't afford to go on strike, but with an offer like this, can we afford not to go on strike? We must all come out to the union meeting on Sunday, March 13th, at 2 p.m. at the King Edward Hotel. We must get a large strike vote.

We must vote for strike and we must also start on-the-job actions right now to let this Company know that this is no bluff, that we are serious. Possible on-the-job actions, such as grievance campaigns and/or work-to-rule will put teeth into our strike vote. And let's not forget, because of the job we do, we are in a powerful position.

It is time now to vote for strike and to back it up with action.

-Concerned Union Members:
Janice McClelland, G. Larter,
Helen McCubbin, N. Nicholls
(CUC members, Toll Unit 9)

Points to Ponder leaflet by concerned union members.

Grassroots activists supported the strike threat and distributed a leaflet called *Points to Ponder* signed by concerned union members: Janice McClelland, George Larter, Helen McCubbin, and N. Nicholls, CUC members in Toll Unit 9. The leaflet urged operators to go to the strike meeting on March 13 at 2 p.m. at the King Edward Hotel, and to vote for a strike and advocate for job action to support bargaining demands.

Another flyer, entitled *Promises; Promises* and signed by Helen McCubbin and other concerned CUC members, exhorted members to read the proposed contract before voting on it. "Except for a few minor changes, our new agreement seems so much like the old one. Is this the best our union can do for us? After six months of negotiations we were hoping for something far better." [27]

At the CUC union meeting held on March 13, 1977, grassroots activists distributed a flyer printed on yellow paper that asked operators to vote for Janice McClelland and Ann Newman on August 23 and 24:

Re: Bell's Offer

You Have A Right To Know
WHAT WE STAND FOR!

1. Complete information to all union members.
2. Monthly union meetings run in a business-like, democratic manner.
3. Quick, thorough fighting of all grievances.
4. No discrimination against anyone because of their colour, age, language, sex, or sexual orientation.
5. No discrimination against night[-]shift or part-time workers.
6. Complete protection for all in the face of TOPS.
7. Democratic control of the union by the union members.
8. In the future, one union for all Bell Canada employees.

The grassroots activities in Toronto were coalescing, had developed a platform to rally behind, and were looking toward the CWC as the future bargaining agent.

George Larter reflected on the factors that catalyzed this union campaign:

> One factor was the lack of representation. The company association was not speaking for the workers. Instead, they were acting on behalf of the company. Real union representation and the democratic principles of CWC were very appealing. Fred [Pomeroy] lived by them. The union had not much money but the principles were more powerful.
>
> I always said the beginning of the union is about money and the end of the union is about money. At the beginning of our union, operators were making less money than others in Canada. Because the unit was primarily women, upper management could exploit the female workforce. Most operators did not feel they had rights. There was a lot of pent-up anger from the disrespect shown to Bell staff; for example, the card system of asking permission to go the bathroom. There was a lot of indignity caused by that system. Only one operator at a time could leave the switchboard and the lineups led everyone to monitor everyone else's whereabouts. And if you had to go to the bathroom a lot, everyone knew.
>
> So it was also working conditions and representation. It was a time when women started to feel as though they could be treated like an equal, and women's liberation had a lot of effect on working-class women. Feminism later became about middle-class women breaking the glass ceiling, but working-class issues were part of the conversation at that time. This changed later.[28]

CUC rhetoric used the strike mandate to whip up the anxiety of the membership as well as the company. However, no strike preparations had been made, and the last hours before the strike stirred up emotions only, not action to make good on the strike threat. To the amazement of no one, the company produced a new offer minutes before a midnight strike deadline, after which the union would have been in a legal position to strike.

Ann Newman recalls, "CUC would go to the bargaining table at the last minute. Usually right before the strike deadline the company called to let the operators know we had a contract."[29]

The company offer failed to meet expectations and there was widespread opposition. To be fair, the poor terms of the contract were more the result of the Anti-Inflation Board guidelines than the performance of the CUC Bargaining Committee, but hostility to the union was growing daily.

The ratification vote was held in May; 55 percent of the membership voted in favour and 45 percent against. Because of the dissatisfaction and the close vote, many members felt the vote was fixed and asked the Labour Board to investigate irregularities in the voting procedure. Despite the announcement that there was an offer, and while they were waiting for the results of the ratification vote, Dufferin Street operators walked out on Friday, May 27. The next morning toll operators at 15 Asquith walked out, too. Operators in Montreal had already walked out.

Ann Newman remembers this walkout:

> At one point during CUC negotiations there was a walkout by operators at Asquith and Dufferin. The union didn't tell us we were in a legal position to strike. The talk was that we were going to be suspended for it, but it was legal. CUC had gotten a strike mandate. We went to vote at the Westbury Hotel. People who were still working were let off by the company so they could come, too, and vote.[30]

To stem the tide of walkouts the union told staff in other locations that the operators who had walked were a bunch of radicals and communists and that the other operators should continue to work. By Wednesday, the CUC had succeeded in talking the Asquith operators into going back to work, but the Dufferin Street operators stayed out until after the union counted the ratification votes on Friday, June 3. Being on strike for a few days released a lot of suppressed frustration but achieved nothing in terms of improvements to the settlement. The contract was signed on June 6.

The Labour Board investigated the claims of irregularities in the ratification vote but could not substantiate them.

Unsuccessful at meeting the raised expectations of its members, and unused to dealing with a bureaucratic body like the AIB, the CUC did not foresee the long-term fallout from this series of negotiations. The ramifications for the union were imminent, however, and potentially life-threatening to the organization. Having a legitimate trade union within the company, one that had achieved substantive gains in its first contract, led operators to begin to explore alternatives to continued CUC representation.

Activist groups of operators that had formed in Toronto and Montreal began looking to move to the CWC. The Montreal group called themselves Force Action and Toronto operators at Asquith called themselves Positive Action. A group also formed at Dufferin Street to pressure the CUC to respond to membership demands and counter CUC passivity in dealing with management and day-to-day-issues.

The CUC reacted in its usual way to all this discontent and grassroots activity by admonishing and trying to guilt the activists and members. They were not very skilled in the art of spin, and tried to pull attention away from the fact that they had negotiated a poor contract by making the women feel guilty for not appreciating the work of their bargaining committee. In the report from the June 21, 1977, General Council meeting CUC leadership spun the contract as a major achievement.

> The newly signed collective agreement was, in the opinion of the bargaining committee and the executive officers, one of the most progressive the union has written, containing as it does changes to many important articles which give protection to people in various areas of change.... I am sure the Bargaining Committee is deeply disappointed as they observe the selfishness with which their work has been regarded."[31]

As in the past, the CUC leadership regarded grassroots activism as a threat. Now more than ever, they saw communists and terrorists everywhere, about to whip up the membership. "We have watched wanton destruction, profanity and actual terrorist activities create an atmosphere of fear and this we cannot condone," said in the General Council report.[32]

So the CUC leadership, just to reinforce the message that militancy and grassroots reform was undesirable and subject to recriminations (and even expulsion), put forth a draft motion at their general meeting on June 21, 1977, to allow the executive to take disciplinary action against members.[33]

Motion for General Council

RESOLUTION

We the duly elected representatives of Communications Union of Canada in the Toronto Region desire that the affairs of this union be conducted in an effective, orderly and united manner at all times, in strict accordance with our Constitution and Bylaws; and out of concern for the preservation of the unity of all regions of our union, our chief source of strength in negotiations with Bell Canada, we respectfully request our District Chairperson to present the following resolution to the next General Council:

Be it resolved by this General Council, in accordance with section 3 of our Constitution, that any member, including representatives and District Chairpersons charged with conduct designed to undermine the union and its officers, or behavior detrimental to the interests and general welfare of the union, be subjected to the process of expulsion as provided in our bylaws, at the earliest possible moment after the alleged offence has been committed; and such offences under section 3 of our constitution shall be deemed to include:

a. Leading or encouraging by either their supportive acts or by their silence, any unauthorized walkout or strike at any time;
b. Supporting or encouraging by either their supportive acts or by silence, any raid on this union by any other union;
c. Willfully disobeying or failing to comply with any lawful decision or order by the union;

d.   Willfully violating the constitution and bylaws of the union;

e.   Such other offences, equally serious, that tend to bring the union into disrepute.[34]

There is no record that the motion passed. It was just appended to the minutes of the June 21 council meeting, and was presumably tabled until the next General Council meeting. It didn't need to be passed to have an effect, however. The message was clear; grassroots dissent was not to be tolerated.

Emergence of Grassroots Leadership

The usual summer lull hardly happened at all. Grassroots activists decided to become CUC representatives, if they weren't already, as a way to get power and legitimacy for future struggles. Grassroots activism was in full swing in Montreal. Michelle Brouillette was a CUC district chairman in Montreal. She led a campaign similar to the Exodus campaign that had happened with the craft unit a couple of years earlier. The Montreal operators took to wearing buttons with the message It's Time to Move.

Meanwhile in Toronto, grassroots activists Janice McClelland, Dorothy Fernando, and Diane Ward ran for local union officer positions in the Manulife office. Their election pamphlets urged their colleagues to elect a slate of strong union leaders who promised to represent the membership and to not be sweet-talked by management. They also promised to work with other grassroots activists like Ann Newman and Shirley Monaghan at Main Square Toll Unit 13. One pamphlet stated that the slate supported a CWC organizing campaign. The vote was held on August 23 and 24; runoff elections were held August 28 and 29. The slate was successful, and the election of these activists signalled that regular CUC members were getting ready for change.

Ann Newman recalls her early days with the union:

> I started at 15 Asquith Toll Unit 9. I used to say I was not interested [in union affairs]. I was turned off the CUC because talking to the CUC was like to talking to management.

The first grievance I filed had to do with scheduling. I filed it with the CUC steward. The next day three managers were waiting for me in the conference room and they interrogated me about why I filed a grievance. I learned I could not trust the union. That's why I was so antagonistic when Janice started talking to me about organizing. She was at Asquith and had started talking up moving to CWC. A lot of people thought she had come to organize for CWC.

I was a CUC steward for a bit. The CUC were not very nice to us. We got branded as shit-disturbers.[35]

Who Was Janice McClelland and Why Was She Fired?

Janice McClelland was already known as an activist. She was fired in Kingston, fought to get her job back, and then decided to move to Toronto in November 1976.

In 1975, Fred Pomeroy sent a letter to Ray Van Eenooghe, McClelland's boyfriend at that time, saying he heard Ray's girlfriend was a service advisor in Kingston. Pomeroy said the CWC was having a meeting in Kingston on May 3 (a meeting for craft employees); he enclosed some leaflets for McClelland to pass around at Kingston work locations.[36] Van Eenooghe lived in Toronto and was active in the United Food and Commercial Workers. Although Pomeroy and the CWC were in formal talks with the CUC, they were fishing for contacts in the Traffic bargaining unit for if and when they would mount a campaign in the future.

Many operators emerged as leaders in this campaign, but McClelland emerged as the leader of the Toronto organizing campaign and later became its first local president. A soft-spoken, petite blond woman then in her late twenties, she was politically astute and doggedly determined. She recalls:

In the spring of 1973, after finishing four years at York University in Toronto, I was worn out studying and decided it was time to get a permanent job rather than go on to teachers college. I had worked at Bell during the summers as a directory assistance operator in Sault Ste. Marie and as a PBX (switchboard) instructor in London. That prior experience was helpful in obtaining a job as a service advisor for Bell in Kingston. This job was considered a first-level management position (although no one reported to you). It involved training switchboard operators in companies and institutions, and helping those companies assess the service provided by their Bell switchboards and systems. One day, while working in this position, my direct manager said to me, "Your shoes are inappropriate, your clothes are inappropriate, and your hair is inappropriate." I managed to look "more appropriate" as required. However, fitting this image and selling Bell every day was not what my heart was telling me to do. When I was transferred to be a manager in the Kingston operator services office (a position that I viewed as more of a "traffic cop" position), I took advantage of the opportunity and asked to go back to the board as an operator. The move back to the board was approved by the upper level manager, who thought that the job of telephone operator suited women very well!

So in May 1975 I became a long-distance operator in Kingston, a position that offered the protection of a union, albeit a company union.

On a shift during the weekend of July 1st in 1975, I was assigned to straight CAMA, [Centralized Automatic Message Accounting], which meant that I had to ask customers (who did not yet have automatic number identification) who were dialling long-distance, "Your number please," and then quickly key in their seven-digit number so their long-distance call would go through. As compared to completing long-distance calls, which required more operator involvement, this was a very boring task. To relieve the boredom, operators would spell each other off. One day after trading off CAMA job tasks, I was reprimanded. Within two weeks I was fired for alleged incompetence. I had at least four years of seniority and I knew I wasn't a total screw-up.

I then grieved my firing with the union. Recognizing that the CUC was more a company union than a real union, I organized a protest about my firing outside the Bell office, hoping to bolster the union's desire to fight my case. (One thing that I learned from this protest [the many women who called me or joined the protest] was how many operators had been unjustly fired in Kingston before me.)

Vice-President Shirley Nicholson of the CUC came to Kingston and interviewed me in a hotel room under a bright light. It really felt as if I were being interrogated. However, the union did get my job back. A small suspension remained on my record.

Within ten weeks of my dismissal, I had my job back. I learned from my co-workers that, in an attempt to discredit me, the company had told false stories about me while I was gone. For example, they said that I had held a meeting in the Bell cafeteria about abortion. It was good to be back at work, although it was not easy to re-establish relationships in an environment that the company had done its best to poison. I asked for a transfer to Toronto, where my boyfriend at the time was living. Management in Kingston did not appreciate anyone who questioned authority, no matter what the reason. In November 1976, the company granted my transfer to Toll Unit 9 on Asquith Avenue in Toronto.

While I was still in Kingston, craft workers (technicians) were organizing into the Communications Workers of Canada. I had met some of the rank-and-file organizers in Kingston before I was fired. At that point I thought that organizing into the CWC would be good for the craft unit. At that time the technicians were in a milquetoast company union called the CTEA, and they did not even have the right as individuals to vote on their own collective agreement — the district chairmen voted for them. The CWC would give them the strength and expertise of a real union.

The campaign to organize the Bell technicians across Ontario and Quebec into CWC was successful. In April 1976, a majority of the twelve thousand Bell technicians voted for CWC representation. Later in 1976, Glen Dundas, a senior technician from CWC Local 26 in Toronto, contacted me at my home in Toronto to see if I was interested in helping to organize the operators into CWC. I told Glen that it made sense to me to have as many Bell employees as possible within the same union — more bargaining strength.

Glen Dundas may have passed on my telephone number. After the legal walkouts of operators over contract negotiations on the weekend of May 24 in 1977, I received a telephone call at home from a very pleasant woman in Montreal, Claudette Doyon, who was an operator. She told me that operators in Quebec had signed petitions while they were on the picket lines saying that they wanted to join the CWC with the technicians. She thought that Ontario operators should do so as well. I replied that there was a different situation here in Ontario. Operators didn't talk much to the technical staff. The technicians had run a rank-and-file campaign called Exodus and had assessed their options for joining a real union. But nothing similar was happening with operators.

I wanted to help myself and all operators improve our lot, so it was important to think tactically and strategically. You might have goals, but you also have to deal with reality. I had to get others involved. I remember talking to Ann Newman at the beginning.... I had to learn to tailor my approach and not to give up on someone. It didn't take too long before Ann Newman, George Larter, and I were willing to take leadership in order to improve the working conditions for the operators, and to also help move forward the cause for joining with a real union, the CWC. Our co-workers supported us (no doubt due to the leadership and solidarity that we showed on the May 1977 picket lines) and we were elected as CUC union reps within the structure of the CUC in September 1977.[37]

From then on, McClelland devoted most of her spare time to getting legitimate union representation for Bell telephone operators and dining service employees. Readers will meet other grassroots and union leaders as the story of the campaign and strike evolves.

Technological Change: TOPS

The recurrent theme of the technological change that perennially threatened the job security of telephone operators reared its head once again in the early eighties.

Writing in 1982, Marion Pollock in "Under Attack: Women, Unions and Microtechnology" prophesied:

> If the present trends continue, however, the computer age may become the decade of despair, as employer-introduced computers in the workplace drastically change women's lives. One major aspect of this transformation will be a displacement of women from the workforce. Other probable effects include deskilling, an increase in monitoring by supervisors, more shift and part-time work, increased isolation, and a growing gap between men's and women's wages.[38]

The company introduced the Traffic Operator Position System (TOPS) into Toronto long-distance offices early in 1978. The system would eventually replace the old plug-in long-distance switchboards throughout the company. While this affected primarily long-distance operators, an automated system for directory assistance operators was in the planning stages.

CUC union representatives had been first informed of the upcoming changes in labour-management meetings. A booklet called *TOPS and You* was distributed in early 1977. A second, *More about Tops and You*, was distributed in July 1977, informing long-distance operators about this momentous change to their work:

> The customer with TOPS available can dial directly to [twenty-seven] countries from homes and offices as well as coin boxes, restaurants, hotels and motels.... For the

operator it represents the end of the plug-in system. Replacing it is a comfortable chair, more space, a modern keyboard and TV-type video units. What does the operator do? As always, help the customer.[39]

As much as their union representation frustrated some operators, much more threatening was the change coming to the work itself. Although they felt they were underpaid, telephone operators experienced a certain amount of camaraderie on the job. As they faced the toll switchboard sitting shoulder to shoulder, they could converse when there were no calls. Although Directory Assistance offices were configured differently, there were always lulls in the call traffic that allowed some fraternizing. Computerization threatened to change all that with a different type of work station, closer monitoring, and quicker call times called "average work time benchmarks" (AWTs).

The booklet *More about Tops and You* informed the operators that TOPS in Toronto was less than a year away. It went on to provide an update on the progress of the system's implementation and preview the new operator chair (historically the source of pain in the operators' work life). This booklet identified the office openings and closings that would result from this new technology and system. It specified how many operators would be required after implementation, how the company would place staff into new offices, and how many operators would become redundant and be displaced because fewer would be needed.[40]

In 1978, when the turnover from switchboard to TOPS occurred, a major change took place, with offices opening and closing and operators placed in temporary offices across the city. Once implemented, TOPS was full of issues and defects. The "comfortable" chair tended to break and was hard on the back.

The new keyboard and video terminal produced more stress, boredom, and eye strain than the previous equipment. "More space" translated into partitions between workers that made casual communication difficult. And computerization brought even closer electronic monitoring of the time to execute a call. All in all, Pollock reported in 1983, the change produced unhappy workers.

At BC Tel, for example, a computer keeps track of what every operator is doing. When one call is finished, the next one instantly appears. A "call waiting" button is always on. The machine paces the operator rather than the operator, her or himself, controlling the work flow. Each operator is expected to process at least 120 calls per hour. Operators who do not meet the company-set pace are reprimanded.[41]

The rollout of TOPS occurred over time. As word spread to those not yet integrated into the system about its problems, operators awaiting the transition experienced a high level of anxiety and frustration. Despite these problems, for those in the industry the promise of any job was still something to be held on to. As Pollock noted, "The report of the 1982 Canada Task Force on Microelectronics and Employment has forecast the possible disappearance or modification of jobs due to microelectronics. It cites the elimination of clerical positions, reductions in typing and secretarial jobs, a significant drop in the numbers of telephone operators, and a substantial cutback of bank tellers."[42]

I got caught in this technological change, too. During the winter of 1977 I was working as a part-time long-distance telephone operator at Dufferin Street when TOPS arrived. Since I was a student, my job just disappeared. They transferred me to the Special Operator Services Traffic office at Asquith Avenue; I made the move in late spring. However, during my summer vacation I worked on average only a half day a week. After living on my own for three years and attending university on my Bell wages and a little government funding, I couldn't survive on what I was now making. Over the summer, I realized I could not return to school in the fall as a full-time student.

The CUC took little action to reduce the impact of this new technology and co-operated with the company instead of mitigating its effects.

Their attitude toward technological change remained the same as always. Their position, which remained the same as in 1970, is discussed in the TEA's 25th anniversary commemoration booklet:

> But to telephone operators, automation is no stranger. They have been made aware that while automation brings concern it is a sign of progress. In a young country such as Canada, engaged in a fight for economic survival and reaching as we are to the great north, more and more sophisticated equipment will be required. The telephone operators and their associates will be training to use this equipment effectively to share in the building of Canada. Bell Canada is determined to give good service to its customers.
>
> If Canada's economy continues to expand at its present rate, there is no reason to believe Bell will require more operators than it has today.[43]

Wishful thinking like this did not change the fact that after the move to TOPS, Bell Canada would in fact need 40 percent fewer operators. Many rural locations were to be shut down completely, and operators were forced to move to keep their jobs.

> In September 1977, before TOPS was introduced, there were 1,048 toll employees in Toronto. One year later, in October 1978, there were 664 toll operators — a 37 percent reduction. Unlike northwestern Ontario, where operators lost their livelihood, in Toronto the reduction was accomplished mainly through attrition, and by transferring a minimal number of operators into clerical jobs.[44]

The realization that the company was slowly phasing out their jobs radicalized operators more than any other issue. When their union failed to put up any kind of fight, operators went looking for an avenue to channel their frustration.

Merger Talks Just a Smokescreen

Once the CWC became certified as the agent for the craft and services bargaining unit, discussions about a possible merger began between the CUC and CWC. A dance went on between the two organizations for more than three years, with the CWC trying to avoid organizing the CUC membership and the CUC trying to prevent a takeover of their organization.

But these merger talks went nowhere. Fred Pomeroy recalls the merger discussions:

> Mary became evasive when the merger was to progress. Montreal blew up as operators there got increasingly disenchanted with CUC. Quebec voted as a block on union matters, and Quebec operators became the official opposition in the union, and had some sort of walkout during the spring of 1977. There was media coverage of that walkout, and I got the names of operators that had been in the paper. I met with Michelle Brouillette and Claudette Doyon. René Roy and Marie Pinsonneault of the CWC staff were with me. We had a good discussion with them on July 7, 1977. All the sevens in the date are why I remember it so well.
>
> People were starting to agitate in Toronto. The grassroots racket in Montreal and Toronto caused them to ask me to speak at their convention about the idea of merger.[45]
>
> At the time however, the CUC could not figure out who their opposition was. Soon after, though, Shirley saw me at the airport in Montreal waiting with some Montreal operators.
>
> I gave up the idea of bringing in the CUC in peacefully.[46]

The CUC responded by pretending to their membership that they were entering into merger discussions with the CWC. At the June 21 General Council meeting of the CUC, the leadership put forth a motion to explore the possibility of a merger with CWC. To support the decision-making process, they provided the local CUC reps with worksheets to explore positive and negative factors involved in a merger. However, the worksheets identified the negative factors without the reader having to think for themselves, while framing positive factors as questions. The leadership was obviously hopeful that their decision makers would be hard-pressed to name the merits of a merger and would fall back on the negative factors. But the grassroots representatives could think for themselves and approved the merger discussion with CWC.

The CUC and the CWC met to discuss a merger on June 29, 1977. The CUC then set up a CUC-CWC study committee that carried out membership meetings during July and August across the CUC membership in Ontario and Quebec. These meetings were not well attended, so they distributed a questionnaire to members at the meeting locations. The questionnaires supposedly went to 75 percent of Ontario members and 90 percent of Quebec members. Approximately 35 percent of the members polled returned their questionnaires. The CUC found that 49 percent of its members were in favour of a merger with the CWC, even though most members knew very little about the union.

Another merger discussion meeting was held on November 29, 1977 between delegates of the CUC and the CWC. The CWC had previously provided the CUC with a set of ten principles for merger. They required that the merged organization adopt the CWC name and constitution. This demand provided the CUC with a convenient way out. Additional results of the CUC poll done the previous summer were printed in the December 1, 1977, issue of *Connection* (the CUC newsletter) and showed that a majority of CUC members were in favour of one large union for all Bell employees. However, only 2.2 percent of the CUC membership favoured a merger under the CWC name.[47]

Merger discussion meetings ended abruptly at the November 29 meeting when Mary Lennox told the CWC that they were a long way from a merger. The CUC announced they had polled their membership and that the majority of members were opposed to a merger under the terms and conditions laid down by the CWC. Additionally, the CUC put forth a demand that the CTEA be included in any merger or federation between the CUC and the CWC.

On December 1, 1977, Mary Lennox sent a letter to Fred Pomeroy thanking him for organizing the meeting and stated that "the meeting was interesting and if it accomplished nothing else, at least clarified to some extent contentious problems which have arisen between our two unions since your union was certified in 1975." She wanted input into the format of any future meetings and said she would be in touch after the next General Council meeting scheduled for February 1978.[48]

Facing up to the fact that the merger wasn't going to happen and having to report on the merger talks at the CWC convention in the spring, Fred Pomeroy wrote a letter to Mary Lennox on March 9, 1978:

> Since the formation of CWC we have had ongoing contact with you and your officers. We have attended your General Council meetings and have had you and your officers as guests at our conventions. We feel we have been through a reasonable familiarization period and we have no apprehension about joining together with CUC members....
>
> However, if the name of the organization is an obstacle to merger we are prepared to go through whatever legal complications are necessary.

Pomeroy went on to say that an annual convention was coming up in May 1978, and his members would want a report on the merger discussions. Eleven months had elapsed since the CUC's 76th General Council had passed the resolution to explore a merger with the CWC, and there was no progress. "I fervently hope," he continued, "that we will be able to report to them that meaningful progress toward a merger under terms which would be acceptable to the members of both organizations has been made."[49]

Merger discussions were just a delaying tactic for the CUC leadership, who wanted to look like they were seriously entertaining the idea while they hoped it would appease grassroots demands for reform.

In December 1977, for my Women's Studies course paper, I interviewed Mary Lennox and found her distracted. When I asked about the merger with the CWC she replied that she would join those Americans over her dead body. By Americans, she meant the CWC, which was once part of the Communications Workers of America.[50]

---

* * *

In 1977, the CUC claimed 8,500 members.[51] The May 1977 financial statement showed income from membership dues of around $200,000 a year with employee salaries of $71,000 and investments of over $400,000. Soon this membership number would decline to 7,400, and redundancies from technological change would later reduce the bargaining unit from 7,400 operators to none in 1999.

As the seventies moved along, the telephone operators at Bell Canada were always the prime target of the Bell System's version of scientific management, which timed every call as well as the time to answer a call. Operators faced increasing workplace stress, close monitoring by supervisors, and more picayune workplace rules. It was not much longer before those operators would seek dignity in their workplace.

Chapter 5

The Pre-Campaign

ANTI-INFLATION BOARD (AIB) Submission

The year 1978 came in with a whimper. On January 9, 1978, the CUC submitted an appeal to the Anti-Inflation Board. The union pleaded its case by claiming that throughout its thirty-year history there had been only one unauthorized walkout, in 1969, and one unauthorized strike, by some of its members, in 1977. They reported that the union had used dues to practise hard-nosed, fair, and responsible bargaining, but now found itself vulnerable to a union raid by the CWC: an aggressive, militant men's union that had successfully taken over Bell's craft bargaining unit in 1975.[1] The appeal asked that members' wages reflect the award given to clerical employees represented by the CTEA. It went on to complain that the AIB decision severely affected the CUC's members, and stated that dissidents were going to use the decision in the propaganda war when the raid by the CWC began. They informed the AIB in no uncertain terms, "You will be helping to destroy our union!"

In playing the role of victim, the union did not play from its strength, and in adopting that stance, it certainly didn't seem to pose any threat to the power of the Canadian government. Its requests reflected this weak position. It did not even dare ask for the award given to the craft union, but requested only what the other company union had managed to wring from the AIB.

Conditions were now ripe for change on the union representation front. Telephone operators in Toronto looking for an outlet quickly found one in the Communications Workers of Canada. They began to organize to raise awareness among telephone operators and dining service bargaining unit colleagues, and to build a foundation for later organizing efforts. Meetings of key organizers in Toronto began with an afternoon meeting on February 18, 1978, with CWC Ontario organizer Bill Howes.

Who Was Bill Howes?

Bill Howes was a native Torontonian, born June 7, 1943. He went to school at Vaughan Road Collegiate Institute, and at nineteen he started working at Northern Electric in Bramalea, Ontario.

Bill got involved with organizing for the United Electrical Workers at that plant. Shortly after, he moved into the office part of Northern Electric, which had a company association. He became active and was one of the leaders of a strike by Northern Electric office workers in 1966, the first successful strike ever at Northern.

Coming out of the strike, the association members realized they needed a legitimate union, and Howes was on the committee that interviewed all of the unions with a connection to telecom. They chose the United Auto Workers (UAW). Howes became involved in organizing with the UAW and was active in that local for several years.

Howes left Northern in 1972 and went to work with the Canadian Labour Congress (the umbrella organization for many of Canada's unions) to organize white-collar workers. He organized the first chapter of the Association of Commercial and Technical Employees (ACTE). Knowing his background in organizing telecom, the CWC asked that Howes be put on loan from the CLC for its organizing drive. The CWC eventually hired him, making him National Representative responsible for organizing in Ontario in 1974.

Howes remembers that early on he met with Janice McClelland and George Larter. The union assigned him to work with them to develop an organizing committee. His organizing strategy was to develop a committee internally first, before going public.

Bill remembers:

> People tend to go shy once a campaign goes public. We would meet after work for something to eat. The circle got bigger over time. People told their experiences. They were informal meetings where we bounced ideas back and forth and engaged in mutual problem solving. We invited people that the small organizing committee had identified as potential leaders for a campaign.
>
> On the agenda for the meeting would be updates, what was happening with technician bargaining, and the CWC. We would talk about how to organize when the time presented itself and began to lay the groundwork for the campaign. I would teach the organizers how to get information on the staffing in their offices and identify organizing targets, determine who the opposition was, and share information on identified supporters.
>
> These meetings developed the key organizers. I had to impress upon them that they needed to get names. We needed surnames to build a database of the workers in the bargaining unit. They could do this by circulating petitions, removing shift schedules from the garbage cans, and copying Christmas card lists
>
> After the campaign began we started holding coffee meetings in homes and restaurants where we could openly recruit everybody and did not have to be secretive.[2]

Usually about eight people attended the organizing meetings. The core group of organizers, Janice McClelland, Ann Newman, and George Larter, sought out colleagues who were potential leaders. McClelland remembers meeting in Nicholson's restaurant (no relations to Shirley). Bringing potential leaders to a meeting with Howes was a way to calm their fears, show them that the CWC was serious, and educate them about the labour movement and organizing. This was only the beginning of the campaign for the core group, however. They still had a massive amount of work ahead of them. If they had really known how much, they might have given up then and there.

Who Was Ann Newman?

I was born in Texas and was an only child. My father fought in World War Two and my mother worked in a plant like Rosie the Riveter. I lived with my grandmother. Then when I was around three, the family moved to Dallas and then Chicago. My father was an engineer, someone who worked on underground pipes, while my mother returned to the home and worked as a housewife after the war.

I went to school in Winnetka, Illinois. After I finished high school, I went to a teachers college and became very involved in the civil rights movement. In Chicago I met an old white guy, a French Canadian who worked on the trains. He said there was no racism in Canada. I believed him and decided to go. I got there and found there were no blacks in Toronto. There was one fellow on the news who was originally from Philadelphia. I was so happy to see a black person on TV. I lived with a Canadian family for a year. I got adjusted and then applied at Bell in 1967. When I retired I had thirty-one or thirty-two years' seniority. I ended my career on December 31st, 1999.

As long as I can remember, I had a passion for the labour movement. I am not sure how old I was at the time, but my earliest memories are of my grandfather listening to the news and in particular of John L. Lewis signing off for the United Mine Workers of America. I do believe I got my love of the trade union movement from my grandfather and my nightly dose of John L. Lewis. There was no TV in those days. My grandfather read the paper aloud each evening, thereby giving the children in the household a nightly update on the world news. My grandfather was well-informed and had a strong impact on my life.

I had relatives that were trade unionists, although I do not remember which unions they were members of. None of my relatives were passionate for labour like grandfather or me. I lived through the Jim Crow laws in the South during the war years, and I can still remember the racism that African-Americans experienced in that era. I lived with my grandparents because my father fought in the Second World War and my mother had to work in the city. My grandfather was African-American. My parents informed me when a child that he was part Native. My great grandparents had already died when I was born, so I have no memory of them. I have seen photographs of two of these grandparents, and they do seem mixed race.

However, I did not know much about unions at the time of the campaign. I had high expectations for what we could accomplish. I expected to rectify some of the injustices and working conditions, Ma Bell's paternalism, the way operators would confide their personal business to managers. It was a rule that we had to go to the Christmas party. It was so hard to go into the office the next day and face our manager who would get drunk every year.[3]

Newman and the other operator members of the organizing committee faced a daunting challenge. First they needed to know exactly who were the employees in the bargaining unit. A target for card-signing had to be set, but no one knew the exact number of operators and dining service employees. Furthermore, as the company implemented TOPS, fewer operators remained than the year before. In 1977 the CUC had claimed 8,500 members. No one knew the number in 1979.

In November 1980, Janice McClelland drafted figures for Peter Klym, the CWC Ontario vice-president, confirming that on September 22, 1977, there were 1,048 long-distance employees in Toronto. By October 4, 1978, after TOPS came in, there were 664, a 37 percent reduction.[4] The declining number of operator jobs, although not easily quantified, was obvious to the workforce and caused a great deal of anxiety for those who remained and motivated many to seek change.

Employee lists were the key intelligence documents for the future campaign. They were vital to naming targets for card-signing and tracking progress. This was similar to election campaigns, where organizers need to target and qualify voters. Address lists were even more valuable because operators could be approached at home where they would be more comfortable than in the workplace. Organizers spent much of the pre-campaign period acquiring employee lists surreptitiously. The campaign needed organizers in every office to get these documents.

Howes shared his primary organizing principle in an interview with the author:

> I hold the toss-in-a-pebble philosophy for union organizing. Toss in the pebble and the ripples work out. Start with one key organizer, and build a team you can trust. I worked with people until they were comfortable to go out and work with others. I built trust with them as I was a worker too. I had no outstanding credentials, but early on decided that unions acted in my best interest as a worker. I told people my story, that I had seen some injustices, and with a union had won some benefits.[5]

Howes put his organizing principles into action as he pulled together a grassroots team that had already started organizing in their offices within the CUC. They were now ready to join with CWC leadership and staff organizers to make never-before-seen changes in the workplace.

Bell Operators Newsletter #1

Bill Howes's diary records his first meeting with traffic and dining service activists on February 18, 1978. But before this meeting, Janice McClelland, Ann Newman, George Larter, and Christine Nugent (another operator organizer) had already organized into a grassroots reform group and sought attention by putting out *Bell Operators Newsletter #1* dated February 3, 1978. A number of the Toronto organizers had already established a relationship with Fred Pomeroy. This newsletter marked the beginning of the pre-campaign. The purpose of the newsletter was to announce that change was coming, prepare operators for it, and begin the recruitment process by grassroots organizers.

Janice McClelland relates the origin of the newsletter:

> Writing the *Bell Operators Newsletter* was a successful tactic. George Larter, Ann Newman, Helen McCubbin and I were the key writers and we ran it off on a Gestetner copy machine. We included information that we had learned from the CWC, such as operator wage rates from across the country. We focused on the rank-and-file operator point of view.
>
> The company union used its money to run a campaign against us. In imitation, they put out their own Bell operators newsletter. At first, I was upset, but then I realized that this imitation was a compliment. The very fact that they felt compelled to put out an imitation showed how effective our newsletter was. There were lots of scare tactics so we had to stay on top of our game and address the propaganda from the CUC.[6]

The newsletter opened with a message from CUC District 15 chairman Joyce Curtis, but declared at the top of the first page that the newsletter was produced and paid for by Toronto organizers.

Janice McClelland, who was the CUC rep in Toll Unit 9, wrote the first article, "AIB Rollback News." The article reported that the AIB had rolled back operator wages by 6 percent and reduced all overtime pay to time and a half instead of double time. This was infuriating, as double time had been secured in the last contract. She went on to report on a district-wide membership meeting held on December 19, 1977, that had passed a resolution: "We the members of CUC District 15 request a city-wide meeting as soon as possible with all Toronto CUC members and districts present for the purpose of discussion of the AIB rollback and what future actions are to be taken."

District Chairman Joyce Curtis reported in the next article, "CUC Wage Reopener," that on November 24 the CUC had submitted bargaining demands to the company.

Ann Newman, the CUC rep for Toll Unit 9, authored "Do I Have a Grievance??" and provided examples of grievances filed in District 15. One example was:

> An employee with 15 years of service was threatened with dismissal for mishandling her keys. A grievance was filed under Part 2 Article 1 of the collective agreement and was settled at the first step. In the grievance hearing the Assistant Manager Operator Services [AMOS] stated that they would be insane to try and fire anyone for mishandling their keys. In front of the grievor and the union rep, the AMOS tore up the statement of discipline from the employee's record and removed the incident from the "black book."

Newman explained that group grievances were often filed around scheduling issues, and policy grievances around issues that affected the office. With this article, she was educating the workforce, identifying problems that employees suffered because of unjust management decisions, problems that in the past no one would have talked about openly. By raising awareness and educating members as to their rights, she was encouraging operators to file more grievances and make use of the rights they already had. This was a threat to the status quo, as filing of grievances happened rarely.

Another article, "Bell Workers Struggle against Compulsory Overtime," was written by Christine Nugent, CUC rep for Toll Unit 7. She reported that the December 19 meeting had passed a resolution opposing compulsory overtime. Management had informed operators that they were going to use compulsory overtime if necessary during the transition to TOPS. Nugent explained how the company could avoid hiring new workers and save a lot of money by using overtime. She informed the audience about the struggles of CWC craft workers to limit overtime use by Bell.

Additional articles in that first newsletter included "Those Were the Days" by Helen McCubbin, CUC member in Toll Unit 9, talking about the operators' strike in 1907 and the Royal Commission. Christine Nugent also wrote "Seniority Rights of Operators Are Being Violated by Bell Canada." George Larter, CUC member in Toll Unit 9, made his first appearance with "CWC Wage Reopener," reporting on progress by the CWC in negotiations for the craft unit and lack of progress by the CUC in bargaining for operators, with no date set to resume negotiations.

In this first newsletter, McClelland wrote another article exploring "The Merger Question??" She said that the December 1, 1977, issue of *Communiqué* (the CUC newsletter) reported that a majority of CUC members was in favour of one large union for all Bell employees.

She went on to report on a merger discussion meeting held on November 29, 1977, between delegates of the CUC and the CWC. The CWC provided a set of ten principles for a merger, the last being that the CWC constitution and name would be adopted. After the CUC poll, when only 2.2 percent favoured a merger under the CWC name, and it looked as though that lack of support might become an impediment to moving forward, McClelland went on to argue, "What's in a name, when inflation of 9.5 percent is wiping out recent wage gains?"

This newsletter threw down the gauntlet and signalled that a battle was brewing. Grassroots organizers were critical to the success of the campaign. Staff resources within the CWC were minimal — primarily Bill Howes in Ontario and Marie Pinsonneault in Quebec. These staff organizers' first priority was to recruit and develop grassroots organizers who would undertake the bulk of the card-signing. The *Bell Operators Newsletter* was the primary communications tool of the activists. By providing a voice from the grassroots, it would complement the official union voice and enhance the official CWC campaign.

Who Was George Larter?

George Larter was born on March 15, 1950 (known as the Ides of March and the day Julius Caesar was assassinated). Larter grew up in the City of York and is still living in that West End community in

Toronto. His family was first-generation city folk from East Garafraxa, Ontario, near Orangeville. His father operated a gas station for eighteen years, and then worked for Avro, the aviation company renowned for building the Avro Arrow. The company laid him off when Prime Minister Diefenbaker cancelled the contract for that Canadian-made plane. Larter's father then worked as a mechanic for the provincial government. After his father was laid off, his mother had gone back to work as an X-ray librarian at Toronto General Hospital. Larter is proud to say he is from a working-class background. He grew up on Florence Crescent and went to Lambton Park Public School, then Runnymede Collegiate Institute.

After graduating from high school, George went to the University of Toronto to study math, physics, and chemistry. He stayed only one year, then got a degree in philosophy and dramatic arts at the University of Guelph, finishing with a general B.A.:

> I found philosophy is a game with no winners. Got involved in dramatic arts, did some training with Second City's comedy troupe. John Candy was my mentor. John then went to work on *The David Steinberg Show*, so my training ceased.
>
> While studying improv, I worked at Bell. I started working at Bell in the fall of 1976. I worked on the night shift as a telephone operator at 15 Asquith. I was operator number 9055. Then I was operator 327 in the electronic era. They had told me I had to do the night shift for a year, then I could get a transfer. After six months I was a top performer. But after a year when I asked for my transfer, the company refused. I then talked to a union rep, maybe it was Janice. I filed a grievance and won it at third stage and then went on the day shift.
>
> I started looking at the company and the union out of self-interest. Janice filled me in on the way things operated with the company union. Janice was at Asquith, too, and formed a small group called "Positive Action," which was committed to unionizing the telephone operators in Ontario and Quebec. She was getting some urging from

CWC. She started writing a newsletter which we all contributed to. Then we started meeting with CWC at restaurants. I remember the first time I met Bill Howes and Peter Klym, and maybe Fred. It was pretty impressive to have the entire leadership sitting in front of you. Soon after, they formed a larger committee.[7]

Bill Howes recorded his meetings with Toronto organizers during this early period in his diary:

March 2/78	Ontario Regional Council. CUC at 6:30 in Mayfair Room
April 18/78	5:45 Janice McClelland
April 24/78	5:45 CUC
May 18/78	5:00 & 7:30 CUC meetings
June 1/78	5:00 CUC at office
June 13/78	Janice McClelland in
June 14/78	6:00 CUC Committee
June 21/78	6:00 CUC Committee meeting
June 24/78	CUC school at 25 Cecil St.[8]
June 28/78	6:30 CUC meeting [9]

In between these formal meetings, more supporters and organizers would be identified and nurtured. They would be invited to the meetings to see how transparently the CWC operated and to be encouraged to join the campaign. From meeting once a month or so, the campaign organizers began meeting every few days. The campaign start was only days away.

CUC Turmoil

And what did the CUC do? Not much. In fact, they began fighting among themselves. An interesting piece of personal correspondence, to Mary Lennox from Diane MacDonald, Quebec vice-president of the CUC, dated May 16, 1978, demonstrates the developing internal tensions in the company union.[10]

Diane MacDonald wrote many pages chronicling a litany of issues. She cited that neither senior officer of the CUC lived where 40 percent of the membership resided — Quebec — and neither had any proficiency in French. Diane was hired in 1977 to bridge that gap, but the position apparently did not come with as much power as she needed. She wrote that when she acted to move a grievance forward to arbitration, Lennox reprimanded her and told her not to act without Lennox's approval. No guidelines existed to give direction to staff; instead they needed to get approval from either Lennox or Shirley Nicholson.

When MacDonald wanted to take grievances to arbitration, she discovered that the union had never taken a case to arbitration in Montreal. Nicholson denied MacDonald permission to take part in radio news shows. The shows would be in French and MacDonald was the only French speaker. "Miss Lennox indicated to me that my inexperience would not allow me to describe our union well or the union's attitude about negotiations to come."

MacDonald reported that she was not involved in the drafting of the new constitution and no discussion was held with any Quebec reps, even though by this time Shirley Nicholson had read a draft of the new constitution to Toronto reps. "I had meanwhile forgotten that the union did not yet belong to the members but that it was the property of Miss Lennox and Miss Nicholson. These two officers chose me to be Quebec vice-president because I had a docile air without doubt. All of that had been done with skill using the unanimity of Ontario against the division of Quebec which was helped along with accusations and gossip." She then went on to describe efforts to terminate her, but she later submitted her resignation as of June 1, 1978.

* * *

Although internal tensions continued within the CUC, the union got busy laying the foundation for the organizing campaign to come by churning out a rebuttal to the first *Bell Operators Newsletter*.

The propaganda war began with an undated leaflet with CUC letterhead.[11]

???? You've got nothing to lose????

If Communications Workers of Canada (some of them from our own ranks) tell you that you've got nothing to lose by singing a CWC raid card — DON'T YOU BELIEVE IT!

WITH A STROKE OF YOUR PEN:

1. Your fall bargaining will be stopped in its tracks — for months and months until the CLRB conducts a referendum of our members.
2. Your next pay raise can be lost for months and months. (The flyer shared timing of CWC campaign for craft and the signing of the first contract with Bell Canada 18 months later.)
3. You can lose:

   - TAXIS
   - CONSECUTIVE SATURDAY PAYMENTS
   - CONSECUTIVE SUNDAY PAYMENTS
   - TRIPLE TIME FOR CHRISTMAS AND NEW YEARS
   - DAYS OFF WITH PAY
   - AND OTHER BENEFITS

   All exclusive features of your CUC contract that have been fought won over the years.

   ONLY CUC CAN GUARANTEE THAT YOU'LL BE ABLE TO KEEP WHAT YOU'VE GOT.

   Only the CUC can guarantee you what thousands of other women in Canadian unions dream of achieving — EQUAL RIGHTS WITH MEN — EQUAL STATUS WITH MEN.

4. Your will lose your majority:
   In CUC WOMEN ARE THE MAJORITY. In CWC women will be the minority. You'll be outvoted on strike votes! You'll be outvoted on bargaining demands! You'll be outvoted — period.

DON'T SIGN ANYTHING

A formal CUC newsletter of June 8, 1978, using the union logo had some positive news to report, announcing some communities move to a higher wage zone (upzoning). On June 1, 1978, operators in Welland, Peterborough, North Bay, and London, Ontario; as well as Thetford Mines, Sorel, Saint-Jerome, and Chicoutimi, Quebec, had gone from wage zone B to A. The newsletter's congratulatory tone changed to smugness by announcing that CWC craftsmen in these areas did not get a similar increase.

Despite the good news, the union also wanted to warn its members of potential dangers that could threaten their new-found position. The following phrases are taken from the newsletter:

- Don't sign anything — it may be a CWC raid card in disguise;
- Proof — not promises promise promises;
- How CWC men bargain for traffic women;
- CWC bargaining for Saskatchewan operators gets them $20.80 a week less than BC operators;
- In the CUC women are the majority;
- Federation, affiliation, or merger;
- That was and still is our objective;
- Nothing to gain by one big union. In such an arrangement, we women would not be lost among the wolves. We would retain our status — equal to the CWC men.

* * *

Despite the early efforts of the CUC to stave off the inevitable CWC campaign, the grassroots operators were still getting the opposition message out. Ann Newman recalls her early days as an organizer:

> When I had to transfer because of TOPS coming in, Janice told me to go to Main Square because there were lots of operators in the building. I met Marg McColl there. She was dynamite. I always had a card with me. You always took

phone calls. People had questions. We had to constantly counter the CUC. There were some strong CUC people. Ev Johnson was the CUC steward for Main Square and district CUC chairperson. Just before the organizing campaign I ran against her and won the election.

You know, the company did us a favour by transitioning to the TOPS system. It helped the campaign.[12]

Profiles of disgruntled operators started to appear in grassroots media. In June 1978, an article entitled "Switchboard [o]perator" by Jen Francis appeared in *Upstream* (a feminist paper).[13] The author interviewed anonymous operators about what it was like to work for an unnamed major corporation.

Here a switchboard operator describes her physical working conditions:

Operator:

The switchboard was designed for petite women. If you are bigger then your knees hit the top of the board. Also you're very close to the two people on either side of you — close enough to bump elbows — and you can't get away because you are plugged into your board. So if the next person has been eating garlic or whistles under her breath or has any other annoying habits, you just have to put up with it. It's very claustrophobic, two people jammed on either side of you or your board in front of your face. Your nerves get worn out really quickly.

We even have to ask permission to go to the bathroom. If someone is out already, the supervisor asks her to wait until the first one comes back so that there aren't too many away from the board at one time. Also the time you spend in the bathroom is recorded and if at the end of the month you've spent too much time in the washroom, according the company's ideals [standards] you get reprimanded. So you could understand that if a call is taken by someone who has just been denied permission to use the washroom, that very basic frustration gets directed to the handiest one around, which is very often the customer.

Author:

"How would you suggest going about combatting these conditions?"

Operator:

The way things are now, it'll never happen. As long as we consent to be passive victims of the company's policies we'll never be able to do anything but gripe. We have to stop turning our frustration back on ourselves or directing them towards third parties, like the customers and direct them to where they'll do some good — against the company. But we need the unions too — that's where our strength comes from. And to have the unions fragmented the way they are plays into the hands of management. We have so much strength, if only we could get together to use it.

The toll office in the sixties and seventies.

Bell Operators Newsletter #2

The grassroots organizers were keeping a little distance from the official organizing campaign that was to start in just a few days; they launched *Bell Operators Newsletter #2* on June 28, 1978. Although this issue was produced by CUC members, there was no opening message by a CUC district chairperson. It mentioned that TOPS had come to District 15 and operators were now scattered everywhere. The newsletter also issued a thank you to the one hundred–plus operators who paid for the previous newsletter. Despite its CUC credentials, this newsletter was to help launch the CWC card-signing campaign.

The first article appealed to the economic self-interest of its readership by comparing the wages of telephone operators across Canada for 1978.

Province	Weekly Wage	$/week + or − Toronto top rate
British Columbia	$252.80	+58.51
Saskatchewan	$232.00	+37.31
Alberta	$221.62 $241.55 effective Dec. 31, 1978	+27.33 +47.26
Toronto and Montreal	$194.29	
Manitoba	$194.25 $196.10 effective Sept. 1979	-.04
Zone A (Ont and Que)	$191.21	-3.08
Newfoundland	$181.50	-12.79
New Brunswick	$180.00	-14.29
Zone B (Ont and Que)	$179.90	-14.39
Maritime Tel	$179.00	-15.29

Toronto operators working at Bell Canada could not help but notice that Sasktel operators organized by CWC were making $37 more a week.

Janice McClelland identified herself as a CUC member in Manulife Office 11 in Toronto and wrote: "One union in Bell — Strength for bargaining." It brought out into the open the fact that she and others were working to bring in the CWC to represent the operators and dining service employees.

The second article then presented the future in "Working Conditions in TOPS" by Judith Chrusoskie, CUC member at Main Square, Office 13 in Toronto. The article discussed the health effects associated with the cathode-ray tube technology used in the TOPS systems, including mental strain, visual problems, and emotional hypertension (anxiety). She also presented the work process changes that came with TOPS, including holiday assignments, with the system changing from being a voluntary one, to one where management assigned holidays.

The next article was by Michele Brouillette, CUC district chairman, District 6 in Montreal. Entitled "CUC Wage Reopener News," it began by reporting on CUC membership meetings held in Montreal on April 26 and 27. The CUC reported that there was no movement by the AIB, no progress on the wage reopener (CUC could not move forward because of AIB restrictions), and that the CUC was proposing a union dues increase. Brouillette then delivered a personal message from Montreal operators to Toronto:

> The girls in Ontario might like to also know what the operators in Quebec think about the letters we have received from the CUC. Many girls here say for years we have never received anything from this Union and now all of a sudden we get all these letters. And the letters are not even signed. The latest one is from the CUC information committee. Who's that? There's not even such an elected committee.
>
> In my office, on Belmont St. in Montreal, most of the operators are wearing buttons that say, "It's time to move — CWC". Other offices are now asking for the buttons.

The fact that Montreal operators were in cahoots with Toronto operators must have sent the CUC and the company into spasms. Traditionally, with the "language question," the two employee groups lived in a separation that mirrored that of Canada. The 1970s was the decade that gave birth to the Quebec separatist movement and the Parti Québécois, yet these anglophone and francophone working-class women were building relationships and joining together to fight one of the biggest companies in the land.

George Larter, a CUC member in the Special Operators Services Traffic (SOST) office, contributed "CWC Wins 9.41 percent Settlement in Wage Reopener." Helen McCubbin, CUC member at Main Square Office #13, wrote "Unions and Who Needs Them?" to answer the question: Who needs a union today? She replied that in Canada, we all do.

Ann Newman and Janice McClelland, in "Is Remote Monitoring Back?", reported on a consultative meeting between Bell Canada and the CUC where the company outlined the process of "non-adjacent monitoring." Monitoring was when mangers listened in on operator calls. The article ended with a warning that managers can hear conversations between operators even between calls.

The section "Supporters of This Newsletter" included the following names: Janice McClelland, Ann Newman, George Larter, Diane Ward, Joan Roberts, Barb Mercury, and Judith Chrusoskie.

I remember sitting down beside George Larter one day in the SOST office after I had finished my 3rd year at the University of Toronto (probably in May). We started chatting and I told him about what I was studying — labour history and sociology of labour. George then told me that an organizing campaign was starting right there with telephone operators and my former dining service colleagues. He told me I needed to make history, not study it. What an idea!

I was really shaken up by what George said, and the company provided me with some added motivation by cutting my hours from thirty-five per week to four. The turnover to TOPS hit me hard financially and I decided not to return to school full-time, but to join the campaign and learn first-hand about working-class struggles and what it takes to form a union. I was now involved!

CWC Support

At the CWC convention in June 1978, the union passed a motion authorizing the CWC to undertake an organizing campaign for Bell telephone operators and approved a $10 assessment for each member of the Bell craft and services locals to help fund the campaign. Bell resisted implementing this assessment. The company agreed to put the assessment on pay cheques only in February 1980, after the filing of a policy grievance.[14]

The pre-campaign consisted of several volleys across the newly demarcated battle lines drawn between the CWC and the CUC. Two Bell operator newsletters, a great article in a local feminist paper, and a core local organizing committee laid the foundation for a lightning-fast three-month card-signing campaign, though whether it would be enough to ensure success was unknown. The CUC demonstrated its strategy and messaging in an undated flyer and a June 8 newsletter, emphasizing that Bell operators would lose their status as a union dominated and led by women, as well as face delays of months for their next raises.

Would the work be enough to build a successful campaign for the CWC? Only time would tell.

Chapter 6

The CWC Card-Signing Campaign

Organizing Campaign Gets Underway

The CWC launched its organizing campaign on July 4, 1978. The union had three months to get the majority of the bargaining unit to sign an application for membership and pay a small fee. The union had very little lead time and very little groundwork had been laid, except for small groups of grassroots organizers in Toronto and Montreal. No one even knew the exact number of members of the bargaining unit. The union needed basic information on membership numbers in all the locations of telephone operators and dining service employees working in Ontario and Quebec. The campaign had to gather basic structural intelligence as well as recruit and build organizing teams in all work locations.

Fred Pomeroy, the president of the Communications Workers of Canada, was deep in preparations for bargaining for the craft local, but he fit in appearances and speeches when needed. He had a great deal of sympathy for telephone operators. He recalls the beginnings of the union's connection to the operators:

Because we were successful with the craft drive, we were more confident, and it gave us an in to the company. A number of operators were associated with technicians in some way, through marriage or family, so we could build on those ties, too. Traditionally operators did more bargaining with the company; the technicians never pushed the company.[1]

In Ontario, Bill Howes was on the job organizing full-time with Ed Seymour and still servicing some craft locals, doing his primary work of education while in between organizing for the operators' campaign. They worked out of the United Steelworkers Hall at 25 Cecil Street in downtown Toronto. A three-storey modernist brick building with a large gathering space on the basement floor, it was the focus of major activities and events for Toronto's labour movement. The CWC rented a few small offices on the third floor with one small office providing the space for organizing this campaign.

Pomeroy comments again:

> While working for the CWC, I organized a telephone answering service for doctors in West Toronto. Although eventually successful, many of the operators who worked there had issues that might have kept them from a more public type of work. Knowing this, their employer preyed upon their embarrassment, urging them to think they could not find work elsewhere. It was real exploitation and the women would be scared that the company might see they were signing cards. Those women were just wonderful, got over their fear and developed a successful union.[2]

Janice McClelland's files show her thoughts at the onset of the card-signing campaign. Notes dated June 9, 1978, identified the organizer's estimates of employees in Dining Services at 153 staff and the number of long-distance operators in TOPS offices at 715. These are numbers just for Toronto. Most telling was that there were no estimates for the Directory Assistance (DA) offices. Historically, there was little interaction between Traffic (long-distance) and DA offices even when they were in the same building. Long-distance operators in Toronto were usually the militants and DA operators were generally a more complacent group unperturbed by the job done by the CUC.

McClelland's files contain numerous handwritten notes with many updates of staff estimates. From the following quotation, you can see how much time went into gathering intelligence on bargaining unit composition.

> People would call me at the CWC office at 11 p.m. at night to ask me for a shift trade because they knew that's where they could find me during my off hours. While doing my volunteer organizing activities, I would strongly encourage people in different offices to take the outdated work schedules from the previous week from the garbage basket in order for us to collect staff names and numbers. Some were frightened.... I had one support, the use of e-time. E-time, or excused time, was unpaid time off when the calls were slow and it was available to all operators. As the campaign wore on and I took on more responsibilities, I would take as much e-time as I could get and the CWC would cover my loss of salary at my operator wage rate.[3]

Success could be achieved only if a majority of the bargaining unit members signed application cards. Without an accurate estimate of these numbers, it was difficult for the campaign leadership to set targets for the number of cards needed for a win. The company was under no obligation to provide employee lists to the labour board or the union until the union filed the application for certification. There were several large challenges for the three-month campaign to overcome: geographically dispersed locations; few connections to Directory Assistance offices; and a weaker grassroots structure in Ontario than Quebec, which had about 60 percent of the target employees.

Despite the obstacles, McClelland and her team got down to work. In one note she recorded that the card-signing campaign actually started on July 1, 1978, although the official start date was July 4. The note also stated that organizers could not use work time [but] could do their organizing work in cafeterias, lounges, washrooms, and locker rooms. There were regular organizer meetings, but little documentation remains of the informal meetings before and at the beginning of the campaign.

The campaign kicked off in Toronto with a meeting attended by a small group of operators, some of whom were also CUC union representatives like Janice McClelland, Ann Newman, and Diane Ward. Those in attendance signed their applications for membership in the CWC and paid a $2.00 government-mandated membership fee. On August 18, 1978, these new members received a personalized letter of welcome from the CWC, enclosing an official receipt for the membership fee.

Although undated, the first official media release of the campaign must have been issued in June 1978. It announced an organizing campaign targeting Bell Canada telephone operators and dining service employees. The release also announced that the organizing campaign followed repeated requests for CWC representation by a cross section of operators from Ontario and Quebec.

Local organizers were not only talking it up at their home offices but were also helping the CWC build internal support for the campaign within the craft and services unit. After all, the financial resources to organize the traffic and dining service employees would be coming from the existing CWC members. The application fee of $2.00 was not going to cover much.

Ann Newman remembers the austerity of early organizing:

> Before the campaign, we went to the CWC convention in Montreal to get a mandate from the CWC membership. We asked the Quebec operators to book us a cheap hotel. Janice McClelland, Shirley Gill, and I went in Janice's old boat of a car. Well, we only got to Newmarket before it died and then we had to take a bus. We got to this hotel in Montreal somewhere on St. Catherine Street. It was so filthy. There was vomit on the floor in a corner.... I could not stay so I got on the train and came home.[4]

Delegates to the CWC convention in May responded with a unanimous resolution to undertake a campaign. Existing members understood the value of a larger union membership, especially with the same employer. Merger talks between the CUC and CWC had broken down earlier after months of effort. A campaign was now the only way forward.

"Fred Pomeroy did everything he could to get the CUC to merge with the CWC. This is apparent from the evidence in the archives. Mary Lennox and Shirley Nicholson had little understanding of what they were up against."[5]

The media contact person on the press release was Ed Seymour, national representative of the CWC at 25 Cecil Street in Toronto.

Who Was Ed Seymour?

Ed Seymour was born in Channel-Port aux Basques, Newfoundland, on July 30, 1940. He grew up in North Sydney, Nova Scotia, during the Second World War. His father was in the merchant marine and later the Navy. As he was able to get to North Sydney more often than Newfoundland, the family settled there. Seymour left Grade 12 in 1958. Two weeks after his eighteenth birthday, on August 17, 1958, he left home to seek fame and fortune.

In the following paragraphs Seymour shares some of the key moments of his early life:

> As a magazine salesman, I travelled throughout Ontario and the Atlantic provinces. When we got to Cornwall approximately two weeks after I was hired, I was informed by my boss that my sales were inadequate, and that if they did not improve he would send me back to Sydney. I suggested that he send me to Galt [now part of Cambridge] where I had relatives. He informed me that because I was not twenty-one years of age he was responsible for my well-being and as such he had to pay my way back to where I was hired. But there was no way I was going home as a "failure" and my sales improved substantially.
>
> From that job I went into a factory — Franklin Manufacturing in Galt, Ontario. They were represented by

the International Association of Machinists & Aerospace Workers Lodge 1246. This job totally changed my life.

My first day on the job, a steward by the name of Elmer comes over and says, "If you have any problems, let me know and I will help you."

Later that day a supervisor tells me to come over and says to me to speed up on the job. Then Elmer the steward comes over and tells me to slow down. I tell them both to make up your fucking minds. The two of them got into a big argument. Elmer was not there for a week after. I thought I got him fired. I had to work twenty-two days before I could join the union. On my twenty-second day Elmer came over with union material and coaxed me to come to a union meeting.

Finally I went. I was captivated with the meeting. All these people were fighting with each other over motions and debates, but after the meeting they were buddy-buddy and playing euchre.

I operated a plastic injection moulding machine for my job. While waiting for the mould to form, I had a couple of minutes in between and would read. Max Saltzman, the NDP Member of Parliament, kept telling me to go back to school. So I went to Glenview High School and registered for Grade 13. I was married and had three kids. The only thing I passed was history. I was going to quit. I was twenty-six years old but my younger buddies convinced me to stay. I finished Grade 13, got to university, and got eleven credits in three years while working full-time.

Because I worked nights, when examination time came around I needed time off to study. Often that was refused and I would then go to see the dean of the political science department, John Wilson. He or someone else would write a glowing letter about my progress, after which I would be granted the time off. That worked until the final examinations in April 1970. We were in negotiations for a new agreement at the time and a strike was imminent. I went into the personnel manager's office, with my chief steward, Stan Stewardson (I was a steward at the time). The personnel manager listened to Stewardson's presentation on my behalf without saying a word. When Stewardson finished, the manager leaned over his desk, got right up to my face, and said, "Seymour, I don't give a f— whether you are going to university or not. You are not getting the time off to write your exams and if you want to write them, then quit."

As it turned out, on April 9, 1970, I found out that I had been hired as the Education and Publicity Director for the Textile Workers Union of America, a job I had applied for in January. The plant went on strike the next day, April 10, and the strike was not settled until January 1971. On April 11, 1970, I commenced my exams. Someone was looking out for my interests at that time. I started my new job with the Textile Workers on May 4, 1970. Regarding the back pay, that also had a story. One day when I was at work, I was on my lunch break, reading something related to one of my courses, as I usually did on my breaks. My foreman, Bob Oliver, sat down beside me and asked, "Why are you reading that? You are never going to get out of here." It was something he said often in one way or the other. On this occasion I looked him straight in the eye and said something to the effect of "I will get out of here and when I do, I will never so much as step on this property again." I never did. The plant closed, one of the early casualties of the Free Trade Agreement. As I recall I would have been fifty years old at the time it closed. I shudder to think what my prospects would have been if I were still there at the time.[6]

Seymour met Bill Howes when Howes was working with the Canadian Labour Congress. They worked together on the grape boycott led by Cesar Chavez. When Seymour was interested in leaving the Textile Workers, Howes convinced him to apply for a job with the CWC. Seymour remembers:

It was an unbelievable opportunity, as I did education work for the CWC. All these new union members — craft members who came out of CTEA — had never received any trade-union-based education. I had an allocation of a million hours of education time to make sure every union officer and every steward in Ontario would take union training courses. The union negotiated one million hours of training and Bell could not tabulate it fast enough. By the time we were done with that first round of training, stewards were submitting grievances faster than the company supervisors could figure out what to do with them. We won some major decisions in the time the company spent figuring out how to deal with real grievances.

In addition to education and publicity, I serviced four locals: Barrie, Newmarket, Orillia CWC Local 40; Owen Sound-Walkerton Local 41; Huntsville, Bracebridge, and Parry Sound Local 39; and Peterborough-Lindsay Local 29.[7]

McClelland's files include some notes in lieu of formal minutes of a CWC Traffic organizing committee meeting held on July 26, 1978. The notes record a motion by Ann Newman to ask the CWC national office to get some research on TOPS from Geneva. There were directions to phone long-distance if necessary. Calling long-distance was still costly, so this admonishment was to send the message to the CWC that the cost was worth it. The meeting participants identified and gave assignments to local organizers. The notes recorded that they were to organize coffee meetings. It was at this meeting that the organizing committee decided to publish another *Bell Operators Newsletter*.

On July 1, the *Globe and Mail* printed an article titled "One Bell Union Seeks Other's Membership." The article framed the campaign as an inter-union battle that came about from the failure of merger talks, with the aggressor being the CWC, the Canadian Labour Congress affiliate, while the independent union CUC was the victim. Shirley Nicholson of the CUC stated that the merger talks had failed because of the CWC attitude, "Here we are you lucky girls, give us your union." She went on to say the women wanted to maintain their independence, which the CWC failed to discuss.

This article outlined the respective messages and themes used by the opposing unions throughout their campaigns; the CWC offered legitimate trade union status and bargaining clout, and the CUC provided a female-dominated membership and a female-led bargaining agent. Themes and messages for both sides resonated with the female bargaining unit members, and both sides used lots of conversation and reading material to persuade converts to cross the battle lines.

Labour Movement Support

To gain credibility and spread their organizing message across Ontario, the CWC sought the support of the labour federations. On June 19, Terry Meagher, secretary-treasurer of the Ontario Federation of Labour (OFL), issued a letter to all affiliates, labour councils, and staff associations notifying them that the Communications Workers of Canada was launching an organizing campaign with Bell Canada telephone operators in Ontario and Quebec. Meagher requested that the letter be read at local union meetings and asked the members to give assistance and encouragement to Bell operators to join the CWC. Contact information for the CWC was included.[8] The OFL also developed an article called "Don't Hang Up" that was included in the OFL newspaper and mailed to all the unions in the province. The article ended with the admonishment: "Remember someone helped make it possible for you to enjoy the benefits of a union. Now you can return the favour by helping Bell Canada employees join a union."

Securing the support of local communities was important, as Bell Canada was generally seen as a benevolent employer whose employees and retirees were staunch community supporters and leaders. Managers especially often held positions of local leadership in communities. Local labour leadership was essential to offset this influence and build support for telephone operators to organize.

CWC Bulletins

Once the official campaign started, the CWC used its resources to print flyers designed to overcome fears and recruit operators and dining service staff to sign union application cards.

Janice McClelland recalls the relationship with CWC staff with fondness.

> Working with leaders and organizers of the CWC was a pleasure. Bill Howes wrote leaflets that explained things in a simple but powerful way. The CWC leaders and organizers listened to us and dealt with everyone with the utmost respect. Linda McCrorie and other secretaries in the CWC office would volunteer to come in on Saturdays (for free) and would run off leaflets for the campaign.[9]

The CWC had to work to convince operators and cafeteria staff to sign up. Except for the key organizers, every potential CWC member needed persuading. The union and leadership recognized that many Bell staff had never been exposed to different expectations and ideas for union behaviour and accountability, so the union undertook an intensive education campaign. The core tool of this mass education campaign was the CWC bulletins. CWC leaflets appeared weekly, usually printed on legal-sized paper, with a marine-blue banner heading; they were double-sided with a tear-off on the bottom asking the reader to join, help in the campaign, or ask for more information. CWC bulletins dealt with the legality of the organizing campaign, why the campaign began (failure of merger talks), advantages of joining the CWC, and what plant employees had gained by joining. The bulletins also provided status reports on the progress of the membership campaign.

Janice McClelland recalls a conflict over the CWC bulletins. "I had one very small conflict with Fred when he wrote a newsletter with very small type. I got into a discussion with Fred emphasizing that operators needed the type to be big enough to read. I even shed a tear. But that was it."[10]

The first bulletin, *Organizing Campaign Starts July 1, 1978,* announced the start of the campaign and presented the case for joining the CWC. Articles included:

1. Resolution passed at CWC convention in May in Montreal-mandate;

2. Current Traffic contract guaranteed by law;
3. Leadership and training;
4. More democratic control of your union;
5. No dues to the U.S.A.;
6. Affiliation with other unions.

The second bulletin, *Merger Talks Failed — Now the Members Must Decide*, provided a history of merger talks, telling how a merger study committee was formed by the two unions but it met only once, as the CUC wanted to include the CTEA in the merger. The CWC took this demand to mean the CUC was not interested. The CTEA was just another company union, and the bargaining agent that the craft and services unit had just left.

The third bulletin answered the readers' question, *Why Join the CWC?* In-depth answers explained that there would be greater strength in bargaining, stronger action on grievances, more efficient use of dues, better leadership and training, and more democratic control of the union. The newsletter emphasized that no dues would be sent to the United States, and that the CWC affiliated with other unions through the federations of labour and the Canadian Labour Congress.

Another full-length bulletin, *What Did Plant Workers Gain?*, identified the achievements of collective bargaining: The list was quite extensive:

1. Wage increases;
2. Retroactive pay;
3. Elimination of two wage zones;
4. Double time for overtime;
5. New shift differentials;
6. Job upgrades;
7. Stronger grievance procedure;
8. Protection against unjust discipline;
9. Increased number of union reps (stewards);
10. More effective job transfer procedure;
11. Health and safety;
12. Non-discrimination;

13. Benefit plans;
14. Improved sickness and absence benefits.

This bulletin ended with the slogan "It's time to make a move" with a tear-off to mail back to the CWC to request more information. After that, the campaign included tear-offs on most bulletins.

When there was no internal organizer or employee list, union organizers and operators from other locations would leaflet a Bell location that had operators or dining service employees. This meant being on the street between 6:00 a.m. and 6:30 a.m., but it was an effective technique to meet bargaining unit members, put out the word, sign up supporters, and develop contacts who were potential internal organizers.

Recruiting Organizers

In Toronto the early leadership and impetus to move to the CWC came from long-distance operators in locations like Adelaide, Dufferin, and Asquith. Leaders such as Ann Newman, Janice McClelland, George Larter, and Diane Ward were all long-distance operators. Directory assistance operators were historically much less militant, and for some reason the local CUC leadership, including Regional Chairman Liz Baker, were all directory assistance operators. Contacts were sparse in Directory Assistance offices, even when they were located in buildings where there were long-distance operators, such as 15 Asquith.

Bill Howes identified the qualities he looked for in a potential organizer: "Honesty. Workers have built-in bullshit radar and smell dishonesty right away and do not trust easily. Organizers need a certain amount of ability to express themselves and their ideas and a gut commitment to the notion of organizing. They need to have that spark of recognition that organizing is the right way to go."[11]

As the campaign progressed, the organizers developed more contacts in Dining Services and Directory Assistance and tailored specific CWC bulletins and articles in the *Bell Operators Newsletter* to target these groups.

CWC Bulletin # 5: Working in DA, announced that the next step in technological change for Bell operator services was Daisy, a computerized directory assistance system designed to reduce DA jobs by 25 percent. The bulletin reported that, as with the TOPS system then in its implementation phase, the new system would reduce customer contact, making the job more boring, creating more stress, and centralizing DA jobs in the big centres. *CWC Bulletin #5a,* "Dining Service and the CWC," advocated for a decent standard of living for dining services staff. The bulletin suggested they talk to caretakers and janitors and see how the CWC worked for them.

Janice McClelland recalls:

> It was really helpful to get one operator on board who would then organize office colleagues. With this kind of outreach, the 2nd time around we got our majority.
>
> Another challenge was the dining service employees. The contract made a provision for wage zoning. For instance, Kingston was in the Wage C zone where telephone operators were the lowest paid in Bell. But the lowest pay was in Dining Service. They were located mainly in large cities, in buildings with a cafeteria. We got a majority of them to sign up the first time around. Signing up with the CWC required the employee to fork over $2.00 as a sign of seriousness, as per the rules under the Canada Labour Code. Even $2.00 made a dent for them so it was tough going back to ask them for another $2.00. They would ask "What did you do with my $2.00?" I had to explain it was held in a trust fund and that the union didn't spend it and that the union could not give it back under the government rules, (because then it would appear like a loan) *and* they still had to pay another $2.00. Despite the hardship, they came through.[12]

Changing Minds

Print materials such as the newsletters and bulletins opened the door to conversations with grassroots leaders. Organizers had to create opportunities for one-on-one conversations and group discussions. These discussions could occur in the workplace on switchboards and in cafeterias if the work was slow (and there was no chance of being overheard by management or snitches). But card-signing had to take place away from the workplace.

Irene Anderson one of the operator organizers shares her recollections:

> I remember trying to convince one friend to join. I just wore her down. I just talked to people, sharing my thoughts and talk[ing]about the organization we were trying to bring in. It was a hard sell to women as the CUC was all-female and the CWC was mainly male. I argued that it was better to be part of the larger organization and not part of a union that was too close to management. Organizing involved answering questions and trying to convince them to make the decision. It was face-to-face. No Facebook then! To change someone's mind you have to appeal to their values so they can see a reason to change their behaviour.[13]

The process of conversion might be slow or very quick. Organizers often had no idea of people's backgrounds or beliefs. The most opinionated person in support of the CUC might still be willing to join the CWC if they could sign a card at home. In that case, organizers went to the potential member's home to accommodate them. Card-signing prospects could also approach an organizer after work and sign a card, or they might call the CWC office.

Another operator organizer, Laurie Cumming, describes how she recruited colleagues:

> I'd bring up hot-button issues like putting up a card to go to the bathroom (called a short) when talking with people. We started to tell the people that we don't need to do that anymore. That was such a brave act not to put up the Snoopy [short] card. It was so stressful. At break time after I went to the bathroom without putting up the card, I would tell my co-workers that I did not put up a short card and I was not disciplined. Small of acts of defiance like these fomented dissent.

We also had information sessions and coffee parties with some of the CWC staff. They were really well-versed in what companies do when you try to organize the workers. It would provide the organizers with ammunition when operators got nervous when managers started to make life difficult for us. We could counteract it. If there were people not signed up, I would approach them in private. I would feel nervous approaching the older women, but most of the time they were waiting for me to come to them. I had to shift my preconceptions.

We had dinners, too, didn't we? I remember Ann Newman's cannelloni. I still have her recipe.[14]

Some of the tightest workplaces — those where key organizers had been for years — signed up early in the campaign. That left those organizers free to concentrate on different outreach and organizing methods for the harder-to-reach.

Linda Young, an operator organizer based in Orangeville, Ontario remembers her leadership style:

I was always organizing, talking honestly to people, giving my opinions, listening to what they had to say. I would let them know if they were talking rubbish but always kept up communication. When the schedule went up, I would notice which operators got the short end of the stick and I would let them know that it was unfair. They valued the principle of seniority. I know I can influence people. People will follow me. It still astounds me.[15]

Who Was Linda Young (Wilton)?

Linda Young went by her married name, Linda Wilton, at the time of the campaign. She was born in 1946 to an unwed mother in London, England. They lived in social housing with her grandmother and uncle. She was the oldest. Her father worked twelve hours a day delivering bread and her mother worked at Nestlé in the evening. Young went to public school but was not in the top level. She explained that as a working-class kid you knew you could not pass the exam. She finished five years of high school and at sixteen got a job as a copy typist in a bank. Young remembers that her parents thought she was in the big time because she was not working in a factory. She shares her background and arrival in Canada and Bell Canada:

My first husband lived across the back from us. We had one room when we got married. Furnished housing. We moved in with his parents. There were no rental flats and you got three opportunities with the social housing provided by the local council. If you turned down the third choice then you were without housing forever. My husband was doing his apprenticeship. We could have lived in a company town. One night we found an ad for tool designers in Canada. He was twenty-three. I was twenty-two. He got a job right away. And I came over shortly after — three months later.

* * *

When I came to Canada my husband worked in Brockville. I got pregnant again and then we moved to Scarborough. I was babysitting five extra kids. Then I decided to go to work. Bell was advertising for telephone operators. I applied and went for an interview. I told them I could not work days. They trained me in the evening. That was September 1971.

I noticed when I was working at 76 Adelaide Street how the women were treated with such disrespect. I remember this single mother wanted the day shift but they would not give it to her.

In 1974 we bought a house in Orangeville and I quit my job in Toronto. And then when I was getting my phone installed, the installer told me there was a local Traffic office. Orangeville was 24/7, seven days a week so we did all shifts. Management played favouritism with the hours of work.

I didn't know we had a union until they came to the office and took me out back to have a chat. The two supervisors were the CUC union reps. I was an outsider and kept asking how they were running the joint. Bell hired me as a temporary, which meant I was not guaranteed any hours. I had to have babysitters ready for any kind of shift — half shifts, whatever they gave me. If you didn't go then you didn't get called any more. One night I was in my nightclothes, with curlers in my hair, ready for bed. They wanted me for three hours. I went. That went on for a year or two. Because I was temporary, I was not involved in the office dynamics. When I got part-time, there were issues around the hours the supervisors would give me. They seemed to give more hours to young kids. I had paid my dues getting the bad shifts. I needed the money. I thought, why should some high school student get more hours than me? We were in zone 3. The lowest. Sometimes it cost me more to go to work than I earned on the shift. I still had to go.[16]

Coffee Parties

Coffee (sometimes called tea) parties were small events held in the homes of operators or dining service employees for the staff at a particular office or location. Ann Newman recalls sending out personal invitations on the grapevine. One person in an office would tell another and you never knew who would show up. Sometimes CUC reps came, and Ann Newman remembers even a Bell manager turned up once, just to listen.

Irene Anderson recalls her coffee parties: "I probably had a number of coffee parties at my place. I remember having Bill and Ed, maybe Fred at a coffee party and the stories they told. Particularly Bill. He had walked with Cesar Chavez on the walk to Salinas. It was thrilling to hear their stories."[17]

CWC officers always attended coffee parties. A national representative or a local leader would open with a few words and then answer questions. They provided an informal atmosphere where employees could get together and feel uninhibited about asking questions. It was away from the workplace, from the prying eyes of management in particular, and promoted bonding and collegiality. Most amazingly, the president of the

CWC often attended these events; for many operators, close contact with a union president diminished a lot of their opposition.

Linda Young remembers Fred Pomeroy sharing his knowledge: "Fred Pomeroy was a big influence on me. I think he had a vision. I always remember him saying when we were just going onto VDTs [video display terminals — i.e. computer screens], "Do you know how many operators they have in all of Germany? One thousand." I knew then our days were numbered."[18]

Many of the leaders remembered one particular event, a tea party. Ann Newman recounts the event:

> It was Denise Foster's tea party. There were so many people there crowded on top of one another. Even CUC people were there, and a Bell manager. Denise lived on Secord Avenue in the East End. I organized it. I've always been good at getting people out.
>
> That's where we met Marnie Veale for the first time. Fred Pomeroy was sitting in the middle of the room. He was so relaxed. People liked him. We were lucky Fred had charisma. They loved Bill too.[19]

Janice McClelland remembered the same event:

> I remember a meeting in the living room of Denise Foster's townhouse. When I got there, the place was so packed, there were people standing outside. Fred Pomeroy sat on the floor in the living room and calmly answered questions and explained what the union could and could not do. People signed cards. Steve Karpowech, the president of the downtown Toronto craft local, Local 25, was there. (Steve almost got into a confrontation with Pierre Denault, a paid CUC hired hand, who barged in uninvited to the party.)[20]

Fred Pomeroy remembered the card-signing events and meetings too:

In Ontario we had regular meetings at our offices on Cecil Street. Janice had sessions for signing people. [He is speaking about coffee parties for card-signing in the summer of 1978.]

We had one in my new apartment on the West Mall near the subway. It had no furniture but it was easy to get to, so we asked people over anyway. The operators were quite curious as to why I had this empty apartment and wondered, "What's with this guy?"

We had semi-formal organizing meetings once a week with CWC staff and grassroots organizers where we plotted strategy. This was a practice we began with the craft organization. Then we had neighbourhood meetings close to the Traffic offices. Bill Howes would hold meetings, too.[21]

Who Was Irene Anderson?

Irene Anderson was born in Dundee, Scotland, in 1954 and came to Canada at the age of fourteen in 1968. She came to Toronto as her sister was already there. She and her mother emigrated for a better future. She went to North Toronto Collegiate Institute in Toronto. After high school she studied English for two years at Victoria College at the University of Toronto. She wanted to become a teacher but ran out of money for school.

Irene Anderson remembers going to work at Bell Canada:

I had worked two years [retail] at Simpsons and Holt Renfrew before I started at Bell when I was twenty-four or twenty-five. In 1977 I started at 50 Eglinton. The company told me I was overqualified, but I said I needed the job. I worked in Eglinton DA3, until Christmas of 1978. While an operator I worked at a number of different locations. I worked as a CAMA [centralized automatic message accounting] operator for two weeks at Asquith. [The job was to ask callers for their phone numbers.] I went crazy doing that. I went to Adelaide as a service analyst. We called Adelaide "the big house," as it looked like a prison. I transferred to the Adelaide TOPS office.

Service analyst was a quality-control position. We listened to calls and graded them on a set of criteria and sent back the reports to the offices. We all had to be trained on all the different operating functions. We also monitored central office — the functioning of equipment for the incoming networks. There were several people in the local who thought the position was quasi-management and that it was not a union job. I thought it was about giving quality to the customer. There was quite the controversy early on in Local 50. Janice Crook signed me up when I joined in 1978.[22]

Leafleting

By midsummer, organizers had gotten signatures on the easy cards and the goal became to reach out to locations where there were few or no supporters. If the campaign organizing committee could find anyone from an office or cafeteria location and they had contact information, then that person would be contacted, not only to sign a card, but also to glean intelligence and be nurtured as a local leader (just as Bill Howes described with his pebble analogy, mentioned earlier in Chapter 5). George Larter recalls, "I was up at 5 a.m. leafleting and talking. I was able to talk to people and sell ideas."[23]

Many of McClelland's files contained the copious paperwork that included continuously updated lists of contacts from the various offices around the city. Organizers would add names as they met their colleagues. Getting that first person to sign was the way into a location and more cards.

Laurie Cumming remembers how George Larter recruited her:

One thing that drove me crazy was taking a short. To go to the bathroom we had to take a Snoopy card and look out over the office to see if anyone else was out. Somebody started to talk about how stupid this was, asking why grown men and women have to do this.

Then somebody — maybe George Larter — gave me a bunch of cards to sign people up for the card campaign.

At first blush it went well, but there was a fifth of the people who were really afraid to even talk about it. People I was friendly with began to avoid me. Some women were openly hostile. They did not think it was right to be signing people up on company property. There were a few of us organizers in the office, maybe Helen Middlebrooks. Connie Graham was another organizer.[24]

Who Was Laurie Cumming?

Laurie Cumming was one of the younger organizers along with Helen Middlebrooks and the author. She was born in Toronto in 1958. Her mother was English and was from the Gaspé Peninsula and her dad was from Marathon, Ontario. They lived in Newmarket, Rexdale, and then The Beaches. Both parents worked. Her father was a credit manager for a pipe-fitting manufacturer and her mother was a secretary for Imperial Oil and then Standard Chemical. She recalls:

> At that point [the time of the campaign and strike] I had finished Grade 12. I had started Grade 13 but stopped. I started working at Bell in 1977, I think. I was eighteen. I had a couple of jobs in between. I worked on the front desk in hotels. One friend got me a job at the Sheraton Centre where she worked. She then worked at another hotel, and then went to Bell and told me to apply, too.
>
> I worked at 76 Adelaide as a long-distance telephone operator on the tenth or eleventh floor. I moved to 15 Asquith for a year or so in long-distance directory assistance.[25]

There were some work locations, however, where the organizing committee knew no one, particularly those where there were no long-distance offices. Furthermore, Bell had cafeterias in office locations where there were no Traffic offices; a few were really large cafeterias with more than twenty employees. Leafleting outside the work location when people left work was the only way to meet the potential dining service members and recruit a potential leader.

Ann Newman (black coat with placard) and Marg McColl (white coat) leafleting 393 University Avenue.

Fred Pomeroy remembers that card-signing went a little slower with telephone operators than the craft unit employees: "Operators would feel loyalties to certain organizers and would only want to sign with their closest organizer. These friendship ties made card-signing a little slower. I used to tell them just get the cards signed, it doesn't matter with who."[26]

Ed Seymour was responsible for the Orangeville office outside of Toronto and recalls his activities:

> Whenever I went to a local meeting during the campaign, I would leaflet various offices where operators worked on my way to and from the meeting. All the national reps who were not directly involved in the campaign did the same thing. In many cases we did it hoping to make the first contact with a potential supporter at that particular office.
>
> That is what occurred with Linda Young [Wilton]. On the same day I met Linda, I had a meeting at Local 40 in Barrie. Later in the day, before the meeting, I leafleted the

Barrie office. It started to pour rain. I was about to pack it in when I looked up and saw a couple of people looking out the window. I thought it was a couple of operators and I said to myself, *There is no way I am leaving now.* I was drenched.

Later, at the meeting, Bob Ascott, a CWC local executive member, came over to me and told me it was him who was looking out the window. He had taken one of the operators, a CUC supporter, over to the window and asked her "if she thought a CUC rep would do that?"[27]

Orangeville is a small town about fifty miles northwest of Toronto. It became part of the Toronto local and its organizer became part of the Toronto strike committee.

Linda Young remembers her recruitment as an organizer:

Working in Orangeville isolated us at the beginning from hearing about the campaign. There was this woman who lived in Grand Valley. We started having coffee together. We could talk about all kinds of issues. The next thing I know she asked me, "Do you want to go to a meeting?" I was clueless. I went to this meeting in Barrie. She introduced me to people. Fred Pomeroy spoke.

One day there was a guy from CWC downstairs. It was Ed Seymour. My friend almost killed him by backing up her big car into him. From then on, I was the organizer for the office.

I stepped up to the plate. I took on the challenge and signed all the operators except for three. I got them two or three at a time. At the beginning, they were terrified and did not want to be beat up by the CUC. I would pose questions to them like, "Do you think these things are right?" No one knew who had signed a card. Then I put up a note congratulating all the staff who had signed. Those three weren't on the list.

Management asked me to take it down. I replied I was sorry and that I did not know I was not supposed to post it.[28]

Dining Service Staff

Dining service employees presented another challenge. The lowest-paid staff worked in Dining Services. This workforce was primarily women, though men were also employed as cooks and dishwashers. The workforce in the cafeterias was the most diverse, with people who had immigrated from all over the world. Cafeteria service was a perk for operators and office staff. It was a leftover from the paternal approach when the company provided many on-site services, such as a matron to iron clothes.

> *As I had worked in Dining Service, I often leafleted at dining service locations. Sometimes I had worked during the summers at these locations so I might be remembered and the staff might be more likely to trust me than an operator. I was never one to miss an opportunity to expose my younger siblings to something political and dramatic. I took my fifteen-year-old sister to help me leaflet Wynford Drive, a modernist building that housed no operators but was home to a very large cafeteria. She felt like we were doing something illegal, but later in life, as a member of the [Ontario Secondary School Teachers' Federation, she realized she got a good lesson in organizing that day.*

Dining service staff did not buy into the union quickly and no one emerged to organize them. They worked steady shifts from 7 a.m. in the morning and worked hard sometimes to the point of exhaustion by the end of their shift. Operator organizers had to fill the gap. Janice McClelland remembers signing up some of the dining service staff.

One day Joan Roberts and I went up to Wynford Drive to speak with the cafeteria staff. We started talking with them during a work break and they started signing cards. When the break was over, they invited us into the kitchen and we signed more cards next to the turkey and meat-cutting machines. The manager came along so we immediately went back out to a table in the cafeteria area. The dining service employees then organized themselves and sent one worker out at a time, with her identification and money, to sign a card. The manager stopped that, too — because of course, we were not to sign cards on work time. Joan and I came back on the next break and signed the remaining dining service person in that cafeteria.[29]

Meanwhile, the CWC organizing committee put together *Bell Operators Newsletter #3*; it came out on September 5, 1978. McClelland led the reports with a scathing critique, "CUC's Presentation to the AIB or Why We Were Rolled Back." She reported that the AIB had just informed the CUC that there would be no increase for CUC members. McClelland was unforgiving of CUC's complaint to the AIB that its "decisions are being used politically as a weapon against the CUC and can be expected to play a prominent role in the propaganda that will accompany the CWC raids on our union this spring." She stuck a knife into the CUC by announcing a newsflash that the AIB had granted a raise to operators in Nova Scotia who were working for Maritime Telephone and Telegraph, bringing their top wage up to $183.00 a week. The fact that East Coast operators were making more than Ontario operators was galling and just too much to swallow.

An article by service analyst Janice Crook, "Comparisons of Wages and Working Conditions for Telephone Operators," included a great chart tracking operators' wages in major Canadian telephone companies. Up to 1974, Bell operators had always been in second place. But SaskTel had moved past Bell in 1974 when it was organized by the CWC. The article also highlighted working conditions of operators at other telecoms. For instance, in BC, day shifts were only seven hours long, with six hours for night shifts and better overtime arrangements.

Ann Newman provided a critique of CUC spending in "Where Do Our CUC Dues Go?" She discussed the high rent paid for CUC offices at 365 Bay Street, a very prestigious location for a union. She reported the rent as $2,300 a month. She then listed the salaries of union officers:

Mary Lennox at $32,000 plus expenses; Shirley Nicholson at $25,000; Helen Kyrtow at $15,000; and Barbara Morgan, financial director, at $15,000 (she was Mary Lennox's niece). In contrast, the top-paid operator was getting less than $10,000 a year.

Newman went on to announce that the CUC had hired a public relations expert, a Mr. Bob Legge, at a weekly salary of $375. She also reported that in March 1977, the CUC had hired the management consulting firm of Stevenson Kellogg to assess its organizational structure, and had also retained Pierre Denault as their latest management consultant. She additionally raised concerns about the substantive investment made by the CUC in Bell Canada as well as International Nickel Company of Canada, Hiram Walker & Sons, and Gooderham and Worts.

Newman compared CUC dues with CWC dues and pointed out that the CUC assessed their dues on premium pay, but that was not the case with CWC dues. She talked a little about how the CWC spent their dues and mentioned that the CWC had a strike fund. She refuted accusations that the CWC was an American union.

Another article, "Who Is Mr. Pierre Denault?", got right into the nitty-gritty of the work of the new CUC consultant hired to counter the CWC campaign. The author, Debbie Bernier, was an operator at SOST-Intercept — the name for the service that dealt with intercepted numbers, i.e., disconnected and changed numbers. She said that the consultant got paid $300 per week plus expenses. She reported that he was wining and dining operators, and organizing boat cruises, dinners, and such. Denault reportedly said, "We'll get together and have fun and talk." He exhorted operators to "bring your friends." The author wondered why this spending was approved by the union but they could deny a request from members for a decent meeting space to discuss amendments to the constitution.

Bernier reported that Denault was giving the operators the impression that CWC supporters would be investigated. The newsletter authors did some investigating and found that Denault had sat on the management side at the bargaining table for Uniroyal and Standard Paper Box in Montreal. This left readers asking why any union would hire a management-side specialist.

George Larter, CUC union rep, composed "The Constitutional Question." He reported that the CUC had announced it was now ready to amend its constitution and bylaws. The amendments would allow members to elect representatives, who would then elect district chairpersons, secretaries, and delegates to General Council and nominate members for vice-presidents for Ontario and Quebec.

Larter pointed out that the proposals did not include the right to dissent or to hold member meetings, whereas in the CWC each local is guaranteed the right to have a minimum number of local meetings annually. He then went into detail on the rights and organizational structure of the more democratic CWC.

The most heartwarming piece was "Notes from All over Ontario and Quebec re CWC Organizing Campaign," which included greetings and updates from Brantford, Windsor, Kitchener, Ottawa, and local offices in Toronto, Special Operators Services Traffic, Crossways, Main Square, and Manulife. The section ended with a message from Quebec: "Let us show for once in our lives what real solidarity is. Let us remove the barrier that is keeping us apart — the CUC. All together, let's join the CWC — a step towards democracy and solidarity." They signed off with "Fraternally. Your sisters in Quebec," followed by the signatures of sixteen Quebec operators and a number from Toronto.

Voices of other operators emerged, not only from Toronto, but also from around the provinces of Ontario and Quebec. Now readers could sense the momentum that was building and see point by point the case that was being made for change.[30]

As the campaign progressed over the summer of 1978, CWC members of the craft bargaining unit prepared to go on strike for their first contract. The possibility of a strike by the craft and services unit made everyone very uneasy and gave the CUC lots of ammunition to spread rumours and foster fear.

To counter CUC fear-mongering, the CWC issued some undated bulletins to develop focused answers to what might happen if the craft unit had to go on strike. Irene Anderson recalls the emotion: "People feared going on strike most of all. We tried to convince people that even though we were going to a real union, we did not have to go on strike. Ma Bell tried to teach us a lesson, but not the one she wanted to teach us. There were a lot of principal breadwinners, single moms, and single women. For single women, a strike was a big fear."[31]

One such undated bulletin, *Bargaining — the Key Issue*, compared the wages of CWC and CUC members and compared the results of bargaining by both bargaining agents. This leaflet announced that if there was a strike by CWC craft members, the CWC would not ask operators and dining service workers to respect picket lines. The bulletin ended by asking readers to compare "then vote for the union that gives you facts — not excuses."

Another undated leaflet was titled *Let's Talk about Operators Wages*. This leaflet addressed what operators in SaskTel were able to make with the CWC as their bargaining agent. It compared the top rates between SaskTel and Bell Canada and addressed the issue of cost-of-living differences — and the CUC statement that, because the provincial government owns Saskatchewan Telephone, they can afford to pay more. The brochure highlighted features of the CWC contract in Saskatchewan and ended with "It pays to belong the CWC" plus a tear-off to sign up.

The leaflet *About CWC Dues* addressed how much dues were in the CWC, who set them, how the union spent them, and the process for financial reporting to the members. Another document, on CWC letterhead but not in bulletin format, asked some questions about dues, and provided answers:

> *How much are CWC dues?*
>
> Dues are set by a vote of the members of each local union and can only be changed by a vote. Bell locals pay .8 percent of basic wages.

> *How are dues spent?*
>
> The national union's portion ($6.25)
>
> - Spent on affiliation fees
> - Office expenses itemized
> - Organizing expenses, etc.

The local union's portion:

- Itemized list of local union expenses

The document ended with: "We hope that the above has been of help in answering questions about our dues structure and how our dues are spent. Additional details are available on request from your national representative."

In a CWC bulletin entitled *The choice is yours*, the key message was stated clearly in its sub-title: *As a member of the CWC you will be better off because:*

1. You will be stronger in bargaining.
2. You will have more democratic control over your union.
3. Your dues will be used more efficiently.
4. You'll be part of a union with a proven record.

The brief leaflet concluded with the message, "It's up to you!"

Another undated bulletin, *CWC — A democratic structure*, explained how the CWC structure was better, how the locals were set up and financed, how a CWC local was different from a CUC local, and how locals communicated with each other.

Education

One of the benefits of joining the CWC as a local union leader was the access to union education. This was a big issue for many local CUC leaders; the company union provided very little education on contract interpretation and filing of grievances. The union did not believe in encouraging the filing of grievances, so education on how to do so was of little use.

Ed Seymour was responsible for education, and explained why the CWC invested in education for telephone operators and dining staff who had not yet paid one cent in dues. "We had education sessions in remote locations because it was difficult for people to leave at night. We wanted to build camaraderie and community and get people to know one another as individuals instead of trade unionists. When we had education sessions, we had social events in the evenings. We took voluntary collections from class participants (usually $5.00 each) and purchased refreshments. Eventually shop talk comes into it and it resonated with people."[32]

Ed Seymour also recalled a training session outside of Toronto:

> Don Milligan was a CWC Local 47 member from Chatham and prior to working at Bell he had studied for the priesthood. He attended one of our courses which was held in a remote location. The facility was an old farm that had kennels. It was in the Tillsonburg area.
>
> Part of the sleeping quarters were the old kennels. Like cells. Those cells triggered bad memories for Don. We were probably doing steward or officers training. Later after the strike we did arbitration and early retirement training.[33]

The French-English Issue

Prior to the CWC organizing campaign, Toronto operators had a history of some activism and militancy. Yet from the strike of 1907 to the walkout of 1977, there was almost no grassroots activism there. The seventies brought an upsurge in discontent but there was little organized opposition on which to build the CWC campaign. This was not the case in Quebec. They were raring to go to the CWC and had much more of a history of militancy. But since Quebec only held 40 percent of the bargaining unit workforce, Quebec operators knew they needed Ontario if they were to win a CWC majority. As mentioned before, Quebec and Ontario operators were in constant contact and would visit each other to show solidarity in the fight against the CUC.

Even in the midst of the Quebec separatist movement, bilingual francophone operators, most with clear separatist leanings, reached out to anglophone Ontario operators, most of whom were unilingual. Janice McClelland recalls, "As with any cause there were tensions within the movement. Looking back, it is not surprising that there were tensions between Ontario and Quebec — with two different cultures within one federal bargaining unit."[34]

Quebec operators came to Toronto on September 27, 1978, to build solidarity and drum up more cards. They developed a leaflet in letter format (shown below) and distributed it throughout Toronto offices, inviting operators to meet with their Quebec counterparts. Toronto operators met with them at the Roehampton Hotel and discovered they had more in common than previously thought.

We the operators of Quebec have been called "separatists"

The reason why, is to provoke confusion within the ranks of our fellow workers. We want a stronger union; we want solidarity with the rest of Canadian labour; we want unity with Bell employees; we need stronger ties between all workers.

THE CUC HAS ALWAYS KEPT US IN THE DARK

1. It was at the request of both parties (Bell Canada and CUC) that conciliation commissioner Dufresne suspended bargaining.
2. We have nothing to lose. We are completely protected by Canadian law when changing unions. The technicians have done what we are doing now and lost nothing. Just ask them!
3. In the first two weeks we signed over 3,300 cards; 4,000 cards is a clear majority even using the expanded list.

UNITE WITH THE NEW MAJORITY
COME AND MEET US
BE INFORMED
DEMAND YOUR RIGHT TO A VOTE
VOTE FOR UNITY

Signed: your guests from Montreal.[35]

Campaign Windup

One of the last campaign bulletins was titled *Asquith DA Has Joined the Swing to CWC*. This was a breakthrough, as the Directory Assistance offices had been solidly behind the CUC up to that point. The CWC announced that a majority of employees had signed cards at Wynford Drive Dining Services, Overlea TOPS, Oakville, and other Ontario locations. The leaflet concluded by announcing that the CWC would be applying for certification early that week. They were still urging the undecided to commit by stating that a clear majority would mean the government could order a vote without delay, and that an earlier vote would mean bargaining could be completed sooner.

Another bulletin on letter-sized paper trumpeted *CWC to Apply for Certification on Wednesday*. It announced that cards signed by midnight on Tuesday would support the application, and every card counted toward the majority needed to win. On October 4, 1978, the Communications Workers of Canada filed an application for certification for the traffic and Dining Services bargaining unit.

But before we move on to the next phase, the forthcoming chapter will document the counter-campaign waged by the CUC as it tried to protect its organization from obliteration. I will also describe a debate between the CWC and the CUC that was held on September 7, 1978. Despite the drain on resources and a growing membership with demands for information and support, the CWC never wavered from its goal.

Chapter 7

The CUC Defence

The Propaganda War

While CWC campaign organizers were developing all kinds of communication documents, including the *Bell Operator Newsletters* and CWC bulletins, the CUC mounted a counter-campaign of propaganda. The company union was slow to respond, and when they did it was often with amateurish print materials. CUC propaganda documents were often undated, fear-based missives full of commands like "Don't Sign Anything," and they were often just photocopies of handwritten documents that contained accusations.

This undated CUC flyer had CUC logos on each side of the page:

WE'RE THE FIRST

CUC... WE WERE THE FIRST UNION IN THE TELEPHONE INDUSTRY TO WIN THE SEVEN-HOUR DAY FOR TRAFFIC DEPARTMENT EMPLOYEES.

CUC... WE WERE THE FIRST UNION TO WIN CONSECUTIVE SATURDAY AND SUNDAY PREMIUM PAYMENTS.

CUC... WE WERE THE FIRST UNION TO WIN TRIPLE TIME FOR HOURS WORKED ON CHRISTMAS AND NEW YEAR'S DAY.

CUC... WE WERE THE FIRST UNION IN BELL CANADA TO WIN A DISCIPLINE CLAUSE THAT AFFORDED PROTECTION TO THE EMPLOYEE.

CUC... WE ARE THE ONLY UNION AT BELL CANADA WITH A STRONG JOB SECURITY CLAUSE.

COMMUNICATIONS UNION CANADA
FIRST NOW ... FIRST TOMORROW

Lacking ingenuity, the CUC mimicked the format of CWC bulletins and the Bell operators fact sheets. In the undated document below, it mimicked a Bell operator's fact sheet developed by local Toronto CWC organizers.

BELL OPERATORS FACT SHEET

When you compare bargaining ability, you will see that the following <u>CWC demands are already contained in CUC's collective agreement!</u>

- Wage increased based on length of service rather than on merit.
- Shorter work week (CWC's demand is that the present 39-hour work week will be reduced to 36 — CUC has a 35-hour week)!
- Birthday off with pay.
- Job posting.
- Management prohibited from doing bargaining unit work.
- Bereavement leave to include grandparents.
- Union security.
- Permanent involuntary transfers to be made on basis of strict seniority.
- Disciplinary warnings must be in writing!
- Dismissal grievances to be submitted at District Managers' level for faster settlement!
- Overtime pay to be included on same paycheques as regular earnings (instead of 2 weeks later)!
- Arbitrators to have authority to:
    - Uphold company's decision.
    - Reverse company's decision.
    - Vary or alter penalty.

CUC MEMBERS HAVE THESE BENEFITS — CWC MEMBERS DO NOT!
DON'T SETTLE FOR SECOND PLACE
STAY AHEAD — STAY CUC

Who Was Helen Middlebrooks?

Helen Middlebrooks was a native Torontonian who finished high school and joined Bell Canada at the age of seventeen; she worked in Directory Assistance at 15 Asquith. Her father's maternal grandmother, Granny Mitchell, was a union organizer for the staff at the King Edward Hotel in the 1940s:

> Operators weren't sure about the CWC. CUC supporters said lots of bad things about them. Management would say the odd thing, too.
>
> I think the quality of the organizers made the difference. They identified the benefits and were able to discuss the pitfalls of company unions and the benefit of joining with the craft unit — creating a larger bargaining unit. We could see we would have more power.
>
> The company had seventy-six ways they could monitor a DA operator including on-site and off-site printouts and direct intrusion into the call. We became aware of health factors related to VDT terminals. We started to see during the organizing campaign management becoming more abusive to staff. Especially people who had work-performance issues such as older workers. Those operators would be under the average wait times or length of call times.[1]

The Problem of Eglinton

The power base of the CUC in Toronto was located at 50 Eglinton Avenue East. When she wasn't on union business, Regional Chairman Liz Baker worked there in Directory Assistance office #3. Other strong CUC representatives like Carol Wooten and Dorothy Petty worked in the same office.

There was a long-distance office at Eglinton, but they stayed quiet under the watchful eye of the CUC cabal in DA3. Estimates done on June 1, 1978, postulated that there were 373 bargaining unit people at Eglinton.[2] The same document estimated that the total number of employees in Toronto offices was 1,607. This meant the Eglinton location contained over 23 percent of the total number of bargaining unit employees and could not be ignored. Most of the Toronto CWC organizers were long-distance operators, so the organizing committee did not have the resources to organize the DA offices in Eglinton. The long-distance office staff at the sole Traffic office at 50 Eglinton was intimidated by the CUC leadership cadre in the building, yet to the CWC organizers the site was strategically important for gaining supporters to sign CWC cards.

During the summer of 1978, I continued to work at the SOST office at 15 Asquith, but the company cut my hours from full-time to just four hours a week. I was volunteering a lot of time to the campaign and slowly fell into the role of an organizer. I was due to go back to university in the fall, but after having made so little money during the summer I decided to "make history," as George Larter suggested. However, the SOST office was due to convert to TOPS that fall, so I had to make a move. SOST management presented moving into DA at Eglinton as an option for a transfer. Knowing how weak we were at Eglinton, and without good self-preservation instincts, I moved to DA3 in Eglinton at the beginning of September.

I lay low at first, trying to learn the job, not needing to alienate everyone all at once. Tension was super high in the office and the main CUC supporters like Liz Baker, Carol Wooten, and Dorothy Petty would sit close together and watch over the office like a wolf pack keeping their prey under surveillance.

After maybe a couple of weeks, I decided it was time to stir the pot. I walked in with a CWC button. I was out of the closet and the CUC knew there was a traitor in their midst. I was under constant surveillance and my co-workers were afraid to speak to me.

It was a start, but not soon enough to get much support before the campaign ended abruptly.

The CUC Counter-Campaign

CUC strategy consisted primarily of countering CWC bulletins with their own material and scaring the operators and dining service employees with rumours, threats, and innuendo. Irene Anderson recalled her feelings about the CUC material: "I believe in honesty and authenticity. The CUC material was rather desperate. The literature for the CWC appealed to me. As well, I felt connected to the larger union movement. Anyone from Scotland learns by osmosis the value of the labour movement."[3]

The most creative and threatening piece of campaign literature the CUC managed to produce was a fake *Bell Operators Newsletter*. It was a perfect replica using the same type of formatting, fonts, and photocopied legal-sized paper.

McClelland's copy notes in her handwriting that "the articles aren't signed. Imitation is the highest form of flattery and the CUC was defending themselves against their own members by confusing the issues. Why?"

The fake newsletter, dated September 25, 1978, and titled *Bell Operators Newsletter*, started off with a table of contents similar to the first two genuine Bell operators newsletters.

What's inside:

1. Operator's Rights under the CWC Constitution
2. What's in the Saskatchewan Agreement?
3. Operator's Wages in BC and Saskatchewan
4. The Truth about Our CUC Dues!
5. The CWC Organizing Campaign
6. Critical of the CUC? .... Read On
7. Newsletter Supporters

The fake newsletter began with this introduction:

Back by popular demand — newsletter #4 is here. We're really pleased that our newsletter has been so popular and we thank you for your support. We know that operators want to know the truth about their union and the alternatives available to them. The information in this newsletter hasn't always been published in the past, and even now some operators are not hearing the truth from their representatives. This newsletter is the truth.

Saying that newsletter was the truth was interesting. It certainly was what CUC leadership believed, and by emulating the successful channel of communication developed by the Toronto grassroots leaders, they effectively put their version of the truth out there. It was damaging to the CWC, and on her copy, McClelland made additional notes, refuting the points, and began to formulate speaking points she could use when talking to organizers, operators, and group meetings

In the first article, "Operator's Rights under the CWC Constitution," they urged that operators interested in joining the CWC read through the CWC constitution and compare it to the recently revised CUC constitution. They stated that the CWC Executive Board had much more power than the CUC Executive Council. They asked about what happened to the funds when a local's charter was revoked, and presented the possibility that a local union could have its charter revoked because of noncompliance with an Executive Board order. This was to counter the CWC claim that it was more grassroots-focused than the CUC.

This bogus newsletter also asked whether there would be separate locals for operators. The CUC designed the question to evoke fears that the operators' interests would be subordinated to those of men — a very common complaint of women everywhere. The article went on to discuss whether plant locals would support striking operators. They suggested CUC members interested in local autonomy would have a better method of ensuring it through amendments to the CUC constitution. McClelland's note: "Experience shows otherwise. CUC didn't mention appeal procedures."

In the next article, "What's in the Saskatchewan Agreement?", the unnamed authors tried to score points by saying that the SaskTel agreement did not provide for permanent shifts, vacation differentials, bridging layoffs, part-time operator job postings by seniority, and sick pay. McClelland's angry response: "This is not true: the SaskTel contract just used a different type of language."

The next article discussed "Operators' Wages in BC and Saskatchewan." McClelland asked, "Where is the comparison of CUC wages with Saskatchewan and BC?" The thrust of the article was that there was a gap of $20.80 per week in operators' wage rates between Regina and Vancouver. The article asked, "Why has CWC not been able to close that gap?" McClelland noted that they were comparing different stats and made the point that while the CUC negotiated wages, they fell further behind.

Another article was "The Truth about Our CUC Dues!," a response to disdain expressed earlier in an authentic newsletter by the comment "Why Does CUC Invest in Companies?" It had come to light that although the CUC never went to arbitration or saved any money for a strike fund, they were sitting on a substantial nest egg.[4]

The article explained their reasoning:

> Unless a person prefers to keep his money in a mattress, it is only common sense to invest his savings in an institution such as a bank, trust company, credit union or corporations (via the stock markets). This is also true of unions.... CUC made $29,234.00 from its investments. [The article goes on to talk about their financial advisors and their wise investments in Hiram Walker and Bell Canada.]
>
> In short, our investments have been made carefully, wisely and profitably. Where does CWC invest its money? twenty- or sixty-day term deposits?... If the CWC is so financially naive to think that none of its money ever reaches corporations, operators should think twice before trusting their dues to such a union.

These opinions and attitudes toward investing union dues illustrated how far removed the CUC leadership was from the legitimate trade union movement. Instead of using their financial resources to maximize the benefits to membership through union activity such as collective bargaining and the filing of grievances, the CUC preferred to invest the dues from its membership. The article also stated that CWC dues were set by convention and not by the locals, and mentioned how in a sisterly manner the CUC donated $500 to the CWC in their struggle with Northern Electric. The article noted the cost effectiveness of the CUC union dues, being only one-seventh of 1 percent of wages. It also reminded readers that dues could be increased only through a referendum with the support of a majority of CUC members; in comparison to the CWC, where part of the CWC dues was decided by a CWC convention, and the members had no voice in setting this amount.

McClelland's notes exclaimed, "What about 1.5 percent of CUC dues that go to the U.S., and that 20 percent of the convention can have a referendum vote on any dues increase by the national union?" Her notes also commented that the CWC does not invest in companies it represents, so there is no conflict of interest.

"The CWC Organizing Campaign" article sought to dispel the half-truths and rumours spread by the CWC campaign. For example, answering its own question: "Has the CWC proven that dangers exist in the use of the cathode-ray tube?" the article explained that the Canadian Standards Association had approved all units used by Bell Canada for X-ray emission.

That did not satisfy Janice McClelland, however, who scribbled in the margins preparing to rebut the accusations, "What about European standards? Why would CUC take Bell Canada at its word?"

Elsewhere she wrote: "How can the CWC guarantee higher wages for Traffic and Dining Service employees?" In fact, wages are determined though collective bargaining and no guarantees can be made by any union.

Despite all of this, McClelland wrote indignantly that CUC bulletins were full of lies. "Why doesn't CUC campaign on their record? Rates of pay, length of vacations, splits, shorts, overtime?"

The newsletter ended with the section "Critical of the CUC?... Read On ..."

It seems that some CUC members have become disillusioned with their union and have acknowledged the only alternative is the CWC. Is the ONLY way to register criticism with our union to sign a membership card?

We believe not!... There are means within the CUC to

change. The recent constitutional referendum, in which there was 70 percent acceptance of the proposed revisions, is an indication that the CUC is innovative, is active, is strong and is concerned with and receptive to the wishes of its members.

LET'S ALL LOOK BEFORE WE LEAP

The newsletter ended with over one hundred signatures, the last being Regional Chairman Elizabeth Baker. That many signatures indicated real support. The CUC was fighting back with gusto. But the CWC countered with messages to reduce the impact it might have on readers and sow suspicion among members about the CUC.

In a letter from CWC spokesperson Ed Seymour to Cheryl Hamilton dated October 11, 1978,[5] Seymour reported:

> We have checked into some of the signatures that were placed on this newsletter. Many of the people did not know their names were going to be used as supporters of the newsletter; in fact, some of the people had signed a petition of support for CUC and because their names were used in this manner, angrily joined the CWC. We have also been informed that one person whose signature appeared on this newsletter is presently in hospital, and is so ill she doesn't recognize her own family and is no position to sign her own name.

These revelations served to counter the impression that the CUC still had substantial support among the bargaining unit.

Office Politics

In CUC strongholds like Directory Assistance offices, tension was very high as CWC organizers went about spreading the CWC message and signing up operators. Wearing a CWC button was enough to draw cold stares from CUC supporters, and active organizing could draw violence.

Helen Middlebrooks remembers the tension in her building 15 Asquith Avenue:

> The CUC was very active in DA at Asquith. Their rep was named Phyllis Beckett, a tall attractive black woman in her thirties who worked in the building. Phyllis was always around. She lived in the area where I grew up. I would meet her on the bus. She was always talking up how bad the CWC was. That we would end up going on strike. Well we did go on strike but we got a nice raise.[6]

Linda Young experienced more than verbal abuse: "The CUC supporters were scary. One spit on my face. Another would tear up flyers in my face. It was stressful because I had to work with them. They were schoolyard bullies. They were losing control of the office."[7]

Agents Provocateurs

Cheryl Hamilton, as a CUC staff person, was one agent provocateur who attended meetings and pretended to be an operator. She would ask the provocative questions that regular operators would not know to ask, because the CUC had acquired interesting intelligence that could be used to discredit the CWC. Organizers for the CWC remember that Cheryl enjoyed the role until the CWC exposed her as a CUC staffer. The disinformation was effective, but came too late to do much damage to the campaign, which was in its final phase.

CUC decision-makers were not above making personal attacks on CWC organizers, especially those that were also CUC representatives. Ann Newman remembers:

> One of the rumours the CUC spread about me was that there is a big black Jamaican woman at Main Square who was going to intimidate you. The campaign made me really tough. It was hard for me as a black woman. They came at me more than others. I was called "a commie." Management, too. This one manager named Sharon Spinarsky was always after me, saying "You have an attitude."[8]

CUC flyer attacking Ann Newman.

Newman was even attacked by the CUC in print. A CUC flyer took her vote out of context and painted her as against progressive reform and more local control of finances.

The CUC Public Relations Campaign

The CUC, not feeling confident that their existing staff and leaders could fend off the draining away of their members to the CWC, decided to hire a public relations expert, Pierre Denault. Denault ran a feel-good campaign attempting to associate warm, fuzzy feelings with the CUC as he said repeatedly, "We'll get together and have fun and talk." He had a substantial budget to hold events for operators so they could be influenced and persuaded of the merits of remaining with the CUC. Below is an invitation flyer to one of Denault's events promising fellowship and facts, facts, and more facts.

RALLY 'ROUND YOUR UNION!

AT THE KING EDWARD HOTEL

ON WEDNESDAY, AUGUST 30TH FROM 5:00 PM ON

☆ WINE ☆ CHEESE ☆ MUSIC ☆ FELLOWSHIP

AND FACTS, FACTS FACTS

☆ COMPARE CONTRACTS WITH THE CWC AND CTEA
☆ LATEST WORD ON A.I.B.
☆ THE TRUE STATE OF OUR UNION
☆ QUESTIONS AND ANSWERS ON EVERYTHING

SPOUSES AND FRIENDS WELCOME

CUC invite to a rally.

Of course, once in the room with CUC leadership, operators were told mistruths and intimidated; as reported in the *Bell Operators Newsletter*, Denault left the impression with operators that the company would investigate CWC supporters. Ed Seymour remembers attending this event:

> We went to a classic meeting where CUC members could bring their spouse. So the operators' organizers brought Bill and me. Janice Crook took somebody. Every CWC rep was there and took on the CUC in the question period of the meeting. What a laugh!
>
> At the end of this evening everyone on both sides were well-fortified with CUC-supplied wine, and as we were leaving, Janice Crook was trying to persuade everyone to get along — and she has Bill Howes on one arm and Shirley Nicholson on the other. We were trying to get her out of there and were pulling her apart in the process.
>
> One time later I was in Geneva with the president of Postal, Telephone, and Telegraph International (PPTI).[9] He took me and a rep from the postal workers out for dinner. He

told the story of how one morning around 3 a.m. his time, he got a call from Janice Crook, ... thanking him for organizing the boycott of Bell in support of operators in Canada. It was amazing that she got him.[10]

The CWC Response

The CWC continued to hammer away with regular newsletters and issue-specific leaflets to counter CUC misinformation. The campaign was fought on multiple fronts. Key organizers worked on their own locations, signing up cards and answering questions generated by the misinformation campaign. On August 29, Fred Pomeroy sent a letter to all craft members enclosing two cards and encouraging them to sign up operators and dining staff, too.

To counter CUC propaganda, the CWC issued a number of undated and unnumbered bulletins. To address the accusation that Bell craftsmen earned more than their Saskatchewan counterparts, the union issued a flyer titled *Facts Not Fiction*.

FACTS NOT FICTION

CUC bulletins say Bell Craftsman are further behind Saskatchewan Craftsman, that Bell Operators are behind Saskatchewan Operators ... but the facts don't support their argument....

Saskatchewan craftsman earns	$396.50 per week
Bell craftsman earns	$339.45 per week
Difference of	16.8%
Saskatchewan operator earns	$232.00 per week
Bell operator earns	$194.29 per week[11]
Difference of	19.4%

The fact is —
IT PAYS TO BELONG TO CWC!!

The Debate

The most emotionally charged event of the campaign happened on the evening of September 7, 1978. Fred Pomeroy invited Acting President Shirley Nicholson of the CUC to a debate. She accepted willingly.[12]

The debate took place in the Vanity Fair Salon of the stately King Edward Hotel on King Street. Cliff Pilkey, president of the Ontario Federation of Labour, was the moderator. He acted more like a referee as the evening grew more and more raucous. Fred Pomeroy spoke on behalf of the CWC, and Shirley Nicholson spoke on behalf of the CUC. About an equal number of supporters were in attendance for each side. Jeering and applause rose from the audience as each speaker made their points.

Fred Pomeroy recalls that memorable night:

> Once we got over the idea of merger with CUC I still thought they might give up. I thought they might come in willingly. Even during the card-signing campaign. Then we caught them in a major lie. They were late one day for a meeting with me. It was after the CUC had just settled their contract and the Anti-Inflation Board had just come into being. As far as the CUC was concerned, the contract was signed, sealed, and delivered. I got there for a meeting and they weren't there. I started talking about the AIB with some staffer who said Mary Lennox had written a letter to the prime minister supporting the AIB. I asked for a copy of the letter and the staffer got it for me. Shortly after, despite Mary's letter, they found out their contract was indeed under the jurisdiction of the AIB. Their brand-new contract deal was limited by AIB restrictions and operators were going to get screwed.
>
> So in August of 1978, we challenged the CUC to a debate. They agreed and we negotiated the format with Pierre Denault. It was agreed that the format of debate would allow a chance to the other to respond. So we told

our people to ask Shirley questions first; then I would be able to respond. So an audience member asked Shirley the question, "Was the CUC opposed to the AIB?" and she replied, "Of course, she was opposed." When Fred Pomeroy got a chance to respond, he took out the letter where Mary Lennox had written she was in favour of the AIB. That was one big CUC lie.[13]

Both sides claimed victory, but the CWC was able to sign a few cards and considered it an opportunity to present their case to people who would normally tear up the CWC literature.

CWC Signs a Majority

The card-signing campaign officially ended on October 2, and on October 4, 1978, the CWC filed an application with the Canadian Labour Relations Board (CLRB) for bargaining agent certification with over 4,000 Application for Membership cards. This press release went on to express confidence that the CWC had a majority of employees signed up, but didn't provide a total number of cards. In addition, the CWC put together an un-numbered bulletin announcing that the CWC had applied for a certification vote. The message was clear that the application was supported by CWC cards signed by a clear majority of the employees in the bargaining unit.

The campaign, at only three months old, was not very long to organize two provinces with over seven thousand employees and get a majority of those employees to sign union cards. Card-signing campaigns had previously lasted four months, but the CLRB had just recently reduced the campaign time from four months to three.

Although CWC leadership was convinced they had a majority, they knew the margin would be slim. Even so, local organizers were confident of a win once the CLRB ordered a vote among employees as to their preferred union agent.

Each telephone operator and dining service member who signed a card received a personal letter reporting that on October 4, 1978, the

Bulletin

cwc applies on october 4, 1978 for vote

CWC filed an application for certification to represent
Bell Canada Traffic and Dining Service employees throughout Ontario and
Quebec with the Canada Labour Relations Board (CLRB) on Wednesday,
October 4, 1978.

The application is supported by CWC cards signed by a clear
majority of the employees in the bargaining unit.

NOW UP TO THE BOARD

The application is now in the hands of the CLRB. They can
be expected to take several weeks to compare the signed cards against a
list of all employees to ensure that we have indeed reached a majority before
they order a secret ballot vote to be held amongst all Traffic and Dining
Service employees. We will be co-operating with the CLRB to speed up the
process as much as possible.

CARDS ARE CONFIDENTIAL

By law, all cards signed for CWC are confidential. At no time
are the names of people who have signed CWC cards revealed to either the
CUC or Bell Canada.

CWC members are also assured that anti-CWC petitions which the
CUC may try to organize have no value in determining the choice of employees.
We can expect the CUC to use petitions and other tactics to try to create
confusion among employees.

CARD SIGNING CONTINUES

We are continuing our card-signing campaign for two basic
reasons:

1. Additional cards will help to ensure that a
vote is held and could speed up the process.

2. Cards signed by an overwhelming majority of
employees will mean greater strength in the
critical round of contract bargaining which will
follow CWC's certification as bargaining agent.
Bell Canada, like all other coporations, respects
a UNITED group of employees.

JOIN THE MAJORITY   -   -   JOIN C W C

If you haven't already joined the majority
of Traffic and Dining Service employees,
sign up today.

CWC applies for a vote.

CWC had filed an application with the CLRB and that a vote was expected in the near future. The letter announced that the union would continue signing membership cards and all members needed to keep talking it up. The next steps were to prepare for bargaining and establish a local union structure.

Chapter 8

The Wait

Organizing Momentum Slows

The card-signing campaign wound down when the CWC submitted its application for certification. Organizers didn't know how long the wait would be, but they needed to develop the local structure and leadership of a new bargaining unit. So they continued to sign union membership cards and to prepare for a vote campaign, and began preparations to build a local union structure for operators and Dining Service. During the weekend of January 6, 1979, the CWC held a Local Union Structure Conference for Ontario in Barrie. Local leaders and the grassroots organizing committee continued to issue Bell operators newsletters, and the CWC issued its bulletins. Meanwhile, the CUC propaganda campaign went from denial that the CWC had signed up enough cards to overdrive in preparation for the eventual vote.

Denial of CWC claims of successful card-signing was the CUC's first position. In an undated press release, the union countered the claims of its rival:

FOR IMMEDIATE RELEASE

The claim of a mass defection of our membership to the Communications Workers of Canada is an organized ploy aimed at stampeding our members.

The other labour organization has been raiding our members in Ontario and Quebec for several months. I am confident that the vast majority of our members want the CUC and will continue to support us as their bargaining agent.

Contrary to the false claims by the CWC, Communications Union Canada is alive and well and bargaining on behalf of the telephone traffic and dining service employees with Mother Bell.

Communications Union Canada represents 7,500 traffic and dining service employees in Bell Canada in Ontario and Quebec.

Miss Nicholson countered the CWC claim in a statement issued at the CUC General Council at the Westbury Hotel here. All 21 district chairpersons of the union are attending the meeting which is being held to develop collective bargaining strategy. Submission of bargaining demands will be tendered to Bell Canada on October 17, 1978.

For further information, contact Cheryl Hamilton, Executive Assistant.[1]

The CUC maintained its head-in-the-sand posture. But the campaign must have scared the CUC leadership, for on October 3 Mary Lennox sent a note the General Council of the CUC notifying them "of her intention to retire and resign from the Office of President of the Communications Union Canada effective 31st December, 1978."[2]

Meanwhile, the CWC continued to organize and recruit members. Ed Seymour's files include a letter dated September 13, 1978, from him to a telephone operator in Toronto. He provided her with a copy of the union's bylaws, minutes of the 1977 convention, and union organizational charts. Recruiting and signing new members never ceased, and letters like this illustrate the extent some potential recruits went to get factual information to help them make a decision.

The CWC had to match the CUC's accusations and propaganda with tit-for-tat flyers such as the following undated and untitled piece, which urged operators to get more information.

WHY — IS CUC FIGHTING TO PREVENT A SECRET BALLOT, GOVERNMENT RUN VOTE?

WHY — IS CUC DESTROYING CWC BULLETINS??
WHY — HAVEN'T YOU BEEN TOLD IN YOUR BARGAINING?

WHY — IS CUC SUGGESTING YOU CAN BE FIRED WHEN THEY KNOW THE LAW SAYS YOU CAN'T BE FIRED OR INTIMIDATED FOR SIGNING A CWC CARD?

Perhaps it's because they don't trust you to make up your own mind. Perhaps they are afraid you will find out how CWC negotiates and handles grievances with Bell Canada and you'll want CWC to represent you. Perhaps they're afraid you will find that CWC negotiates better contracts for operators with other companies. For example, in Saskatchewan CWC operators have been earning $232.00 per week since last March 26th. That's a whole year ago and they're in bargaining now for more!! Their working conditions are better too!! Meanwhile CUC is free to bargain but spends its time blaming CWC for their lack of action.

ISN'T IT YOUR RIGHT AS A CITIZEN TO BE INFORMED AND MAKE YOUR OWN DECISION??

INVESTIGATE CWC — WE'RE SURE YOU WILL LIKE WHAT YOU FIND!

Opieu 343[3]
Issued by CWC

The issue of the CUC newsletter *Communiqué* published in October 1978 featured an interview with Shirley Nicholson. (She might have been named president by this time, but the author was unable to access any official announcement of Mary Lennox's retirement and Shirley Nicholson's appointment.) The interview was a reflection on the state of the union and its priorities at the time; dealing with such information would have been part of the president's role.

The interviewer asked, "Does this mean a change in philosophy for the CUC?"

Nicholson replied:

> It isn't a change in philosophy for me. I grew up in a trade union family in Cape Breton. We talked about the union around the dinner table. But there was a time, maybe two or three years ago, when some of us didn't like to think of ourselves as trade unionists. With the AIB and other pressures on our union, that's all behind us. We are going to improve our situation and protect our jobs by working together. Nobody's going to hand it to us.

She went on to promise a constitutional referendum to put districts on a good financial basis and train the representatives in collective bargaining, servicing the collective agreement, and processing grievances.

* * *

Meanwhile the CWC kept producing their bulletins. One, dated October 4, 1978, reported that the CWC had filed an application for certification to represent traffic and dining service employees.

Another bulletin (undated, #14) announced that the Canadian Labour Relations Board had acted on the CWC application, having announced receipt of the application and given notice to Bell of the company's obligation to provide up-to-date employee lists. It also reported that card-signing was ongoing.

The CLRB was slow to order a vote and operators and cafeteria staff were getting frustrated because it had been so long since a raise. Despite the Trudeau government's wage and price controls, inflation was not under control and working people bore the brunt of constantly rising prices for energy, food, and housing. Operators and cafeteria staff were weary of waiting and being penalized by decisions made by the AIB. They had received their last raise in June 1977. Regardless of whether or not they had joined the CWC, the workers in the bargaining unit were very dissatisfied with their income and working conditions.

There was a provision in the contract for a wage reopener for November 1977 to November 1978. Local organizers who still retained their position in the CUC started to clamour for the union to negotiate that raise. The CUC kept deflecting by saying the raid was holding up negotiations. However, the CUC could easily have held negotiations with the company, as there was no legal problem in doing so. But the only option remaining under Anti-Inflation Board guidelines was a raise of less than 1 percent. If the CUC had gone ahead and obtained a raise that low, it probably would have drawn more criticism. Being in a Catch-22, they decided to do nothing.

As with any campaign, once you identify your vote you have to keep it. With a vote and a questionable majority, the CWC and local organizers had to keep people on their side until the CLRB arranged the vote. Local Toronto organizers produced *Bell Operators Newsletter #4*, published on December 15, 1978. It included the short article "Bargaining," by Janice McClelland. She reported that the federal government, including the prime minister and the Cabinet, had turned down the CUC appeal of the AIB ruling and that the bargaining unit wages remained rolled back. She also noted that nothing had happened with bargaining on the wage reopener. She was particularly appalled that Bell Canada clerical staff had received raises that left operators' wages on par with Grade 4 clerks — down from Grade 6.

George Larter wrote a short piece, "The Vote — When Will It Be," about when operators and cafeteria staff could expect a vote on the bargaining agent. He reported that the CWC and the CLRB were checking the cards and were waiting for Bell Canada to submit final lists of employees, which they had done on December 1. George said that with luck a vote could be announced by the end of December.

Meanwhile, supporters were to keep signing union cards. They signed off the mini-newsletter with "Merry Christmas."

The CWC gained a lot of credibility with potential members because of its affiliation with the trade union movement through labour organizations such as the Canadian Labour Congress and the Ontario Federation of Labour. The CWC heard that the CUC was going to try to apply for membership in the CLC. This would meet two objectives: if accepted, the CUC could not be accused of being a company union; and the CWC could not raid another CLC affiliate. The CUC would continue as the bargaining agent for Bell telephone operators and dining service employees.

To make sure that the CUC got nowhere with this idea, on January 4 Fred Pomeroy wrote to Dennis McDermott, president of the CLC, requesting that any CUC application be rejected. McDermott wrote back immediately and said he was willing to agree to Pomeroy's request.[4] The CLC had cut off the CUC strategy before it could even promote the idea.

Local Union Structure Conference

On January 6–7, 1979, the CWC hosted a conference to determine Traffic and Dining Services' local structure at the Continental Inn in Barrie. Representatives from around the province of Ontario came to set up locals for Traffic and Dining Services members. Although the primary purpose of the conference was to take the first steps toward building a local union structure, the union also wanted to build friendships, networks, and solidarity to deal with whatever the future would bring.

The conference opened on Saturday and was chaired by Bill Howes. Seated at the head table were: CWC President Fred Pomeroy; CWC Vice-President, Ontario Region, Peter Klym; Quebec-based National Representative Marie Pinsonneault; and Ontario Region National Representative Susan Edgar. Operators and dining service representatives from all over the province attended. The CWC covered transportation and accommodation expenses. The conference began in a plenary session with representatives sitting with their colleagues from the same geographic area.

Ed Seymour gave an update on the campaign and Pinsonneault shared what was happening in Quebec. Seymour, also the national representative responsible for education, reported that five hundred craft unit members had taken part in CWC courses since September 1977.

Dave Handley, Chairman of the CWC Ontario Regional Council, explained the administrative and educational role of the council. Susan Edgar explained local union finances — how part of the dues money went to the locals as outlined in the constitution — and took questions from the audience.

The national union designed the presentations to educate future local officers and union stewards, and to offer a context for the tough decision-making to come later. Bill Howes, Ontario campaign organizer, was the CWC staffer entrusted with presenting the report to participants. He displayed a large map of Ontario showing the numbers of all the traffic and dining service members working in each city and town. For each area, a handout identified the geographic centres, the current number of plant union members, and estimates of traffic members.

Then he presented three options for a Traffic and Dining Service local union structure:

1. A separate local for traffic and dining service members only.
2. Joint locals with both Bell Canada plant as well as traffic and dining service members represented.
3. A restructuring of existing local union areas.

Howes presented the scenario of operators in Toronto joining the existing CWC locals. He showed which offices would be in downtown Local 25, East End Local 27, and West End Local 26; the total number of members for each local; and the number of convention delegates each reformed local would be eligible for.

This information was redundant for Toronto representatives (including Oakville), as they had already decided on a separate local for Toronto traffic and dining services employees. Other operator groups were still in discussions and needed to hold further local meetings.

> *The conference was a highlight of the organizing campaign. It was the first time I had met organizers from across the province. To me it felt like we connected across vast geographic distances, and were joined together by a vision of a better workplace for ourselves.*

At the conference, some Traffic locals made the decision to merge with existing craft locals. Most offices, owing to numbers of employees, decided to join existing locals. The two exceptions were Toronto and Ottawa, which formed separate locals 50 and 51.

Pomeroy wrapped up the day-long session by emphasizing that the union would change its structure when necessary to keep the unity and solidarity of its membership — but the real issue was winning the vote.

The national union issued another CWC bulletin to celebrate this milestone conference. *CWC Bulletin #16: Report of the Local Union Structure Conference* included summaries of the presentations made at the conference and ended with the key message that local structure was important, but winning the vote was the priority. The bulletin ended with the statement that when the labour board vote was held [the readers would need to] vote for the union that kept them informed.

Throughout January the Toronto organizers geared up for an eventual vote and produced the fifth *Bell Operators and Dining Services Newsletter*. Issued on February 4, 1979, it covered the questions and topics that were percolating at the grassroots level. Although produced by Toronto operators, this newsletter was sent to Bell offices around the province.

The first article was coauthored by Janice McClelland, Marnie Veale, and Betty Wilson from Valhalla TOPS in Toronto. They reported on a CUC general membership meeting on the wage reopener held on January 18. Carol Wooten began the meeting by reading the following text from a written report:

> In view of the raid by the CWC on our membership and the referral of this matter by the CLRB, Mr. Dufresne [the

conciliation commissioner] has adjourned the conciliation proceedings until the CLRB has dealt with the question of the raid.... The CWC action before the CLRB is holding up our negotiations — not only for the 1977 Wage Reopener but also for our collective agreement for 1979.

This was an attempt by the CUC to cast blame on the CWC campaign for the delay in getting any kind of raise. Janice McClelland felt that was incorrect and asked Wooten to read the letter from the conciliator. The last paragraph read: "The conciliation commissioner adjourns the proceedings of the conciliation 'sine die' or until such time as one or both parties requests the undersigned to convene the commission to proceed in bringing the parties to reach agreement in the present dispute."

The article then reports that McClelland confronted Wooten on the blatant manipulation of government correspondence, while Veale grilled Wooten on the activities of the CUC and ended by demanding the CUC resume bargaining.

George Larter wrote the next article announcing that Daisy (the technological change proposed for directory assistance) was coming to Toronto in 1980. Larter reported that he had attended a district union-management meeting on January 17, 1979, at which the Bell Canada representative informed them that computerized DA would be implemented in the latter half of 1980. The company expected to reduce DA staff by up to 25 percent.

He shared what had happened in the TOPS turnover and how the tech change had diminished customer contact and increased job stress. George urged DA operators to seek greater union protection to offset the worst of the impact. "We need a new union that will keep us informed of the latest technology in the telephone industry." With this change, the company helped move the DA operators into the CWC tent.

Next, Ann Newman interviewed Fred Pomeroy about the status of the CWC campaign. Pomeroy explained the CLRB process for deciding whether to hold a vote. The two discussed the CUC claim that the CWC had not signed up a majority of operators. They also discussed what would happen to CUC funds once it was decertified by the CLRB.

Pomeroy emphasized that the union had a right to organize on company premises and addressed why the union was still signing cards. Newman asked for some words of encouragement, as her members were getting impatient waiting for the vote.

The author wrote the next article while working out of DA unit 3 at 50 Eglinton Avenue in Toronto. Titled "How about Dining Service?," it featured an interview with Hubert Graham, who worked in Dining Services at 393 University Avenue in Toronto. Graham reported on the wages of dining service employees. At that time the starting rate was $3.32 an hour or $129.75 a week. The author probed Dining Service satisfaction with their union representation. Graham reported that it was nonexistent, with no grievances ever filed to his knowledge.

When asked about working conditions in the cafeterias, he replied that they were pretty rough. "We work 7 ¾ hours per day. That's ¾ of an hour more than operators. The cafeterias don't have enough people for all the work and so everyone has to work really hard. If someone is sick then we work even harder." Graham urged dining service staff to sign up for the CWC. "Why hold on to a broken broomstick when you can have a new one?"

Diane Ward, union rep at Manulife TOPS 11, was a key Toronto organizer. She wrote about the health hazards that developed with the introduction of TOPS. She shared what had happened with the lovely chairs the company promised. They became a safety hazard as the backs came loose and had to be bolted. She complained about the constant glare from the CRT screens, and that the CUC fully accepted Bell's position that there was no health impact of the screens. She went on to relay some scientific information indicating that operators should get regular eye checks.

Janice Crook, a service analyst and Toronto CWC organizer, reported on the January 10 meeting of new Local 50 to discuss and vote on a local structure. She explained the four options for forming a local that were on the table. She reported that Toronto operators were mostly in favour of one local for all Toronto traffic and dining service members. The local organized a bylaw committee to draft bylaws for the membership to adopt. This committee was receiving nominations and would run the election for local officers. She relayed that the local was seeking nominations for interim officers and that there would be a CWC membership

TOPS office.

meeting to elect the officers on February 21. She concluded with the important point that the officers would get training after the election.

The fifth newsletter included a section called "News from around Ontario." London reported on its election for local officers. Kitchener reported its estimate of how much membership had paid in union dues to the CUC over the previous five years. The figure they came up with was a whopping $2,639,440. It ended the rant by complaining that the CUC had been milking them for some twenty-five to thirty years. The progress reports from out of town were often quite humorous. Here is one from Guelph:

> Hello to all Fellow CWC's ... I've just got through putting my "Rolaids" and my "Excedrin" in the green garbage bag. Why? Because the heartburn and my headache has just left my old worn-out CUC body, and it has been replaced with excitement and the CWC.

I sure hope there are a few more of you out there that feel the same way. It's just not me, it is 80 percent of the Guelph office that has finally seen the LIGHT. Now is your chance to throw away the ball and chain, stand up and be counted. We and I say WE have been held down long enough. Operators have long been awaiting the chance for fair bargaining and a decent raise in pay. Let's put 30 years of unfair wages and working conditions where they belong, in retirement with you-know-who — M.L. Come on, let's get involved and get what we all want, the CWC.

Jean Corrigan, Traffic Dept., Guelph

Marg McColl, a CUC union rep from Main Square TOPS Office 23, contributed an article reminding CUC members that "You Don't Lose Anything" by joining the CWC. She explained there is no reason to think that traffic and dining service employees would accept a contract for less than they had now. The law had frozen the old contract until the new one was negotiated. She emphasized that the union addressed many of the fears and apprehensions expressed by the bargaining unit.

The newsletter ended with an open letter to Shirley Nicholson from Gemma Bourque of Scarborough. She admonished the CUC for shutting down conciliation and urged Nicholson to begin again on the wage reopener. To illustrate the growing support, the newsletter published a whole page of new supporters

The Birth of Local 50

January 1979 witnessed the birth of Local 50 of the Communications Workers of Canada. As the decision had been made at the conference earlier in the month to create a separate local for telephone operators and dining service member in Toronto, the grassroots leadership moved ahead to prepare for the day they would represent the Toronto membership.

Local 50 nominated interim officers at its meeting of January 21. They were:

Janice McClelland, President
George Larter, Vice-President
Ann Newman, Vice-President
Diane Ward, Secretary
Marnie Veale, Treasurer

By nominating and electing officers and drafting bylaws, the local union was developing the infrastructure to function despite not yet being certified as the bargaining agent.

From then on the Local 50 executive met once a month. Bill Howes recorded in his diary that they met on March 21, April 18, and May 16. The local's pre-strike work was primarily preparation for getting bargaining off the ground in anticipation that the CLRB would call the vote and the union would win. July 14 was the deadline for submission of bargaining proposals to the national union. Local 50, like all locals, had to have discussions so that members could formulate thoughtful proposals and build support for a submission.

The CWC issued two more bulletins before the CLRB called the vote. *CWC Bulletin #17* asked the question: "Where Is Your 1977–1978 raise?" It reviewed the history of the wage reopener and reported that for more than a whole year CUC took no action toward negotiating an increase. It ended with this exhortation for after the Labour Board vote was called: "Vote for the union that deals with the facts — not excuses. Vote for the union that has demonstrated it can negotiate effectively. Vote CWC!"

CWC Bulletin #18 asked "Who Is Stalling?" It countered the CUC claim that the CWC application to the CLRB for certification was preventing negotiations on the wage reopener.

Bill Howes recorded that he was in attendance at the weekly Toronto organizing group meetings from January 3 to February 28, 1979. This must have meant that the grassroots organization was from the Local 50 executive, was meeting independently, and may have used their meeting time to build the local's structure — although most of the Local 50 executive would have been on the organizing committee as well.

On February 17, the CWC hosted a local union administration course. Ed Seymour led the course with help from Bill Howes. The CWC prioritized capacity-building, and their investment in developing local leadership helped tie the grassroots to the CWC. The agenda included:

- Duties and responsibilities of local union officers
- How to run a local meeting
- Giving reports
- Taking minutes
- Psychology in the workplace

With training under their belt, local union organizers in Toronto could begin to develop their autonomous local — CWC Local 50.

CUC Wage Reopener

The wait for a Canadian Labour Relations Board decision meant the CWC needed to engage the new membership and shift attention to the incompetence of the CUC. The organizing committee decided to open a new battle with the CUC based on the clause in the expired contract permitting a wage reopener. On February 18, 1979, a cover letter signed by Janice McClelland on behalf of the organizing committee went out around the province of Ontario. She asked for help in getting signatures for a petition to the CUC about the wage reopener. The letter said:

> We have started a petition campaign (see enclosed) to get the CUC to resume negotiations on our 1977–1978 wage reopener.
>
> 1. Why? The CUC is still our legal bargaining agent and they should be bargaining in good faith on our behalf.
> 2. The CWC campaign has nothing to do with this wage reopener. All CUC has to do is send a letter to conciliation officer Pierre Defresne and the negotiations on the wage reopener will be on again.
> 3. Why should we be suffering financially and the CUC not even bargaining for us?

She enclosed the petition form and asked readers to send the petitions back in the care of the *Bell Operators Newsletter* at 25 Cecil Street. She closed with "We will make sure these get to the CUC."[5] The petition form stated: "We, the undersigned Traffic and Dining Service employees, urge the CUC to immediately resume negotiations for the 1977–1978 wage reopener."

Meanwhile, following a mid-February weekend training session, the CUC issued a verbose press release. More than half the release was a rant by Shirley Nicolson about unions losing sight of their social goals and caring about people's personal problems. Then she said she had heard from "a reliable source" that the CLRB had rejected the application by the CWC. She went on to say, "As soon as we hear from the Board we will be getting back to the bargaining committee."[6]

Rejection

In the end, the wait for the Labour Board decision was six months. On February 23, 1979, it handed down its decision: The CLRB denied the CWC application for certification to represent the Traffic and Dining Services bargaining unit at Bell Canada. The CWC would *not* be given a vote because they had failed to get membership cards signed by a majority of employees. They were short by 143 cards when compared to the list provided by the company. CWC staff officers and local organizers felt the list had been tampered with. A list from the CUC gave a count of 7,272 members. The CWC estimated there were 7,321 employees in the bargaining unit, but the company listed 7,658 employees. The CLRB accepted 3,687 cards for CWC membership, but 155 members had quit and 124 had transferred.

There was no way for the union to contest the company list. Later on, the CWC would find that this number was incorrect and that they *did* have a majority. But that knowledge did not come to light soon enough to eliminate the need to begin another card-signing campaign.[7]

The CUC wasted no time in communicating the news to their membership. On February 27, Shirley Nicholson, now the acting president, sent out a letter to members. To emphasize the union's labour bona fides, she started off with a quote from the labour anthem "Solidarity Forever," and then went on to explain exactly what had happened from the CUC point of view. The CWC might brand the card-signing a campaign, but Nicholson called it a raid, saying that a raid is not creative, it is destructive. She called it an "act of treachery."

Nicholson claimed that the raid by the CWC had come in the midst of civilized negotiations between representatives of the two unions to look at the feasibility of a merger so that Bell Canada employees could improve their bargaining strength. She proudly pronounced that the CWC had failed to get a majority of traffic and dining service employees to sign cards. Perhaps fearing that the campaign was not really over, she argued that the CUC was part of the labour movement despite the CWC's descent into silly name-calling. CWC leaders and propagandists had called the CUC "a company union." Those accusations had clearly stung.

Nicholson went on to give two definitions of company unions and said that neither fit the CUC. She maintained that the CUC operated under traditional trade union procedures and had a constitution and regular delegated conventions. She ended by saying the CUC harboured no ill will toward the CWC membership. "We are prepared to let bygones be bygones. We must now close ranks and devote our energies to negotiating our next collective agreement and to building a strong union."

The next day, the CUC sent a note to its reps. It contained official notification of the results of the CLRB decision and announced:

> Now that the raid is finally over, the bargaining committee will resume negotiations with Bell Canada on 6th March, 1979 and proceed with bargaining for the 1978 Collective Agreement.
>
> A great deal of work lies ahead — bargaining, further constitutional reform and the election of executive officers at the special council scheduled for May — and I am certain that by working together and standing united we will be successful in negotiations and in becoming one of the most effective, democratic and progressive labour unions in Canada.
> Yours sincerely,
>
> Shirley T. Nicholson,
> Acting President[8]

As far as the CUC was concerned, now that the CWC raid was over, it was back to work. The CUC was to return to negotiations with the company and move forward with the democratization agenda and structural changes proposed the previous summer.

On March 8, 1979, a CUC newsletter announced "CUC and Bell Canada Return to Bargaining Table." A new round of bargaining had begun on March 6 with renewed demands for retroactive pay and a new collective agreement. Shirley Nicholson told Bell Canada that the current bargaining sessions were the most serious in CUC history.

The newsletter went on to protest that the CWC were poor losers. They refused to face facts. They trumped up accusations of foul play against the CLRB and called for an appeal of the decision against them. Full of righteous indignation, the newsletter suggested that this action by the CWC seriously called into question the honesty of the CLRB and said, "No Traffic and Dining Service members should associate in any way with this slur on the reputation of the Board."

The decision was a severe blow to the grassroots organizers. Everything they had worked for was not to be. They had failed to get enough cards to get a vote. Some had worked for years to lay the groundwork for change. The news was devastating even to those who had recently become involved.

Linda Young recalls her emotions that day: "The loss of the application for certification was my low point. I thought, *Holy Shit how could this happen?* You can't be serious. I have to do it again. I thought, I'm done for. *I got scared. Now what is going to happen to me?*"[9]

But when you have worked so hard for something, sometimes you can't give up. Despite having their noses rubbed in dirt and feeling both humiliation and personal failure, the organizers grieved for a day or so — and then got back up and tried again.

Chapter 9

The Second Card-Signing Campaign and the Vote

The Canadian Labour Relations Board decision to deny a vote for certifi-cation devastated both the staff of the Communications Workers and the grassroots organizers. Everyone mourned for all the time they had invested that now seemed wasted. Operators and dining service staff who had come out as CWC supporters dreaded having to face CUC supporters, who wasted no time before taunting them and rubbing their faces in the defeat. CWC organizers and supporters felt Bell had tampered with the company employee lists. This was undoubtedly the lowest point of the campaign for many of the key organizers.

Janice McClelland recalls the pivotal point in the campaign:

> I was considering going back to work within the company union structure, but the CWC decided to do it again. They saw that momentum was with the card campaign. It just ended a little too soon. Despite the outlay of money to continue the campaign, the CWC decided to do it again. And we did.[1]

Ann Newman looks back and recalls the intensity that organizers felt.

Although they had clearly failed to get a majority the fact that they were so close led them to consider doing it all over. "The low point was when we lost the first campaign. We could not believe it. We were angry with the people sitting on the sidelines. We had a meeting at a hotel. The CWC threw out the question, 'Should we give up or try again?' We all said we had to do it. And we only had a month to do it in."[2]

On March 4, the CWC and Local 50 hosted a meeting of about forty operators and dining service staff. After much mutual commiseration over the loss, the group decided that the only way was to go forward.

Ed Seymour remembers how the discussion evolved within the CWC:

> We were short by 137 cards and were told we had to wait six months before we could have another campaign. Then there was an executive meeting on March 5. I saw Fred afterwards and asked him, "Are we in it?" Fred replied with a hand gesture more or less saying, "Up to here." I saw Bob White (president of the United Auto Workers) and told him we were doing it.
>
> Fred sent out an all-staff memo telling us we were having another campaign, but to tear up the memo once received. We had only twenty-six days for the campaign; March 30, we applied again for certification.[3]

For the CWC leadership, two options for moving forward were to work within the CUC to press for a merger, or to give a card-signing campaign another try. Starting another campaign involved a major legal problem. Existing law required a six-month rest period between card-signing campaigns. Since the last application had been submitted on October 4, 1978, it could be argued that six months had indeed passed. However, a counterargument claimed that the six-month rest period had to start from the date of the CLRB decision on the application.

After discussing all the possibilities, the CWC leadership decided to take the risk and began another card-signing campaign.

Ed Seymour remembers Fred Pomeroy's confidence and the reason for it:

The [Labour Relations] Act said the CLRB had the power to direct the vote. Fred was always totally confident. I suspect that Fred went to the board and reminded them of their authority to order a vote in these circumstances. Rather than the board, it would have been the government of the day who would have been embarrassed by denying a group of employees the size of the work unit at Bell the right to vote for representation.

We had the capacity to embarrass the government. He probably pointed out that, "You are a lot better siding with us than the CUC." The consequences to the government would be great if they didn't. The government didn't stop the application despite the ties between the CUC and the Liberals. There was always a Liberal around the CUC.[4]

It was a calculated risk, but still a crapshoot. The campaign had to be quick; if the CUC was able to sign a new contract or went on strike, there could not be another card-signing campaign until three months before the new contract ended. As bargaining unit contracts usually ran two to three years, another campaign would have to be put off for several years. Many variables, including reductions in the workforce due to technological change, made a future campaign even riskier than starting all over again with the CLRB regulatory decision hanging over the campaign. Bill Howes remembers the collective determination: "It was always intense and there was never a stalling point. Even when we lost the first card campaign, we all immediately jumped on board do it again."[5]

A New Campaign Begins

The second card-signing campaign began on March 5, 1979. Organizers — both Bell operators and CWC staff — worked around the clock to sign up members again on new cards and ask for an additional two dollars as required by the CLRB. The CWC kicked off with a new bulletin: "New Campaign Launched." The newsletter stated that in the week since the CLRB decided not to call a vote, operators and dining service employees at Bell Canada had made it clear they did not want to stop. They were unanimous in demanding that solutions be found and action taken to overcome the setback. In response, the CWC officers proposed a concrete plan of action:

THE FIRST STEP IS THE IMMEDIATE LAUNCHING OF A NEW ORGANIZING CAMPAIGN.
IT IS TO BE A LIGHTNING CAMPAIGN.

We must act quickly. Each operator and dining service employee is being asked to sign a new application for membership card immediately and pay another $2 application fee.

The newsletter addressed procedural issues with the CLRB and urged their future members to "make sure every day counts toward a winning vote." It ended with the slogan: "SIGN A CARD TODAY."

On March 11, the CWC held a rally to gain a vote at the Sheraton Centre in Toronto. Leaders reported that 2,300 employees had signed new membership cards. They urged grassroots members to work even harder.

The next day, the CWC issued another bulletin, announcing "The New Campaign Off to a Great Start." The newsletter reported on the campaign rally the day before. It also described how successful the new campaign was, getting 2,300 new cards signed and the $2 fee paid during the first seven days. The goal now was to get 4,000 cards signed as soon as possible.

The newsletter included information about what happened with the list and card-counting in the previous campaign. At the March 11 rally, Bill Howes explained that the CWC fell 143 cards short of a majority with the CLRB rejecting 155 cards, and that the list supplied by Bell had never been verified as accurate. He reported that the CWC was signing 143 cards a day at the end of the previous campaign, so in effect it was only one day short of getting the needed majority.

The bulletin also included remarks by CWC President Fred Pomeroy. He congratulated all the organizers and called on them to work hard in the days ahead. He noted, "CWC is in a race against time because a majority has to be reached before CUC signs a new agreement with the company. CUC is in bargaining now and will be desperately trying to reach a fast agreement to stop employees who are organizing for the CWC. They won't be trying to sort out genuine solutions to the many problems employees have. So we have to go all out every day. Failure to reach a majority in time could result in living under an unsatisfactory CUC agreement for another two years."

The newsletter also included a report on the campaign in Quebec from CWC National Representative Marie Pinsonneault and traffic operators Claudette Doyon, Michelle Brouillette, and Carmen Lantin. The message was loud and clear: the campaign was going well in Quebec, and everyone there wanted unity with employees in Ontario in a new, more dynamic union.

The bulletin concluded with a section called "Let's Look at the Facts," which stated that no one could be expelled from the CUC for signing a card. It referred to Canada Labour Code section 184 (1), which made it an unfair labour practice for an employer to fire an employee for signing a card for either union. The bulletin emphasized that many, many employees had been openly working for CWC with no repercussions. The bulletin ended with the exhortation:

Don't Be Afraid — Stand up for Your Rights — CWC Will Take Legal Action Against Either CUC Or Bell If They Attempt to Violate Your Rights Under the Law.

SIGN A CWC CARD TODAY

While working full-time, grassroots operator organizers dug deep and pulled up reserves of energy and courage to deliver the cards and application fees. As soon as all or nearly all the staff in one office had signed cards, Toronto organizers focused their energies on the offices and locations that had weak or even nonexistent support. Local 50 set up full-time information tables at 50 Eglinton and 15 Asquith Avenue in Toronto. Operators sat at the tables sixteen hours a day, ready to answer questions and sign cards. The CUC was especially strong at 50 Eglinton, and both offices were a good source of new members.

Once card-signing was almost complete in Montreal, organizers from that city came to Toronto to support the campaign and show solidarity with Ontario. This kind of interprovincial cooperation had been minimal in the CUC. Antagonism between the two provinces was subtly fostered by the company, because it served the company's interest to keep them apart. The language issue and Quebec's desire for independence threatened to blow apart the whole country, but francophone and anglophone operators transcended the national division by taking up a common cause against the company and its union.

The second campaign produced a lot more hostility and tension than the first. Time was of the essence and the CUC leaders knew they were very close to losing the right to represent telephone operators.

Campaign Reports — Toronto

In three days the campaign had gotten off to a flying start. In some TOPS offices, such as those at Main Square and Crossways, almost everyone who had previously signed a card signed another. Fifty-five of the fifty-eight who had signed up in Dining Services re-signed. The initial membership base was holding firm. In one TOPs office — Valhalla — even more cards were signed than in the previous campaign. The campaign had gained momentum. By March 9, the campaign in both provinces had signed up 1,733 cards.[6]

From these campaign reports you can see that in just four days Toronto organizers had re-signed 325 Application for Membership cards. The second card campaign was off to a wonderful start; the momentum was building nicely and morale soared.

March 9 Toronto campaign summary report, p.1.

CUC flyer: "Do You Really Think They Are YOUR Meal Ticket?"

Work Location Information Tables

Organizers at information tables distributed literature. CUC supporters picked it up and threw it away while cursing the CWC. Supporters on both sides wore buttons proudly proclaiming their loyalties. Some operators took it too far: they wore so many that they began to look like they were wearing suits of armour made of buttons. The CUC distributed free T-shirts that said "CUC for me" on the front, and "I am an independent woman" on the back. The slogan was ironic, as telephone operators were making a top wage of $194.00 per week — and on that salary could be only independently poor.

With a tight timeline in place, the CUC was unable to produce thought-provoking print material, and resorted to amateurish cartoon leaflets stoking fears that the CWC would be male-dominated and women would be exploited.

On March 8, the CUC issued a newsletter, *CUC and Bell Canada Return to Bargaining Table*. The first paragraph reported that the CUC had re-entered bargaining with the company on March 6 and that bargaining continued daily. Shirley Nicholson, the acting president, called on company officials to bargain in good faith and jointly complete the agreement.

The title of the next article declared that the "CWC RAID IS DEAD." The article went on to say that the CWC leadership were "poor losers" and that they "refused to face facts."

When these messages failed to rouse the membership, their newsletter moved into begging mode. Under the subtitle "Let's All Pull Together," the union pleaded, "We need our retroactive pay. We need to complete a collective agreement covering our new bargaining demands. We need the back pay and we need new conditions without further delay. Let bygones be bygones.… LET'S GO, CUC!"[7]

CUC General Council Meeting

At a General Council meeting on March 10 in Montreal, the CUC leadership faced another card-signing campaign; despite their best efforts to denigrate the CWC, they had to keep up the fight to save their union. But these efforts were more suited to a community meeting than a national union fighting for its existence. Their arguments quickly descended to scolding and the use of guilt. As any mother knows, such tactics fail as children grow up. The membership was growing up and wanted to assume a more adult role in relation to the employer. Realizing that the CWC was not going to give up, the CUC proposed a resolution:

Motion for General Council
RESOLUTION #1

Whereas:

- the Canada Labour Relations Board has ruled that the CWC failed in its bid for a representation vote among Traffic and Dining Service employees at Bell Canada;

- the CWC is continuing to harass our membership, contrary to trade union principles;
- the best interests of our members would be served by a demonstration of solidarity;
- Bell Canada is a powerful monopoly;

THEREFORE BE IT RESOLVED:

That all Traffic and Dining Service Employees join ranks in support of CUC and that the CUC call on Craft and Services employees to join with us in a united front in our negotiations with Bell Canada.[8]

This motion might have sounded good, but by the time it got to employees it was too late to convince anyone who was signing with the CWC for improved wages and working conditions. The second card-signing campaign had begun on March 5. By the time of the council meeting, the CUC must have known that the new card-signing campaign was underway. It tried to up its defence, claiming, "The CWC publicity machine accused CUC of being 'in bed' with Bell Canada. That's our trade union sisters of the CUC bargaining committee the CWC is slandering. This is the kind of insult we can continue to expect from the morally bankrupt leadership of the CWC."[9]

Right after the General Council meeting, the CUC issued a press release describing the CWC as (again) poor losers and calling them on their legal challenges to the ruling. They also ranted at Louis Laberge, president of the Quebec Labour Federation. They called him "the self-appointed spiritual leader of Quebec Labour and protector of trade union principles," but said "he made a grave error in supporting the CWC — a male-dominated union raiding a female union." The General Council passed a resolution supporting the CUC, as well as calling on the federal government to either appoint a conciliation officer or waive that step and allow the union to get a strike mandate. The press release ended with an announcement that the union was going back to the bargaining table that week.[10]

Diatribes, rants, and rumours were the modus operandi of the CUC campaign. While the CUC looked like it was operating on a shoestring budget, led by a number of amateurs, the CWC counteracted every rumour or untruth with well-written and professionally produced newsletters. The *CWC Bulletin* of March 12 directly addressed CUC propaganda with the headline "CUC RECORD STILL PERFECT — THEY'RE WRONG AGAIN!!" The bulletin reported that one of the latest stories being spread by the CUC was that the CWC couldn't legally apply for a vote again. The bulletin diplomatically said, "Once again CUC representatives either don't know the law — or they're lying to their own members."

The CWC reported that they had the "opinion of our lawyers (supported by similar cases) that the Board will accept a new application from CWC." This information was put in context by noting, "<u>PROVIDED THAT A MAJORITY OF EMPLOYEES HAVE SIGNED CWC CARDS BEFORE CUC CAN SIGN A FAST CONTRACT</u>." To get potential members thinking, they posed a question: "Just ask yourself — would CWC be going through all the work involved in a new campaign unless there was a reasonable certainty that the campaign would result in a vote? Not likely!"

As in other bulletins, they urged potential members:

BE PART OF A NEW MAJORITY
SIGN UP TODAY
SIGN A CWC CARD TODAY

Ann Newman, Connie Graham, George Larter, and Irene Anderson sitting at an information table at 15 Asquith.

CUC supporters were getting highly agitated as they saw they were being outmanoeuvered and realized how effectively organizers countered their rumour mill. In Toronto, 50 Eglinton Avenue was the home of many CUC officers and stalwarts, and when the operator organizers set up a table in the cafeteria there, they were livid.

On March 15, 1979, Dorothy Petty, a CUC union steward in a Directory Assistance office at 50 Eglinton Avenue, took action to show how she felt about the campaign.

Irene Anderson remembers one particularly eventful day at 50 Eglinton:

> One memory sticks out. At 50 Eglinton, Ann, Janice, George and I, we were all sitting at a table. Dorothy Petty came down from DA 3. She must have been in her mid-forties. She swept her arms across the table and threw off all our material. We all broke out laughing. It was the worst thing she could have done. It made them look bad.[11]

This incident prompted the CWC to file a complaint with the CLRB the same day to stop the destruction of literature under section 186 of the Labour Code. The complaint letter reported that at 11:50 a.m. Dorothy Petty (an officer or steward of the CUC) destroyed organizing bulletins in the cafeteria at 50 Eglinton Avenue. The letter asked that she cease and desist her intimidation and that she be prosecuted. The letter served notice to the CUC that there were protections under labour law, and that the CWC had a legal right to organize. The complaint was signed by Bill Howes and provided lots of fodder for the propaganda war. These protections of organizing under labour law led the company and both unions to agree on rules for electioneering. This was three months too late for card-signing, but the rules were applied later to campaigning around the vote

Although 50 Eglinton and the Directory Assistance offices were the CUC strongholds, there were still many CUC supporters in some of the long-distance offices.

Special newsletters were developed to offset the CUC rumours. Photocopied rather than run off on a Gestetner machine, they could be undated, as was this example for Crossways, a toll office located in a high-rise at Dundas and Bloor Streets in Toronto.

Joan M. Roberts

"SPECIAL MESSAGE
FOR OPERATORS AT CROSSWAYS"

It has come to our attention that the CUC has been using threats to try to prevent operators from re-signing cards in support of CWC.

The threats have been:

1. That operators who sign cards will be expelled from the CUC.
2. That CUC will refuse to represent operators who sign CWC cards.

LET'S LOOK AT THE FACTS

First, CUC has copies of the Bell Operators Newsletters which contain the names and signatures of dozens of operators who support CWC. Not one has been expelled from CUC. (If they expelled everyone who had signed a CWC card, they'd have to expel over 48% of their members!)

Second, the Canadian Labour Code, Section 136.1, requires CUC to represent all employees covered by the CUC contract whether they are CUC members or not.

The Section of the Canada Labour Code is reproduced below:

Bargaining agent to fairly represent employees	**136.1** Where a trade union is the bargaining agent for a bargaining unit, the trade union and every representative of the trade union shall represent, fairly and without discrimination, all employees in the bargaining unit. 1977–1978, c 23, s49.

Either CUC representatives don't know the truth or they are afraid to tell it. The CUC propaganda was so effective in one office that it instigated a number of operators to ask to withdraw their CWC cards.

JOIN THE UNION THAT KNOWS THE LAW AND DOES REPRESENT ITS MEMBERS

SIGN A CWC CARD

opieu 343

The CUC finally began to direct its message to constituencies within its ranks and also the ranks of the CWC. The company union designed one flyer for part-timers. Called *CUC: THE PART-TIMERS UNION*, it featured this information:

Which union — CUC or CWC — best represents the interests of part-time employees? If you think it's CWC — think again! The facts prove otherwise.

If you were a part-time operator in SaskTel, where CWC represents Traffic, you would not:
- Receive sickness-disability benefits!
- Be entitled to take vacation weeks!
- Receive a company pension!
- Be guaranteed a minimum amount of work!
- Be protected from lay-off due to technological change!

CUC PART-TIMERS HAVE ALL OF THESE BENEFITS

The flyer then went on to confront some wording in a letter sent by Fred Pomeroy to the CLRB questioning the veracity of company lists with respect to numbers of part-timers.

CWC President Fred Pomeroy does not respect part-timers. He does not even understand the nature of your work! In a letter to the CLRB dated 9th January [1979], he observed that part-timers are "employed on a casual or occasional basis." Mr.

Pomeroy called your presence on the company lists "very questionable." CWC does not want the Board to allow part-timers to cast a ballot if a representation vote is announced despite the fact that some of you have many years of service in Traffic. CWC also believes "casual employees" should be entitled to vote. CUC can certainly accept this, as Bell Canada does not employ casual employees in the Traffic and Dining Service departments!

Taking their cue from CWC bulletins, the flyer ended with the admonishment, "CUC REPRESENTS ITS MEMBERS — IT DOESN'T EXCLUDE THEM! **CUC, EVERYBODY'S UNION."** This flyer struck a nerve with Bell part-timers, as they had a different classification and protocols than craft and services part-timers, and were at the mercy of managerial favouritism to get enough hours to make working worthwhile.

The following extract is taken from an undated CWC Bulletin as the response to CUC flyer about part-timers.

PART-TIME?

Communications Workers of Canada represents _all_ operators in Saskatchewan, both full-time and part-time, and has applied to the Labour Board to represent both part-time and full-time employees in Ontario and Quebec. The following information explains how CWC, representing these people since 1945, has succeeded through bargaining to work out the differences between part-timers and full-timers and to ensure protection for both.

The next section, "Working Conditions," compared working conditions for part-time operators in Saskatchewan and operators in Ontario and Quebec. A section on "Rights" reported that SaskTel operators have the right to refuse to work any shift that does not suit them.

The CWC also prepared a special bulletin for dining services employees comparing their wage rate structure to similar jobs (such as custodian) in the craft and services contracts.

Wages — Dining Service

Dining Service employees have hours, working conditions, and job problems which are very different from those of Traffic Department employees.

Because the CUC-Bell Canada contract is the only combined Traffic and Dining Service contract in Canada, we must look at different industries in order to compare wages and hours.

The table below shows the top wage rates now being paid to employees in the dining service. It also shows the wage rates now being paid to employees in service jobs for which CWC bargains.

It is interesting to note that out of the 13 jobs which pay less than $200 per week, 10 of them are jobs through which the CUC bargains. Six of the seven jobs which pay more than $200 per week are represented by CWC.

SERVICE JOBS BY TOP RATES OF PAY

JOB	WEEKLY RATE	REPRESENTED BY
Building Maintenance Man	259.10	CWC
Express Driver	247.80	CWC
Utility Man	246.85	CWC
Garage Service Man	231.90	CWC
Apparatus Cleaner	213.75	CWC
Head Cook	208.43	CUC
Senior Cook	188.38	CUC
Cook Attendant	186.84	CUC
Dining Service Storekeeper	178.10	CUC
Elevator Dispatcher, Inquiry Desk Attendant	172.00	CWC
Cook	164.74	CUC

Kitchen Attendant	160.88	CUC
Elevator Operator	159.40	CWC
House Service Woman	156.80	CWC
Senior Dining Service Attendants	156.77	CUC
Traffic Matron-Class III	154.71	CUC
Traffic Matron-Class II	149.31	CUC
Traffic Matron-Class I	147.00	CUC
Dining Service Attendant	147.00	CUC

Dining service employees have not had good representation from the CUC over the years. CWC's policy is to bargain for ALL the employees in the union.

In CWC's first contract with Bell Canada we were successful in up-grading (and therefore getting even higher raises for) several of the service jobs in the plant group. The jobs which were upgraded were: *Garage Service Man, Building Service Man, Building Maintenance Man & Express Driver.*

CWC is now in negotiations for a 1979 contract. Our proposals ask for an upgrading (to a higher wage schedule) for the following service jobs: *House Service Woman, Apparatus Cleaner, Building Maintenance Man & Building Equipment Man.*

CWC is committed to a policy of upgrading the wage rates of services jobs.

Campaign Midpoint

The CUC issued an update for its member on March 16 entitled *Bargaining Bulletin.* In it, the union informed its members that twenty bargaining sessions had taken place since it resumed bargaining. The CUC had made many concessions, but the company was not responsive to any of the union's demands. The CUC was now considering asking for conciliation. Nonetheless, bargaining was to continue in Quebec City, March 20–23.

AREA	POTENTIAL	OCT 4 CARDS	NEW CAMPAIGN CARDS REC'D	NEW CAMPAIGN CARDS IN FIELD	TOTAL
TORONTO	1470	661	423	61	484
BAL. OF ONT.	2999	867	488	202	690
TOTAL	4469	1528	911	263	1174
QUEBEC	3198	2159	1487	457	1944
TOTAL	7667	3687	2398	720	3118

TRAFFIC CARD SUMMARY — ONT & QUE. 10:00 AM MAR 16

TOTAL PER CENT SIGNED (OF 7658) = 40.71 %

March 16 campaign report.

On that same day, and only eleven days into the campaign, the CWC was able to celebrate reaching 40 percent of the total number of signed cards needed for a majority within the bargaining unit.

A handwritten letter on CUC stationery dated March 24, 1979, warned operators that the CWC was about to arrive.[12] The CUC emphasized the length of time it had taken the men to get a contract and warned that if the CLRB called a vote, it would cause additional delay. They asked why the CWC was not bargaining for the men instead of raiding the CUC. The bulletin also asked if the CWC was going to be a better representative for Bell operators then why have four hundred Northern Quebec operators signed Teamster cards — and why have men in Toronto cancel their membership? It also suggested the reader ask if the CWC contract had a job security clause

On March 21 the Canadian Labour Congress formally denied the CUC application for membership in the CLC. The CWC had thwarted their desire for legitimacy.[13] The CUC was not wanted by the mainstream labour movement, and their argument that the CWC campaign was a raid on a fellow trade union could not hold up any longer.

In early April, a CUC release to their members regarding their rejection by the Canadian Labour Congress announced:

COMMUNICATIONS UNION CANADA HAS CHARGED
THE EXECUTIVE COUNCIL OF THE CANADIAN
LABOUR CONGRESS WITH DISCRIMINATION
AGAINST 7,900 WOMEN TRADE UNION ACTIVISTS.[14]

In the release, the CUC claimed 7,900 members instead of 7,400. The company list identified five hundred new members. The CUC collective agreement included the Rand formula, which was a clause that meant it was a dues shop and all employees, including part-timers, had to pay union dues. Even the format of the release was awkward; today's communication norms would consider a flyer in all caps as shouting. (While the CWC also employed all caps on occasion, it did so only in the final statements of its messages, for encouragement.) In this instance, the CUC might have tried to mimic the format of a telegram, attempting to grab the attention of the reader about the urgency of the situation.

Dissipating its energy, the CUC decided to pick a fight with the CLC and accused it of discrimination. Its argument was that the CLC was rejecting it as an affiliate because it was female-dominated, not because it was a company union. It played the victim as well, complaining that a CLC affiliate was raiding it. Its response was to draft the following petition:

We the undersigned are members of Communications Union of Canada, the certified bargaining agent for Traffic and Dining Service employees at Bell Canada. We deplore the action of the Canadian Labour Congress in denying, without explanation, the application of CUC for affiliation to the Congress. We support the Executive Council of CUC in its decision to continue all appropriate action to support affiliation the CUC to the Canadian Labour Congress.[15]

The CUC sent the petition to their local representatives, who were asked to return it by April 30.[16]

The CUC also tried to stir up resentment in the craft locals of the CWC. They drafted a notice that was distributed to craft and services locations.

A MESSAGE TO CRAFTSMEN [undated, unsigned]

A growing number of craftsmen across Toronto are concerned about the time and money that our union is spending on the Traffic campaign. (In case you are not aware, CWC has been trying to organize Bell operators and cafeteria workers since last May.)

The first organizing campaign began in July 1978 and cost over $200,000. The Labour Board refused the application for certification in February 1979 (in contrast to their decision in the 1976 CTEA campaign). Our union is now conducting another campaign which will take a few months. Will the second drive also cost $200,000? Craftsmen could be losing half a million dollars if the Traffic union wins!

We haven't seen our president for months but Bell operators have. Let's get him back looking after us! A Toronto craftsman was told his grievance would have to wait until after bargaining. Why? We pay the shot — we should get the attention.

P.S. Pass this on to a fellow craftsmen — we want all Toronto locals to be informed.

On March 31, 1979, the Communications Workers of Canada submitted a second application to be certified as the bargaining agent for the Traffic and Dining Services employee bargaining unit at Bell Canada. In one month the campaign had signed up 4,027 telephone operators and dining service employees in Ontario and Quebec, who had paid over $8,000 in fees for the right to have legitimate union

Bulletin

---

3 7 5 0   C A R D S   P L U S !!

CWC – On Monday, March 5th launched the "new" campaign to sign up a majority of Traffic and Dining Service employees across Ontario and Quebec.

Through the efforts of literally hundreds of employees over 3750 people have signed up with CWC - in just 3 weeks!

CUC – according to their Bargaining Bulletin of March 16th has held numerous bargaining sessions. According to CUC's own Bulletin they have "made many concessions" while "Bell has made no concessions to any of the Union's demands".

JUDGE FOR YOURSELF

– WHICH UNION HAS THE SUPPORT OF EMPLOYEES !!

– WHICH UNION HAS DEMONSTRATED THE ABILITY TO GET THINGS DONE !!

YOUR CARD COUNTS

As of March 26th we have slightly more cards signed than the Labour Board accepted in the last campaign. The next few days - and fewer than 250 more cards - will decide whether you will stay with the same tired old union or have a new opportunity to achieve decent pay and working conditions.

YOU can't afford to sit on the fence any longer. YOUR card can win a better future for you and your fellow employees.

S I G N   U P   W I T H   C W C

T O D A Y

CWC bulletin announcing the signing of 3,750 cards.

representation. It was a miraculous feat considering the geographic dispersal of staff across small towns in two provinces. These workplace organizers persevered to improve their rights and standard of living, even if it meant giving up all their time, their family life, and a great deal of sleep. More than wages were at stake for these women; their future as workers was on the line. It was a chance to gain dignity after being oppressed for so long.

On April 2, 1979, a CWC press release announced the March 31 filing of an application with the CLRB for certification to represent traffic and dining services employees. The application was supported by over 4,027 Application for Membership cards.[17]

Fred Pomeroy announced in a press release: "This new campaign received a tremendous response from employees. In the space of just twenty-six days, over four thousand employees signed up with the CWC. This ought to make it clear to everybody that these employees want and need a new union." He went on to say that he was optimistic that the CLRB would order a secret ballot vote amongst employees.[18]

The CUC must have been blindsided by the news. It released a bulletin on April 4 that reported negative points about the CWC, but it was not until the middle of the document that the CUC announced that the CWC had applied for certification again. It noted that its legal counsel was sure the application would be turned down. That may have been a strategic placement, as it was not news that it wanted to highlight. Here is some of the text of the bulletin:

AIB ADMINSTRATOR ROLLS BACK CWC 1977 WAGE REOPENER

The Administrator has ruled the craft and services employees were overpaid $250,000 for the period December 1, 1977 to November 30, 1978. The employees must pay back to the [C]rown, $125,000 from their wages. This is the union that accused CUC of having no clout with bureaucrats. While CUC members were rolled back, never have they been in a position of having to pay back any money to the crown.[19]

TEAMSTERS RAID CWC IN QUEBEC

The Teamsters union has applied to the Quebec Labour Relations Board for certification for telephone operators in

Telebec LTD. According to Teamster organizers they have signed up 80% of the bargaining unit. Reasons for the operator dissatisfaction with the CWC are:

1. No representation at the bargaining table
2. Operators do not feel part of the CWC; they feel ignored by the male majority because they are a minority group
3. Grievances are not attended to

CWC ATTEMPTS SECOND APPLICATION

CWC stated in a bulletin dated April 2, 1979, that they applied again to the CLRB for certification. According to our legal counsel in both provinces it is highly unlikely that the CLRB will accept another application at this time.

WHERE IS CWC'S BARGAINING EXPERTISE?

Craft contract stalled

CWC had been bargaining with Bell Canada since September, 7, 1978, and according to its *Bargaining Bulletin #10* (dated March 26, 1979), it had not been successful in forcing Bell to "seriously face the issues in a responsible manner." Many of its "issues" are already contained in CUC's Collective Agreement, e.g., vacation selection by seniority, job posting, union security and others.

GET THE FACTS

See your representative, district chairperson or regional co-ordinators for correct information.

Printed by Communications Union Canada — Toronto, Ontario 5/4/79.[20]

On April 5, the minister of labour announced the appointment of Conciliation Commissioner Pierre Dufresne. Bargaining had produced little progress prior to his appointment. The commissioner set a date of April 17 to resume bargaining.

On April 25, the CWC issued a press release emphatically stating that it was not opposed to any wage or benefit increase negotiated on behalf of traffic and dining service employees by the CUC. The press release referred to a recent communication that blamed the CWC for the breakdown of talks between the CUC and Bell Canada. Recognizing that the employee group had been too long without any increase, the CWC explained that the Labour Code allowed bargaining to continue even with a pending application. The document went on to say that the CWC had taken the position that it would not prevent any bargaining or settlement between the CUC and the company. The CWC concluded by saying that it would be willing to commence bargaining as soon as it was certified as the bargaining agent.[21]

By mid-April the CUC was looking for legal means to stop the CWC application for certification. In a CWC press release dated April 25, 1979, the CWC reported: "Meanwhile the Communications Union Canada which represents Bell's 7,600 operators and cafeteria employees is asking the Federal Courts to prevent the Canada Labour Relations Board from studying a second application by the CWC to replace it as agent for the operators."[22] This tit-for-tat communications war was critical to retaining the members the CWC had signed up. Just because someone had signed a card did not mean they could not be persuaded to vote against the CWC.

The wait for a decision from the CLRB was not as long as after the first campaign. To pressure the CLRB, demonstrations were held outside its office in Ottawa and at Bell regional offices to push home the point that operators had waited long enough.

On May 26, a *Toronto Star* article titled "Bell Operators Must Choose among Unions" reported that earlier that week, the CLRB had ordered a representation vote to settle the rivalry between the two unions. The article reported: "'We'll win the vote but it won't be a shoo-in,' said CWC spokesman Bill Howes. 'The officers of the CUC have no place to go, so they'll be fighting hard to keep their jobs.'" The article also reported that balloting would be conducted by mail and should be completed in two months. The CUC point of view was expressed by President Shirley Nicholson, who said that she was confident the operators would stick with her organization, even though a majority had signed cards with the CWC. "Many of them signed just to get a vote and get the challenge from the CWC out of the way," she told the *Star*.

Rules of Engagement for the Certification Vote

And so another campaign was underway. Despite their weariness, the organizers went back to work writing newsletters and bulletins, setting up information tables, and talking it up. Early on the morning of June 7, a group of Toronto operators decided to hold a sit-in at 15 Asquith to protest the company's actions in denying their rights to campaign for the CWC. They put up a CWC sign and put out CWC bulletins, buttons, stickers, and cards. When ordered to leave by Bell management, they refused.

Conference calls were hastily arranged with all parties and the Labour Board. Not much was accomplished, so the operators — including George Larter, Irene Anderson, and Ann Newman — again set up a table in the cafeteria at Asquith. Within an hour, Bell management called the CWC saying they wanted to negotiate the terms of a settlement. On June 7 and 8, phone calls were arranged between Bell Canada, the CUC, and the CWC regarding electioneering on Bell premises, which resulted in the following agreement (sent by telegram):

1. CAFETERIAS: EACH UNION IS TO BE PERMITTED THE USE OF ONE TABLE ONLY IN EACH CAFETERIA FOR THE PURPOSE OF ELECTIONEERING IN CAFETERIAS PROVIDED THERE ARE NO DISRUPTIONS TO EMPLOYEES.

2. KITCHENS/LOUNGES: AT LOCATIONS WHERE THERE ARE NO CAFETERIAS ELECTIONEERING WILL BE PERMITTED ONLY IN KITCHENS, THIS PRECLUDES ELECTIONEERING IN OPERATORS LOUNGES OR NIGHT KITCHENS.

3. EARLY ACCESS TO BUILDINGS: ACTIVE EMPLOYEES IN THE BARGAINING UNIT WILL BE PERMITTED ON THE PREMISES AT OTHER THAN THEIR WORKING HOURS.

4. ACCESS TO BUILDING BY OTHER EMPLOYEES: ACTIVE

EMPLOYEES IN THE BARGAINING UNIT WILL BE PERMITTED ACCESS TO CAFETERIAS/KITCHENS AT OTHER THAN THEIR NORMAL WORK LOCATIONS. THE NUMBER OF SUCH EMPLOYEES AT ANY ONE TIME SHALL BE LIMITED TO (3) THREE AND THERE SHALL BE NO DISRUPTION OF THE LOCAL WORK FORCE.

5. HEAD SET BOXES: WILL NOT BE USED FOR ELECTIONEER-ING PURPOSES.

6. STICKERS: WILL BE PERMITTED PROVIDED THAT THEY ARE, GENERALLY SPEAKING, ABOUT THE SIZE AND CONFIGURATION OF BUTTONS CURRENTLY BEING USED, HAVE THE TYPE OF MESSAGE THAT WOULD BE CONTAINED ON A BUTTON AND ARE STUCK ONLY ON AN EMPLOYEE'S CLOTHES OR PURSES. NO STICKERS WILL BE PLACED ON COMPANY PROPERTY. THERE SHOULD BE NO PROLIFERATION BEYOND BUTTONS AND STICKERS.

7. T-SHIRTS: WILL NOT BE WORN ON COMPANY PREMISES.

8. SHOULD DIFFICULTIES ARISE WITH ANY OF THE ABOVE, THE PARTIES AGREE TO CONTACT EACH OTHER TO ATTEMPT TO RESOLVE SUCH DIFFICULTIES PRIOR TO TAKING ANY UNILATERAL ACTION

B KELLER, ASSISTANT DIRECTOR LABOUR RELATIONS BELL CANADA.[23]

The rules permitted on-site campaigning and the grassroots organizers continued to set up information tables in Bell cafeterias. The only restriction that the Labour Board placed on electioneering was that it could not be done during working hours. However, Bell Canada posted a notice to employees advising them that the only electioneering that could be done was the wearing of buttons. Bell managers demanded that employees remove CWC stickers, even from their own clothing and purses. Bell managers also tore up CWC bulletins at a number of locations.

The days when Bell Canada staff were acquiescent and passive were over.

Bell Operators and Dining Services Newsletter #6

The Toronto organizing group, now officially organized as Local 50 of the CWC, pulled together *Bell Operators and Dining Services Newsletter #6* with the byline, "as written by Bell Canada Traffic and Dining Service Employees."

It was dated June 6, 1979, and featured:

What's Inside:

1. The Choice Is Yours
2. Information on Bell craft and services negotiations
3. Newsletter supporters

"The Choice Is Yours" was written by Janice McClelland, Diane Ward, George Larter, and Janice Crook. It announced that in a few days, all traffic and dining service members would be deciding to mark an *X* as to which union would represent them. It included a nice chart comparing wage increases won for operators in Saskatchewan by the CWC compared to wage increases won for operators in Bell Canada by the CUC. The chart showed wide discrepancies in wages between the two companies. The authors also noted that the CUC reportedly had met twenty times with the company; the union had made many concessions, but the members didn't know what these concessions were. The two sides had reached agreement only on minor issues such as distribution of seniority lists and definitions.

The authors then included a chart showing the differing hours of work, overtime, and sick pay between SaskTel and Bell Canada. They presented a comparison of the CUC vs. the CWC on membership, size, economic power, and links with other unions. The authors emphasized that the CUC was refused admission to the Canadian Labour Congress on March 13, 1979. They concluded with, "Here are the facts. We respect your ability to make up your mind yourself."

Pat Sautner, president of CWC Local 26, wrote the second article, "Toronto Information on Bell Craft and Services Negotiations." He announced that as of Thursday, June 7, Bell Canada craft and services would have completed conciliation on their new contract and would be in a

PAPER TIGER IN ACTION !

BARGAINING EXPERTISE. CWC's famous, worthless phrase. Craft and Services employees have received dismal bargaining reports since negotiations between CWC and Bell Canada began last September. Reproduced below are excerpts from past reports. We invite you to read the entire set of reports available from the CWC and judge for yourself if that is the kind of "expertise" you need.

Bargaining Report #2 (Nov. 78) admitted:

"We haven't been able to reach agreement on any item to date"

The Bargaining Committee added:

"It is, however, becoming more and more apparent that it is going to be difficult to resolve some of our key items concerning job security, job rights (including seniority, reporting to the work site, transfers and expenses), hours of work and leisure time, safety and health, union security, wages and zoning."

Report #4, issued in December, was no more optimistic:

"real progress is either very slow or non-existent in most cases"

And a further admission:

"We've modified our position on some items... However, the overall message seems clear that it is going to be very difficult to make any fundamental changes in hours of work, vacations, holidays and overtime."

By January, 1979, after five months of negotiations, CWC's Bargaining Committee was able to report:

"We've made some progress... but still have a lot of unresolved issues..."

Later that month, CWC requested conciliation:

"The bargaining committee took this action because there are a number of substantial issues such as job security, hours of work, overtime, holidays, vacations, transfers, travel allowance, expenses, safety and health, job postings, benefits and union time on which we have been unable to make the kind of progress needed... The substantial issues of wages and zoning are yet to be resolved as well."

After sessions with the Conciliation Officer, CWC's March Report laments:

"Bell Canada is proposing either no improvement or an inadequate improvement on every major issue we're after. They don't believe the employees are serious!"

WHERE, WHERE, WHERE IS ALL THAT MARVELOUS BARGAINING EXPERTISE WE HEARD ABOUT?

WHERE IS THE SPRING AGREEMENT THE CWC PREDICTED IT WOULD HAVE? WHERE IS THE $$$?

MORE IMPORTANT, WHERE IS THE CREDIBILITY?

CWC HAS NO TEETH

CUC flyer: *Paper Tiger in Action*

legal strike position. He explained why the bargaining committee had recommended rejection of the company offer. This made the likelihood of a strike very high. He informed Toronto operators and dining service staff what they could expect if there were picket lines. He announced that the craft and services union members recognized that operators would have to cross their picket lines, as operators would not yet be in a legal strike position. He concluded by saying "Solidarity may originate in our hearts but must be administered by our heads."

The last words on the last page urged readers to vote for the CWC in the upcoming vote and listed CWC supporters from across the province of Ontario.

Craft and services negotiations were a weakness in the CWC campaign that the CUC was eager to exploit to stoke fears about striking. The CUC also made sure that its members knew that the CWC craft and services bargaining unit was not making much progress in the negotiations.

Craft and Services Strike

To complicate the vote tremendously, right at the moment when operators and dining service staff were to vote on joining the CWC, their colleagues in craft and services went on strike, playing out their worst fear of all. On June 8, the Canada Labour Relations Board mailed out the vote ballots to traffic and dining service employees. Meanwhile, the CWC was in ongoing negotiations as well as a strike in the craft and services bargaining unit, and had to prepare for both a national convention on June 14 and an Ontario Regional Council meeting on July 21.

From August 13 to September 10, technicians went on rotating strikes for parity with western phone company employees and to cut compulsory overtime. The contract secured both a wage increase and a reduction in mandatory overtime.

Expecting to win the certification vote, the national union staff also supported the new Traffic and Dining Service locals in developing bargaining proposals. Bill Howes recorded in his diary that July 16 was the deadline for the proposals.

CUC Campaign

Meanwhile, the CUC was fighting for its life. If it lost the vote, staff would be out of a job and CUC representatives would lose both their status in their workplaces and the perks of attending union meetings and conferences.

One CUC leaflet announced "Nicholson Confident — CUC Will Win Vote and Bargaining Will Resume Immediately." The following text has been extracted from the original text and is not replicated in its entirety.

an interview with Communications Union Canada Acting President Shirley Nicholson, who has been leading the bargaining committee in negotiations with Bell Canada for a new collective agreement, and who continues to lead CUC's campaign against the CWC raid. This special report brings members up to date on the negotiations and the interruptions which again prevented your union bargaining committee from completing its job.

CUC: When can we expect to see an increase in pay?

SN: Quite frankly, we are further away from reaching the ratification stage than we were few weeks ago.

CUC: What's holding us up?

SN: The second raid by the CWC.

CUC: The CWC publicity machine said that the signing of their cards by some CUC members wouldn't make any difference to our bargaining.

SN: The CLRB's reason for acceptance of the CWC's second application is stated on page 10 of their decision:

"We realize that if we permit CWC to file a new application for certification, the negotiations of the terms and conditions of employment covering the employees referred to in this second application cannot take place until the matter is resolved."

This isn't the first time some of our members have been misled by the CWC.

CUC: What kind of money are you talking about at the bargaining table?

SN: I estimate the retroactive pay demand to be worth up to $2,000 for members with seniority dating back to the fall of 1977.

CUC: When do we get back to the bargaining table?

SN: As soon as the CLRB counts the ballots and announces that CUC has won the representation vote, we'll be right back where we left off — with the conciliation commissioner.

CUC: One final question. Does it bother you as union president that some of your members signed cards with another union?

SN: Of course it does. But those who did sign cards can change their minds. And I'm confident these members will change their minds and vote CUC in the secret ballot vote.

A regular CUC bulletin was issued in July under the CUC logo. It announced, "CUC Receives Unanimous Support." The support came from the delegates to the second annual convention of the Telecommunications International Union (TIU), which unanimously passed the following resolution in support of the CUC:

Therefore be it resolved by the TIU, in convention assembled, that the convention delegates offer their wholehearted supported and encouragement to the Executive Officers and Board of the CUC, headed by President Shirley Nicholson, in their ceaseless efforts to repel the unwarranted and unwanted raid by the CWC, and be it further resolved that the TIU offer its available resources in its election and in the ensuing negotiations with Bell Canada.

The TIU, a sector organization for independent unions in the telephone industry, was reportedly in discussions with the AFL-CIO about TIU affiliation. The CUC neglected to mention that the sector organization faced jurisdictional disputes similar to what the CUC faced earlier in the year with the CLC. Trying to make the CUC look like a progressive trade union, the bulletin went on to say that the TIU convention introduced resolutions in support of a national health care program, and in opposition to mandatory price and wage controls and labour law reform.

The next item about the decertification of telephone operators in Telebec, however, was true — and hurt the CWC's reputation. The article commended "the employees at Telebec for rejecting the CWC on the basis of irresponsibility and wished them well in their upcoming negotiations."[24] But nothing the CUC did could diminish the amazing accomplishment of the CWC and grassroots organizers in signing over four thousand cards in twenty-six days. The momentum for change was now strongly rooted across both provinces.

The Vote

The CWC ran the vote campaign like a well-run election campaign. Canvassing in an election campaign is used to identify committed voters. The CWC knew it had the potential for over four thousand votes and had a recently verified list of names. Now, with the vote campaign as with an election, the CWC needed to make sure those people voted and that they voted for the CWC. And, as with an election campaign, each side wanted to ensure that every vote for its side was valid and could be included in the count. CWC staff worked to prepare forms and contact information for all four thousand potential voters, and grassroots organizers worked to contact all the employees who had signed union cards.

The following canvass list procedures provide an idea of the administrative activities needed behind the scenes to get out the vote.

Joan M. Roberts

CANVASS LIST PROCEDURE

1. On the receipt of a Force Assignment list, compare the total number of people listed against our "Potential" figure. Note the results on the sheet attached to the cover of the "Canvass List" file.
2. Using the Force Assignment list, type a "Canvass List."
3. On the Canvass list mark a "check mark" behind the names of all members using the white index cards. For each member found on the Canvass list, mark a "check mark" on the white card also. Record each member's phone number on the Canvass list.
4. Pull and photocopy any white cards which DO NOT appear on the Canvass List. Re-file the white cards.
5. Check the Status of any member whose name does not appear on the Canvass List bracket (working from the photocopy of the white card). Check first with the Traffic contact for the office or with the member by phone. Record the status (eg. quit, on leave, etc.) on the photocopy of the white card.
6. Provide a photocopy of the marked Canvass List to the Traffic contact for use in canvassing. Record the name and phone number of the Traffic contact to whom the Canvass List was provided.
7. File the original Canvass List with the Force assignment list.
8. To the original Canvass List, add the names of any members who, through the white card follow-up, were omitted from the Force Assignment list. In the "Notes" colum[n] beside each added name mark "omitted from Force list" and give the reason why the name should be added.
9. Destroy the photocopy of the white card.

The Canadian Labour Relations Board counted the votes on July 30, 1979, at its Ottawa offices. The CWC was allowed one scrutineer, and chose Ann Newman. The CWC scrutineer's role was to challenge any ballot for the CUC that could be considered spoiled. Then a returning officer (an employee of the CLRB) would rule on it. This was the board's approach to spoiled ballots in a vote count.

WHAT HAPPENS TO SPOILED BALLOTS?

Where a party challenges a ballot that has been cast, the Returning Officer shall rule upon the validity of the ballot. If the parties accept the ruling, the ballot shall be counted or rejected accordingly. If the Returning Officer's ruling is not accepted, the challenged ballot is sealed in an envelope and is placed back in the ballot box with all other ballots. The ballot box is then sealed and a statement is obtained from the parties as to their reasons for challenging the ballot. The matter then goes to the Board for a decision. [Rule 26(5)][25]

The ballots were then counted by the Returning Officer in the presence of union and employer representatives.

Within minutes of the completion of the count, Ann Newman left the room in a state of total elation to let everyone know that CWC had won the vote. Ann Newman remembers her excitement:

> The highlight for me was when I was selected to go to scrutineer the vote. We stayed in the Broken Arms hotel — another dive. When I could see we had got the votes, I ran out of the building and I could not even share the news — I could not talk. I was so happy. We were so happy.[26]

Irene Anderson remembers the same event: "When we went to Ottawa for the vote. We drove from 25 Cecil Street to Ottawa. I think it was August 1979. That was an incredible trip and an even more thrilling moment when the results of the vote came out. We were celebrating so much. It was memorable."[27]

Bill Howes with results of vote.

The CLRB Certificate of Result of Vote showed the final count. Ballots were sent to a total of 7,408 employees, and of those, 6,351 returned their ballots. One hundred and five ballots were ruled invalid and twenty ballots were spoiled. The crucial numbers revealed the CWC had won: 3,498 ballots for the CWC; 2,728 ballots for the CUC. The CWC had won with 56.18 percent of the vote.

The CWC had signed over five hundred more people than the votes received. Many did not vote, in spite of continuous efforts by the CWC to prevail on its organizers to monitor each supporter throughout the campaign to ensure they remained loyal. Some supporters may have left Bell and would not have been entitled to a vote, but others may have been too conflicted to make a decision.

The CWC issued a bulletin dated July 30, 1979, headlined "CWC Wins Vote!" The bulletin identified all the key issues to be addressed in the transition process:

- The CWC to be officially certified by August 10.
- The CUC to be decertified at the same time.
- The CWC to inherit the contract with Bell for the bargaining unit.
- The CWC to inherit all existing grievances.

- New CWC stewards to be appointed until elections are held.
- The CWC would open negotiations with Bell.
- A CWC bargaining caucus was to be held August 13–17 at York University in Toronto to select bargaining proposals from those submitted by employees. Toronto sent delegates George Larter, Marg McColl, Janice McClelland, and Ann Newman.

The bulletin emphasized that, following the vote, it was "**A TIME FOR SOLIDARITY** and that Certification would give CWC the right and responsibility to represent <u>every</u> Traffic and Dining Service employee." The union declared, "We intend to <u>meet</u> our responsibility to <u>every</u> employee," and added, "IF YOU HAVEN'T ALREADY JOINED THE MAJORITY — JOIN THE CWC TODAY!"

True to his word, on August 3, Fred Pomeroy wrote to the secretary of Bell Canada giving notice of the CWC's intention to begin bargaining with the company on behalf of Traffic and Dining Services, and proposing to meet August 28 in Montreal.[28] The locals had hardly any time to submit bargaining proposals and prepare for the bargaining caucus.

On July 31, articles appeared in both the *Toronto Star* and the *Globe and Mail*. The *Star* article was titled "Operators Switch to One Big Bell Union"; the *Globe and Mail* piece was titled "Bell Operators Vote to Join Communication Workers." The articles noted that the CWC would now represent twenty-seven thousand bargaining unit members, but that Bell Canada operators wouldn't be joining the craftsmen on the picket lines any time soon. By then, the technicians were involved in rotating strikes and company retaliatory lockouts.

John Deverell of the *Toronto Star* wrote a wonderful post-mortem article on August 4, titled, "Ma Bell's Paternalism Under Fire."

> The switch of allegiance by the operators brings to more than [twenty-two thousand] the number of employees who since 1975 have cast aside the in-house employee associations which for decades dealt with Bell on their behalf .... For their part, after [fifty] years of dealing with in-house associations, Bell executives are unprepared for the rising

union sentiment. They're reacting to the Communications Workers as an unwelcome, disruptive and foreign intruder in their long tranquil domain....

Bell itself sponsored the first employee organization in 1928 and helped select its leaders. During World War II, in response to federal labour law, the employee associations took on a veneer of independence. But in structure and outlook, neither the Canadian Telephone Employees Association (CTEA) nor the operator's Traffic Employees Association bore much resemblance to a genuine trade union... Both organizations were avenues to promotion within the company and that showed up strongly in their abhorrence of the adversary system of collective bargaining.[29]

Fred Pomeroy identified the major factor that led Bell employees to seek legitimate union representation: the end of wage parity within the telephone sector: "Until the early 1970s, Bell was in good shape, but then it made the sad mistake of not keeping up with other phone companies," says Fred Pomeroy. "The employees had no choice but to build themselves a union."[30]

On July 30, 1979, the CWC was officially certified as the bargaining agent for the Bell Canada bargaining unit of Traffic and Dining Services employees. "A major turning point was when we cracked 50 Eglinton, which was harder to crack than Asquith. The CUC was entrenched there. When we got a watershed number of votes we knew we were winning the battle. It was pretty grueling as we had tough CUC people to deal with."[31]

Post-Vote: What Happened to the CUC?

On August 2, the third Special Council Meeting of the CUC General Council met to manage the winding down of the CUC. President Shirley Nicholson acted as chairperson. The CUC conveniently forgot to invite all the CUC delegates who had openly supported the CWC. The minutes record the results of the certification vote and show that the council was informed as to the legal responsibilities regarding grievances and arbitrations. The council agreed (although no formal motions are recorded) to close the Toronto and Montreal offices pending wrapping up of their affairs. The council directed Barbara Morgan to continue as chief financial officer until operations ceased.

Council members passed a motion of non-confidence in the president and added a termination allowance of thirty-three weeks' pay. Her regular pay was to continue up to the end of her term, which was December 31, 1980. The union also agreed to assume the rest of the lease term on her car and transfer ownership to her. Thirty-three members supported the motion; ten were absent.[32] An additional motion was passed agreeing to pay out a settlement totaling $19,000 to the Ontario vice-president, secretary, and staff.

After the disbursements were made as set forth in the Special Council minutes, the rest of the money was given to charity. The CWC's law firm advised that there was little the CWC could do to access the funds of the CUC.[33]

On August 7, CUC vice-president Liz Baker sent a letter to G.W. Lemieux, labour relations manager at Bell Canada, advising him that the CUC had forwarded grievances at the fourth step and information regarding arbitrations to the CWC, and that it had advised CUC representatives to transfer their grievances to the individuals representing the CWC. On August 10, Baker wrote to Fred Pomeroy saying that the company had been informed about the transfer of step-four grievances to the CWC, and enclosed the details of a possible arbitration case.

On August 10, the CUC was officially decertified.

Chapter 10

Collective Bargaining and Early Job Action

The grassroots organizers celebrated the death of the Communications Union of Canada and the certification of the Communications Workers of Canada with gusto, but now the hard work of bargaining had to begin. Because of the very long organizing campaign, operators and dining service staff had heightened expectations of improved wages and working conditions. They were frustrated because there had been no substantive wage increase since 1975, during a time of very rapid inflation. The CWC had to manage the expectations of its new members while building an organizational structure and an inclusive and democratic bargaining process. At the same time, its biggest bargaining unit was already on strike. And it was also possible that its newest bargaining unit would strike as well.

Craft Strike and Lockout

The craft and services bargaining unit contract had expired, and the locals were on rotating strikes during July and early August. Rotating strikes continued until September 10. Now operators and cafeteria staff had to cross picket lines established by their fellow CWC members. It was illegal to go on strike with the craft bargaining unit, but many operators walked the picket lines on their time off.

Temporary Stewards

Whenever possible, the national union worked with the local organizing committees to appoint temporary stewards to serve until democratic local union structures could be put in place. Once bargaining got underway, the stewards' role was to communicate with the membership about what was happening at the bargaining table and to represent the union's members in day-to-day dealings with the company. Their only tool when they assumed the role was the existing CUC contract. As bad as it was, it still contained just enough language to enable the filing of grievances to begin the pushback against unjust management decisions.

> *I took on the roles of steward and chief steward and remember taking a grievance to the third step at which the decision-maker was the chief operator. I don't remember what the issue was or who the grievor was, but I remember taking a strip off that manager to the point where she was crying. Management was unfamiliar with adversarial grievance hearings, and was used to a corporate culture where the company promoted the belief that the workplace was an extended family with the chief operator as the mother figure. I can see now that the chief operator was genuinely perplexed at the uppity behaviour of her rebellious children and hurt by my accusations. I now wish I had taken a softer approach that day, but I was angry because of what my colleagues and I had experienced in such a paternalistic culture, where I had to ask for permission to go to the washroom or had calls listened in on by a supervisor.*

Bell refused to recognize the closed-shop clause in the CUC contract, so the stewards had to continue to sign membership cards and dues deduction cards for existing members. Despite the difficulty in signing people up to pay union dues, the union succeeded in signing up over 90 percent of the membership by Christmas 1979. This task was critical in building solidarity for the eventual strike.

On August 10 the CWC sent a letter to acting stewards congratulating them and informing them that steward training would begin as soon as the craft and services strike ended. The CWC staff deserved a lot of credit for always moving forward with operator capacity-building[1] while most of its membership was on strike. At this point, after the outlay of thousands of dollars on the organizing campaign, the union had not received one dollar in dues. True to their word, on September 5, 1979, Local 50 hosted its first CWC steward training course.

The letter suggested that new stewards contact the craft local stewards and build a relationship with them. It advised them to familiarize themselves with the existing CUC contract and to pay attention to the time limits associated with the grievance procedure. Enclosed with the letter were a number of grievance forms and the step-by-step process for managing grievances. The message was clear: Don't wait for a new contract or for someone else to do it; you as the new steward have to submit grievances when necessary. It was a new day in labour relations in Traffic and Dining Services at Bell Canada.

Celebration

Local 50 then did what they were to become known for — throw a party. A really big celebration was due. Social organizer extraordinaire Marg McColl and a Local 50 social committee arranged a wonderful affair for August 18 at the Masonic Temple. Organizers invited all of Local 50 and the Toronto-based CWC craft and services locals, as well as CWC staff and everyone associated with the organizing campaign.

The party helped build solidarity between the two bargaining units, which were both going through difficulties and change. Sometimes social gatherings and celebrations are discounted by those committed to social change, but this accomplishment was momentous and had required so much time, energy, and resources that no one complained. Celebrations are critical to building relationships, recognizing milestones in progress toward a goal, and honouring commitment and devotion to the cause.

Traffic and Dining Service News

In September 1979 the CWC published and distributed a new CWC bulletin called *Traffic and Dining Service News*. The bulletin informed members that on August 6, the CWC had discussed the transition from the CUC to the CWC as the bargaining agent for traffic and dining services employees with the company. It reported on the election of the bargaining committee and the actions taken by the bargaining caucus. It also notified members that acting stewards were now in place, and that bargaining talks had commenced in Montreal on August 28.

The bulletin ended with the news that the CWC had requested the ongoing grievance and arbitration files from the CUC, but the CUC hadn't yet sent them. This could have meant that there were no ongoing grievances (although there had been at least one at the fourth step), or that all staff were already gone, or that they had not kept files. Whatever it was, there was very little administration to take over from the CUC. Everything had to be started from scratch.

On September 17, Bill Howes sent a letter to acting stewards for Traffic and Dining Services, asking them to send a representative to the upcoming CWC Ontario Regional Council meeting on September 29 and 30 at the Sutton Place Hotel. On the first day, traffic and dining services representatives would have a separate meeting room so they could discuss bargaining, local structure, dues card sign-up, and grievance issues. There would be a social in the evening. The second day, the meeting would include both Traffic and Dining Service as well as craft and services representatives.

It had been just over a month, and responsibilities were increasing rapidly for Local 50 leadership. From assuming local officer responsibilities, to assuming steward and chief steward positions, to sending one of their own to the bargaining committee, and then supporting the national union in developing the entire bargaining unit's capacity to manage its own affairs, the local grassroots leaders could never stop long enough to catch their breath.

Within two weeks of assuming the role of bargaining agent, the CWC held a bargaining caucus from August 13 to 17, 1979, with thirty-six delegates from across Ontario and Quebec. Convention delegates had to choose a bargaining package to present to Bell from among five hundred proposals submitted by bargaining unit members. The bargaining caucus also elected a rank-and-file bargaining committee with two representatives each for Ontario and Quebec. The Ontario representatives were George Larter from Toronto and Lisette Sabourin from Sudbury; for Quebec, they were Michelle Brouillette from Montreal and Louise Godin from Quebec City.

George Larter recalls how the experience transformed his way of seeing the world:

> I was on the bargaining committee. When I walked the picket line with Quebec operators, I found the issues were the same. I connected over the two solitudes while rejecting the notion that the English were the enemy. I never accepted the guilt on a personal level, although I accepted the injustice. And I did not like it when Quebecers used guilt as bargaining strategy. Experiencing Quebec connected me to my own country; then I got connected to the world.[2]

Negotiations for a new contract with Bell Canada began on August 28, 1979. The previous contract had expired in November 1978, and the membership was hungry for a raise. The bargaining demands were substantive and were seen as a charter of rights for telephone employees, incorporating the best practices for telephone sector collective agreements from across North America.

Fred Pomeroy was straddling two bargaining processes: the craft and services rotating strikes, and now telephone operators. He recalled working around the clock:

> I was chair of the bargaining committee for craft and services and got a deal at four in the morning — and started bargaining for operators at nine in the morning.
>
> I was really proud of the operator and dining service bargaining committee. We wanted to work with a certain conciliator and he was busy in the day, so we bargained at night. He told Bell that they had an idiot chairing the management side.[3]

A quick settlement, however, was not in the cards for operators. The company had another female-dominated bargaining unit to think about: service and clerical employees. On September 20, negotiations broke down. Bell was stunned by the number of demands presented by the union. The company applied to the federal minister of labour for conciliation assistance. The government, understanding the length of time since the last contract, decided to bypass the first two steps of the conciliation process, and on October 5, appointed Conciliation Commissioner Roland Tremblay.

Despite Tremblay's entry into the negotiations, bargaining remained difficult and did not improve. The company apparently took a hard line in the conciliation process, responding to every proposal with, "We are entertaining no change in this area at this time," and proposing to remove seniority rights that had been in the previous contract. On November 12, the company proposed an offer so poor that the bargaining committee rejected it.

CWC Local 50 News

October 9 saw the first edition of *CWC Local 50 News*: now the Toronto telephone operators and dining service employees would get their news from their local. It was in black and white, poorly copied, and was probably run off on a Gestetner. But the newsletter proudly announced that the local covered the offices in Toronto, Brampton, Oakville, and Orangeville.

This first edition provided a bargaining update, informed members that at the request of the company the government had appointed a conciliation commissioner, and that the bargaining committee had told the company that they were ready to bargain seven days a week. It also reported on the Ontario Regional Council meeting of September 27 and 28, provided reports from the Ontario bargaining representatives, and reported that the craft and services locals expressed support in the fight. The tone of this newsletter was feisty. Articles were unsigned, as the local leadership now presented a collective front. It ended with the names of the Local 50 executive.

The article "What Can We Do?" made the following suggestions to bargaining unit members:

- Submit a dues card. Over half of Ontario employees had done so by October 5. Demonstrates union support to the company.
- Cut out favours to the company. Don't take E-time (unpaid time).
- Discuss all violations of the contract with your union steward.
- Tell your manager you support the union.

On November 30, after fifteen conciliation sessions, Tremblay adjourned the conciliation process to write his report. This report was supposed to be used as a basis for a contract settlement. If the company and union did not reach an agreement, the union would be in legal strike position seven days after the release of the report.

A strike now seemed inevitable. Each local began to take secret ballot votes authorizing the bargaining committee to call for work slowdowns or rotating strikes if a settlement was not reached. As Local 50 officers and members prepared themselves, they knew that a strike would be a public relations battle. They also prepared a leaflet to begin to inform the public of the latest developments and the union's position.

Rotating Strikes

Toronto Local 50 passed a motion to ask the following question by secret ballot at the membership meeting on December 11, 1979.

> Pending the outcome of a formal ratification vote, are you in favour of authorizing the banning of overtime, the banning of E-time and other appropriate action short of a full scale continuing strike? Such actions may be ordered by your local executive after Traffic and Dining Service members are in a legal position to strike and subject to approval by the bargaining committee.

The conciliation commissioner announced the release of his report on December 17. Fifteen sessions failed to reach any agreement. Seven days from the 17th meant that the union would be in a legal strike position at midnight on Christmas Eve. The union saw the report as a basis for settlement, but the company took no position, neither accepting nor rejecting it.

BELL CANADA OPERATORS AND DINING SERVICE EMPLOYEES

ARE AT THE END OF THE LINE!

DID YOU KNOW   That Bell operators and Dining Service workers have been without
a contract since November 24, 1978?

DID YOU KNOW   That Bell operators and Dining Service workers have not had a
raise since 1977? (The 1977 raise was $5.21 per week in Toronto.)

DID YOU KNOW   That Toronto operators start at $145.46 per week and earn a
maximum of $194.29 - regardless of their years of service?

DID YOU KNOW   That Bell Dining Service attendants earn a maximum of $147.00 a
week?

DID YOU KNOW   That Bell Canada is the richest telephone telephone company in
Canada?

DID YOU KNOW   That Bell Canada's employees are the most productive telephone
employees in the world?

DID YOU KNOW   That Bell Canada subscribers pay the highest telephone rates of
all Canadians?

DID YOU KNOW   That Bell operators must have permission to go to the washroom?

DID YOU KNOW   That Bell operators are "monitored" by managers listening in
without the knowledge or consent of either the operator or the
subscriber?

BELL CANADA REFUSES TO NEGOTIATE....

- Adequate protection from the adverse effects of technological
change. (Recent changes have meant 400 fewer operators' jobs
in Toronto alone. The company plans reductions of up to 40%
of operators jobs.)
- Wages comparable to those of telephone employees in western
Canada. (Bell's wages under their current wage offer would
still be $30 - $40 a week behind western wages.)
- Proper union security language.

Bell's current contract offer was made with three conditions:

1) The union must accept all of the company's proposed changes
to reduce existing employee rights and benefits.

2) The union must accept all of the company's proposed contract
language on the union's proposals.

3) The union must drop all of the union's other proposals.

WE'RE STILL TRYING

to negotiate a decent contract. In the event that we are forced
to strike, we hope that we can count on your support.

THANK YOU

Issued by Local 50
Communications Workers of Canada
(CLC)

Local 50 flyer for the public.

The writing was on the wall. Operators would be home for Christmas. This was something that most of them had never experienced.

A note via the phone tree went out to the Local 50 membership on December 18:

> Our legal strike date is :01 AM on December 25th, (one minute after midnight, Christmas Eve).
>
> In the Conciliation Commissioners report there are improvements above the company's original offer, and there are some areas where the report falls short.
>
> As of Tuesday, December 18, 1979 we are awaiting word from the bargaining committee as to whether our bargaining committee recommends that we accept or reject the report. (The report is over 60 pages long.)
>
> As of Tuesday, December 18, 1979 the company has not indicated whether they accept the report of the Conciliation Commissioner.
>
> Local 50 Executive.

Although the legal strike date was December 25, the Toronto membership was so frustrated and angry that staff at 50 Eglinton, Main Square, and Orangeville walked out illegally beforehand.

Linda Young remembers the tension and excitement of leading her colleagues to stop work and leave the office:

> I was home one day and Bill Howes called. He told me that I had a sit-in going on in my office. He said, "Get your ass over there." My husband took me over to the office and I was crying all the way over. My husband advised me to just go in there and be calm. There were eight of them on the board, and the former CUC reps. I plugged in. I went and plugged into everybody and said to each of them, "We are having a sit-in; come with me." We all went to the lounge. After an

hour someone asked how long we have to sit here. I called Barb (another operator that was off) and she called down to Toronto. She said, "It's over, just go home." We all went home. They were all respectful of authority.[4]

On December 21, to avert a strike, the union's bargaining committee accepted the terms of the conciliation report subject to membership ratification. However, the company did not respond. Faced with no other options, the bargaining committee called for a forty-eight-hour study session beginning Christmas Day. No other day to begin a strike could be as auspicious: a strike on Christmas Day was going to hurt the company on its busiest day of the year. Long-distance dialling did not need operator assistance most of time anymore, but collect calls needed operator assistance, as did person-to-person calls. New Canadians used person-to-person calls to reach family members who did not have a phone in the house. Switchboards in Toronto on Christmas echoed with the voices of operators shouting "Pronto!" and asking for Italian and Portuguese names. Operators then had to wait several minutes for someone to run and get the person to answer the call from their loved one. Due to poor pronunciation on the operator's part, the person answering the call often fetched the wrong person. This resulted in more shouting and more dead time on the line. Person-to-person calls were expensive because of this extra service time. Of course, smart customers would hang up when the caller came on the line and call back using direct dialling.

On Christmas Eve, the excitement was palpable. The operators were going to strike on the busiest day of the year; and they — dedicated and reliable Bell Telephone operators — were planning to stay home. It seemed scandalous and incomprehensible that these women could be shutting down the telephone system, and doing so legally. It was difficult to find words to express the excitement.

Linda Young remembers the delight of going on strike on Christmas Day:

When we went on strike, I told them we are taking Christmas and Boxing Day off. I had never had Christmas off. I thought,

"If I am going make them picket every day, I am not going to make them feel guilty about not picketing on Christmas Day." But we did get up to some tricks that day, as Carol, one of the operators, and I were trying to let the air out of the tires of managers' cars. We put eggs on their windshields. We went out in the countryside and took the pay phones off the hook, tied up all the lines. That was fun.[5]

Bill Howes also remembered the community response: "My biggest laugh at that time was at the cartoon in the *Toronto Star* the next day. It showed a Bell executive in a pinstripe suit at a switchboard. The caption read, 'No this isn't Ralphie and we're not allowed to accept dates!'"[6]

Laurie Cumming remembered the pitiful picket line at 15 Asquith: "I remember picketing on Christmas Day. For part of the time I was the only one on the picket line. I was feeling pretty darn lonely. My mom came to pick me up. No one else joined me."[7]

Christmas Eve was almost as busy as Christmas Day, so the switchboards were jam-packed with operators sitting shoulder-to-shoulder. As busy as they were, all of them kept watch on the clock for that elusive minute when they would walk out before their shift was over. Operators

Leaflet: *'Twas the Night before Christmas.*

walked off the job at the stroke of midnight. For almost all of them, it was the first time they had experienced the power of collective action. Ann Newman remembers the bitter cold:

> It was so cold. I've never been the same since. Margaret [McColl] and I were at Main Square. Margaret was off Christmas Eve, but the plan was to walk out at twelve midnight, which was the first legal date we could walk. I walked up to Main Square and walked into my office, and it was like, "rise up." Once everybody saw me, they just up and walked. And then I went up to Marg's office and did the same thing. Everybody walked out. Managers told me to get out. That felt really good. We had power. But I didn't know we were going to be out for over three months.[8]

A few dedicated union members set up picket lines in the morning for a few hours, but the weather was terrible and the whole point of striking on Christmas was to enjoy it. For senior operators, it was the first Christmas they had spent at home during their entire careers.

I remember that Christmas Day because it was my first Christmas as a newlywed. It was also my birthday. I would not have worked it as the CUC contract contained old-fashioned perks like the entitlement to have your birthday off work.

But this Christmas morning I had to get up at 5:30 to get a picket line up and running. I had no idea what to do. It was really cold, too. I seem to remember my husband grudgingly driving me to work and walking the line for a bit, but leaving quickly to return to bed.

A few other diehards and I kept at it until maybe 10 o'clock, when Bill Howes came by and told us to go home. There were scabs in 50 Eglinton making double time, and I was so worried that if we didn't have a picket line that day, they would get used to walking right in the front door as though it was no different from any other day. But we all wanted to be home so badly, we left.

Bill Howes remembers the author calling in a panic: "On Christmas morning, I recall getting a frantic phone call from Joan asking me to teach her how to picket. She reported that scabs were going in to work. I told her to establish a protocol that we didn't let them in until the cops showed up."[9] As president of the local, Janice McClelland might have stayed in some central command post, but she was out on the line and suffered alongside everyone else:

> I remember being on the picket line on Christmas Day at the Manulife building where my TOPS office was located. It's a large, windswept area in the heart of Toronto's commercial district. That was just one cold day on the picket line amongst many from January to the end of March 1980. We organized special mission pickets whereby we would take a very large number of operators to a specific location and surprise Bell with our pickets. Sometimes these locations were garages where the technicians were located, and after the technicians came in to work, we would set up our picket lines to delay them as they were leaving the work centre to go out on their jobs. An operator would drop a mitt in front of the technician's vehicle, and it would take a long time to carefully retrieve that mitt, and meanwhile the lineup of vehicles was getting longer and longer.[10]

For those who showed up on Christmas Day, song sheets had been prepared with new words to well-known Christmas carols.

"Winter Picket Line"

Phone bells ring, are you listening?
In the lane, snow is glistening
A beautiful sight, we're happy tonight
Walking on a winter picket line

Gone away is the bluebird
Here to stay is the new bird

He'll sing a love song as we go along
Walking on a winter picket line

On the picket line, we'll build a snowman
We'll pretend its name is old Ma Bell
She'll say do you give in, we'll say no man
You can take your job and do it yourself

Later on we'll conspire
As we sit by the fire
To face unafraid, the plans that we made
For walking on the pickets Christmas Day

Other songs included "Ma Bell's Blue Christmas," "I'll Be Home for Christmas," and "Have Yourself a Merry Little Christmas." The novelty of not working on Christmas was energizing, and the voices of Bell operators rang out on this very cold Christmas day. On Boxing Day the picket lines were kept up most of the day, and at midnight operators went back to work. The union's plan was to call another study session for New Year's Eve and New Year's Day.

On December 28 the company announced they were rejecting the conciliation report, but had another offer to make. They presented the offer and asked that it be put to the membership. They must have expected the union to cave, assuming that, as in the past, once the operators blew off steam with a short walkout, they would then get back to business. However, when the union bargaining committee received the offer, they saw that the company proposals on wages, tech change, zoning, cost-of-living increases, and language were not even close to the suggestions of the conciliation report. Once they communicated the offer to the members, the reaction was swift. Operators walked off the job en masse in Toronto. By 11 p.m. everyone in Toronto (except for a few scabs) was off the job and stayed out until after New Year's Day.

When they returned to work after New Year's, the operators and cafeteria staff engaged in work slowdowns. Operators slowed down by giving super service to their customers, not paying any attention to their average work times and how close they were to company targets. Customers loved it, as did operators, who felt no pressure to conform to arbitrary time limits. Customers realized for the first time that the reason operators were rude or impatient was that they could not take the time to help as much as they might like. Operators and customers were human once again, and the artificial barrier produced by the automaton-like behaviour encouraged by the company was plain for all to hear.

But rotating strikes and work slowdowns were too much for the company to tolerate. On January 3, 1980, the company locked out Chicoutimi, Quebec. The union bargaining committee had established a policy that if one location was locked out, all locations would be considered locked out. By noon the news had spread throughout Quebec and operators left the job; by 3 p.m. all of Toronto was out.

The company's offer required a vote by the membership. The local scheduled the vote for the following Thursday and Friday (January 3 and 4). Most operators remained off the job until after the vote.

Strike Vote

Tallying the strike vote would take two weeks, so the membership returned to work on January 7. The bargaining committee asked operators to stay on the job until the ballots were counted so they could take home a full paycheque before going on a full strike. There was very little in the strike fund, and most operators and dining service staff lived paycheque to paycheque. Union members were to continue with the work slowdown and refuse to work overtime. But operators worked at a fast pace and found it difficult to slow down. Dining service staff would have to serve the same numbers as before, and a slowdown only hurt the operators on short breaks. Management, taking advantage of being without the restrictions of a collective agreement, harassed workers and made life intolerable for all staff.

Janice McClelland recorded in a handwritten note: "The company began this week to mistreat the operators and dining service and then refused to accept the grievances of our members. Several stewards called study sessions Tuesday in response to this and their offices were locked out."

Notice to Local 50
membership regarding
upcoming strike votes.

Peter Klym, vice-president of the CWC, called a staff meeting for January 14.

The agenda included:

1. Review of meetings and the status of the strike vote
2. Strike preparation and other actions
3. Button and poster program
4. CLC NDP campaign[11]

Many grassroots leaders and stewards were unable to deal with the tension and frustration. They took matters into their own hands and called study sessions (a more polite term for walkouts) for their own locations without the approval of the local or the bargaining committee. The mood was really tense at 50 Eglinton, Main Square, and Crossways; where members believed that it was futile to keep working without a contract, and that the long lead-up time for the results of the vote just gave the company time to prepare for the strike that everyone knew was coming.

Wildcat walkouts in Toronto started January 15. Two offices at 50 Eglinton Avenue walked out, and offices at Crossways and Main Square left the job as well. Those who had left the previous day set up picket lines and managed to keep most of the other staff off the job. The company responded by locking out a few other locations. The situation became highly chaotic and volatile, with locked-out staff putting up picket lines where operators and dining service staff were still working. In order to maintain unit discipline and order, the executive of Local 50 called the whole local out on strike.

In another handwritten note, Janice McClelland reported: "On January 17/80 the company locked out Main Square, Crossways and Eglinton. Local 50 executive is meeting this A.M. in an emergency meeting to discuss the situation and consider appropriate action. All the rest of Ontario is working, doing super service, no overtime with exception of Sudbury who is out until the vote is counted."

This meeting contained a lot of heated discussion, since most of the membership was in Toronto, while the rest of Ontario was still working. Toronto was now out and officially on strike.

Laurie Cumming remembered a large meeting where the CWC staffers managed to keep the Toronto local united:

> There was some big meeting about moving forward with the company for a contract. There was a huge turnout and a lot of dissent. On one side of the room were the "Yes" votes and the on other side were the "No" votes. But more people were supportive of the union campaign. The CWC folks were wonderful. They laid out what we faced on the job; they were calm and able to handle the objections. It was a turning point for me, as I could tell we were winning. Some people were there from my office that were on the CUC side, and that surprised me because they were pretty circumspect in the office.[12]

Here is a handwritten account by Janice that was photocopied for this Local 50 executive meeting:

In Toronto today there was a great deal of confusion amongst members of the local union. Some reported for work today to find themselves locked out by the company. Others were not locked out.

In order to bring a measure of stability to the situation, the local union has asked all their members to the leave the job. They are expected to remain off the job until the results of the strike votes are available this weekend.

Besides the local in Sudbury which has been on strike since December 29, Toronto is the only local off the job.

Although the members throughout Ontario and Quebec have been in a legal strike position since December 25, the union is not asking other cities and towns to join the strike at this time.[13]

This preamble was then summarized in this succinct phone tree announcement:

1. The picketers from Eglinton are picketing Asquith tonight.
2. In order to preserve unity in Local 50, we are asking all stewards to call out their people now.
3. We are out until we hear results of the vote — likely next week.
4. We want to picket.

McClelland started the phone tree by relaying the decision to the Local 50 Executive Committee and key organizers and stewards in every office. You can see from her notes below how difficult it was to communicate the decision and motivate the local leadership and stewards to fall into line:

4:55 p.m.   Linda Pottle notified at work. Will wait until after 5 p.m. Her people want to stay.

5:00   Pauline Stoner notified. No problem, no work tomorrow. (Have signs)

5:05	L. Wilton notified. Upset at stewards but will do it.
5:10	Crook and Anderson gone. Anderson home DA
5:15	Bev Hunter notified. She and Marie both at home so will either go down or get someone else to get them out. Will picket tomorrow.
5:20	Jocelyn Felix DA (doesn't answer)
5:27	L. Evans called, reluctant but will do it.
5:32	Notified Mary MacIntosh at work. She will call all the girls tonight. Should be ok for tomorrow.
5:42	Rena Dakin notified. She will call her girls. Doubts they will go out.
5:58	Janice Crook notified. Will call all her people.
6:05	Notified Eva Chrones. Will notify her people. No work.
6:28	Notified Ruth Taunton. Very reluctant but will call her people.
6:30	Called Joceyln Felix. Call her back in a couple of hours.
6:40	Notified Ann Newman.
6:45	Notified M Vallieres [Madeline].
7:04	Notified J Felix. Says her people will not go out.
6:30	Manulife out.

Once the stewards were reached on the phone tree, they were to activate their own phone trees for their membership. These organizing activities occurred prior to the invention of fax machines and email, so phone trees were an effective tool to get a message out to a lot of people. They relied on simple messages that could be transmitted by a lot of volunteers. The use of phone trees allowed people to distribute information quickly, without placing the burden of work on one person.

Phone trees took time to set up, but could be used again and again. One easy way to visualize a phone tree is as a phone pyramid. One person at the top of the pyramid calls a predetermined number of people, as Janice would call the list above. Then each of the people she called would have a certain number of people to call, who each call more people, and so on, until every person in the phone tree has been called.

By using a phone tree, a number of people shared the work and distributed information very quickly. However, there were very few answering machines at that time, so if someone was out, you had to keep calling until you reached them.

There was no doubt that a full-blown strike was on the horizon. The union membership was already on strike in many places, including Toronto, and the confusion led the company to lock out certain work locations. The walkouts were mere skirmishes in preparation for a larger battle. Every day on a picket line prompted ordinary union members to dig deeper for the resolve to win the war, despite having to do it during a very cold winter.

Chapter 11

Strike

The Inevitable

The union announced the results of the strike vote on January 19, 1980. It was a foregone conclusion that the new union members would overwhelmingly reject Bell's offer. Union members had not spent months organizing into a new union and overcoming fear of their employer to quietly give up their dream of decent wages and better working conditions. As soon as the results were tabulated and the immediate next steps defined, the local activated a union-wide phone tree.

Here is the phone tree script that was released at 5:20 p.m. that day:

1. Bell's offer rejected with authorization to strike by a 90.3% vote.
    > Total Ballots = 5,289
    > Spoiled Ballots = 28 (.53%)
    > Ballots Rejecting = 4,776 (90.3%)
    > Ballots accepting = 485 (9.07%)
2. Bargaining committees for the union and Bell will meet at 3:00 p.m. Monday.

3. The union has set an official strike deadline of midnight tonight. All night shifts should not report tonight.

4. Locations already on strike or locked out should remain on strike.[1]

Any locations not already on strike were called out at midnight. This was the official beginning of a two-and-a-half-month strike. The excitement of Christmas Eve had vanished. Union members now knew what they were in for. They knew about the freezing cold they would have to endure while walking the picket lines. They soon knew the feeling of betrayal as they watched co-workers cross the picket line and go to work inside warm offices. And they knew the stress of the loss of a regular paycheque — and that when it trickled to nothing many of them would be in deep trouble.

On January 21, 1980, the union petitioned the government to appoint a mediator to try to resume negotiations with Bell. The CWC request for a mediator must have been copied to all MPs. One Progressive Conservative MP, Doug Lewis, notified the government of his support. On January 30, 1980, the minister of labour informed the MP by telegram that the minister had appointed a mediator.[2]

Meanwhile, operators and dining service staff created and supported picket lines in front of the buildings in which they worked. Local 50 leaders developed strategies, built the infrastructure needed for picket lines, and executed a public relations campaign to win public support and raise funds.

An article in the February 9 edition of the *Bell Operator and Dining Services Newsletter, Special Strike Edition* (the title now reflecting the composition of bargaining unit) reported that the strike had brought out many talents that had been hidden for years. Every town had its budding picket sign artist. In Kitchener, a songwriter had come up with these lyrics, sung to the tune of "For Me and My Gal."

> The phones are ringing
> Down at Old Mother Bell.
> Her girls are singing
> Cause we think it's swell.
> Everybody is knowing

Our resistance is growing,
And we know it is showing
In each Suzie and Sal.

We're congregating in front of the Bell.
Operators are waiting
And you never can tell.
Someday we'll make a little pact
For one or two or three years more.
It's a phoney land
When you work for the Bell.[3]

Keeping up morale was the primary job of the local leadership; they got creative by writing songs, organizing parties, and strengthening friendships. A handwritten note by Janice McClelland listed her initial thoughts for dealing with the logistics of managing a strike:

> … with 1,400 members on strike in many widely separated Bell offices across Toronto and including Brampton, Oakville and Orangeville — all within the boundaries of Local 50.

- Stewards.
- Picket captain sheets — no padding of books.
- Police — do not fraternize.
- Armbands — borrowed — make list of picket captains.
- Stewards can cancel [picket lines] due to weather and put it on sheet.[4]

Notes taken at strike committee meetings convey a sense of the day-to-day issues in the first month of the strike. They refer to a motion that a fund be set up at each location to provide picketers with beverages. Some locations, like 15 Asquith, had benefactors (a Canadian Union of Public Employees local) that had set up coffee accounts for picketers. The chance to grab a coffee and warm up was a lifesaver for a picketer. On days when it was twenty below you could only stay on the line for twenty minutes. Helen Middlebrooks remembered the camaraderie on the picket line:

I remember the picketing at Asquith. We used to have great picket lines. I was proud of our picket line. We had four hundred operators in the building and really good solidarity when it came to picketing. We were near the reference library. CUPE set up a coffee account for us with a donut shop right around the corner from our office. We could leave our picket signs there and get warmed up. Lots of friendships grew out of that time — really solid ones.[5]

Meanwhile, the national union came up with projects to raise strike funds. A memo on CWC letterhead dated January 16, 1980, went to all presidents of Bell Canada locals in Ontario and all key contacts in Traffic and Dining Service explaining a "Help Crack Bell" campaign. The first project in the fundraising campaign was for all union locals to sell "Help Crack Bell" buttons for a dollar, with the proceeds going to strike assistance for the operators.

Other communication projects included "Help Crack Bell" and "Bell Canada Is Out of Order" posters, which the memo said would soon available for public promotion; as well as *Bell Canada Is Out of Order* leaflets, which would be available for public distribution on picket lines or door-to-door distribution.

"Help Crack Bell" button.

Strike Committee

Someone had to make day-to-day decisions, so Local 50 created the Strike Committee. The members were: Janice McClelland (chair), Ann Newman, Marnie Veale, Irene Anderson, Barb Mercury (chair of membership assistance committee), George Larter, Heather MacLeod, Diane Ward, Laurie Cumming, Joan Roberts, Linda Wilton from Orangeville, and Bev Hunter from Oakville.

No notes remain from strike committee meetings prior to January 23, but some handwritten notes in McClelland's files refer to plans to picket craft locations at Shaw and Sunrise, and Dining Services at 393 University Avenue. The note records that a motion was passed directing Newman and Anderson to prepare minutes for the next meeting. As the committee worked through their many decisions, minutes became an important record as well as a key organizing tool. From these notes and minutes we can glean important information on what was happening. McClelland's undated notes record one motion stipulating that the strike committee meet every Monday and Friday:

Local 50 Strike Committee Meeting Minutes for January 23, 1980

Donations to the strike fund from two unions and $100 from an anonymous donor.

George Larter gave a bargaining report: negotiations broke off on Monday January 21.

Bell Canada refused to accept the Conciliation Commissioner's report. CWC asked for a federal mediator to be appointed.

Picketing update: discussed whether taking pictures of scabs crossing the picket line could be useful to identify scabs. Janice reported on discussions with the Bay (which was attached to 15 Asquith). The Bay has stated that they do not want to get involved in our dispute and they do not want outsiders using their door keys etc. The Bay is aware that if any more scabs come through their premises, we will picket the Bay.

Agreed that Monday 28th be a Special Assignment Day.

That Liz Baker and Carol Wooten[6] addresses and telephone numbers would be printed in the minutes.

Agreed to spend $100 on new picket signs and declared they were unable to pay TTC fares of strikers who go to picket.

The minutes informed stewards of their responsibility for recording who was picketing on picket sheets. They had to record the number of hours that people spent on lines to determine their eligibility for financial assistance. McClelland noted that picket captains needed to be told to make sure that it was not always the same people getting to sit inside, and to make sure to call in every day.

From the first and last lines of the minutes, it is clear how little money there was to run the strike. The secretary recorded every donation for a grand total of three donations. Union members were already hurting financially, but there was not even enough money to cover public transportation costs for those picketing.

Scabs

It is clear that a major focus for the committee was containing scabs. Scabbing was a problem at 15 Asquith Avenue, as they were getting into Bell Canada through a door from the Hudson's Bay store. Helen Middlebrooks remembered incidents involving scabs:

I remember that we had an issue with scabs. We did not have a lot, but one was persistent. We also had an issue with two part-timers whose father was management. The Asquith building backs onto the loading docks of The Bay department store, and The Bay would let the scabs in through side doors. I talked to Janice about it, and the CWC warned The Bay they had to stop it or there would be a picket line outside The Bay. That ended that.[7]

Scabbing was an even bigger problem at 50 Eglinton, as former CUC vice president Liz Baker had returned to work full-time. She and Carol Wooten, a former CUC rep, were the de facto scab leaders. This explains why the committee printed their addresses and phone numbers in the minutes of January 23. This was a subtle way of encouraging a harassment campaign against the two of them. The special assignment day was a mass picket on January 28 at 50 Eglinton. Irene Anderson recalled getting into an altercation with Liz Baker, the former vice-president of the CUC:

I was charged with assault by one of the CUC leaders — Liz Baker. I run into her every once in a while and we have a laugh. I was on the picket line back of 50 Eglinton. The charge was I pushed her into the path of an oncoming car. I couldn't have pushed her much. I was only one hundred and ten pounds soaking wet.[8]

Helen Middlebrooks remembered another incident at 50 Eglinton:

We were walking the picket line at Asquith only during the day, but other offices were open 24/7 and we would help out on surprise pickets. Asquith was really cohesive. The only issue was with the scabs. Sometimes at other locations things would get out of hand. At Eglinton, at a surprise picketing of the building, one of my sisters picketing at the back tried to a keep big transport truck out. The cops had to pull her off the grill of the truck.[9]

Scab Headquarters

The office at 50 Eglinton Avenue was a hotbed of scabbing. Former CUC leaders Liz Baker and Carol Wooten worked there in Directory Assistance Office 3, and encouraged their supporters to keep working during the strike.

By the time of the strike at least 50 percent of the DA operators were still unsigned. I was chief steward of 50 Eglinton and morning picket captain, which meant that I was on the picket lines just about every morning. I did mornings so I could attend strike committee meetings in the afternoon. I was twenty-two and had no experience with leading a picket line that had scabs crossing it every day. But we persevered, and the strike committee picked up the slack when we lacked local supporters and volunteers. Over time, some really strong leaders emerged. One of those was Terry DiNardo, whose husband held a position in a trade union and was very sympathetic.

The high level of scabbing prompted the committee to schedule a special picket on January 28. Picketers were more numerous than usual, and things rapidly got out of hand.

Many of the picketers at 50 Eglinton were older operators who were so hurt at having to watch their colleagues of years and years walk right past them and into the building. They would complain to me day after day about how awful it was to watch, and kept asking if there was anything that somebody could to do — something to ease their pain and stop the scabs from going to work. The bitching began to be a nonstop cacophony in my ears. I felt I had to do something.

I decided to bring a dozen eggs to the picket line. No one advised me to do this. I must have got the idea from something I read. The scabs at Eglinton came to work in company-paid taxi cabs. Although they could have come in the back way, there were a number of staunch CUC supporters who brazenly came and went through the front door, sauntering confidently across the picket line. At five minutes to seven, I put an egg in my pocket and waited for the scabs to arrive. Roberta

> *Cole came out of the building, walking in her fur coat toward a wait-ing cab; I proceeded to smash an egg on her coat and give it an egg shampoo. She looked at me horrified while I called her a scab. This incident is not something I am proud of, as I am now a believer in non-violence. But at the time it was a great release of tension.*

This incident led to assault charges against the author. In addition to criminal charges, the company suspended her for three weeks after the strike came to an end. The union grieved the suspension and took it to arbitration.

The incident was described in the arbitration hearing report:

> Ms. Roberta Cole is an employee in the bargaining unit who was working during the strike. Shortly after 7:00 a.m. on January 28, 1980 she left work after completing her night shift. A picket line which included the grievor was set up in front of the building. As Ms. Cole approached the taxi wait-ing for her immediately in front of the company's offices, the grievor crushed an egg on her chest. The egg splattered over the front of her fur coat and in her hair.
>
> The grievor admits to this aspect of the incident. Ms. Cole, however, testified that when she turned around to go back into the building, she was struck on the back of her neck.[10]

The special picket lasted over three hours, and by 9:00 a.m. the author was involved in another altercation on the picket line.

> The grievor testified that at approximately 9:00 a.m. Ms. Z. Payne, a bargaining unit employee, approached the building to go to work. At the point in time at which Ms. Payne tried to cross the picket line and enter the building, the grievor

was squarely between her and the door. The grievor testified that Ms. Payne took her under the arms, raised her about six inches to a foot off the ground and knocked her into revolving doors. The grievor maintained that she fell to the ground with Ms. Payne landing on top of her, after which, according to the grievor, a policeman pulled Ms. Payne off. The grievor immediately complained to the policeman who told her to file charges in court if she wanted. The grievor filed the charges which were ultimately dismissed. No disciplinary action was taken against Ms. Payne by the company.[12]

The company's failure to take action against Ms. Payne in this case, and in a post-strike incident involving a striker and a scab in the workplace, gave credence to the union's assertion that the company discriminated against the strikers. The company could have discouraged scabbing, as it could have been expected that scabs crossing picket lines might ignite angry reactions. Although the union was almost all women who were socialized to be meek and compliant, being on strike in the bitter cold brought out strong reactions from even the senior union members.

Bill Howes recalls:

I remember getting a call from Joan asking for specific instructions on how many times you could hold back the cars from crossing a picket line. Joan said something like, "We are blocking the cars from crossing the picket line and now the cops are getting angry." I said, "Try two times, but by your third time you are asking for trouble."[13]

My memory is that it was a cold winter day. Most of the strike committee was there that day, and we usually picketed in the front of the building, but this day went out to the back entrance. The picket line might have been between forty or fifty people at the most.

We were around at the back of the building trying to delay the cars entering the parking lot. We had not been keeping a picket line out back, so this must have shocked the company and the police were called. I remember Irad Munro getting the attention of the police because he was one of the few men on the line. They kept shoving him around, while he just kept holding on to his picket sign and using his shoulders to block them from splitting up the line.

There were a number of police cars parked all over the place. All of a sudden, somebody started leaning on one and rocking it up and down. These were some of the older operators in their fifties. Just rocking the yellow police cars of the Toronto Police Service up and down with their bums. This happened to maybe three police cars. Those women were mad and wanted to show it to the cops. Of course, a police car is an extension of a police officer, so this gave the cops cause to pull the women away. But it was how they did it that shocked me to my soul. The cops grabbed us from behind, one hand on each breast and pulled us away from the cars and the line.

At least we didn't get arrested. But I always looked at cops differently after that. They wanted to demean us, as we were women stepping outside our socialization as good little girls.

Eglinton Avenue picket line.

The 50 Eglinton location continued to be a problem for Local 50 throughout the strike and for a long time afterwards.

Day-to-Day Business Continues

Special pickets and regular picket lines were usually organized in the early-morning hours to stop or delay Bell employees and scabs from getting in to work. So the strike committee members would be up at five o'clock in the morning to get to the surprise picket location or their own picket lines, and then would gather for meetings after lunch. It made for long days, especially for senior leaders like McClelland, who would also go to local union meetings at night. After an eventful morning like the one on January 28, it was difficult to concentrate, but the union leaders grabbed a bite and proceeded to the local's temporary headquarters at 25 Cecil Street.

Local 50 Strike Committee Meeting Minutes for January 28, 1980

Raised $100 in button sales

Special assignment day was reported to be very successful.[13]

Plans for membership meeting on Tuesday

1.   Film: Babies and Banners
2.   Go over Picket Guidelines
3.   Stress Picketing

Membership Assistance: The committee will meet Wednesday and Friday 8:00 am to 12:00 pm.

Craft picketing: We will picket Shaw St. and Sunrise locations. Offices to participate include Manulife, Crossways and Valhalla.

Picket captain guidelines: it is important that members report to their picket captains.

Marg McColl and Irene Anderson will co-ordinate a flea market sale.

Lack of money continued to dominate the agenda with the report that button sales had pulled in $100. There were approximately 1,400 employees in the local and $20 was given to people for food assistance. If everyone had taken the $20, Local 50 would have needed $2,800 per week. The membership assistance committee was to meet twice the following week, so the need for funds was increasing. The strike committee was entirely composed of women (George Larter was in Ottawa most of the time on the bargaining committee); so they turned to traditional fundraising tactics like bake sales and flea markets. These were nickel-and-dime events that kept members focused and engaged, but raising $100 did not make much of a dent in the fundraising targets. You can see how desperate the situation really was.

Communication with members was critical, as rumours ran rampant. The local planned a membership meeting for January 29 at Trinity-St. Paul's United Church. McClelland's personal notes, used to prepare for the membership meeting, indicated that the girls were getting jobs, which led to deteriorating picket lines. She identified financial assistance as the biggest issue for discussion. After buying into the CWC, regular union members were hurting much more than they had expected. Many long-term union members prepared for strikes, but the average telephone operator or dining service worker was between a rock and a hard place. They wanted better wages and working conditions, but their biggest fear — destitution — was right in front of them. Many of the new union members prepared to go back to work.

Irene Anderson remembers the challenge of keeping women from returning to work when they began to suffer financially:

> I remember one meeting when we had the whole local out. Imagine fifteen hundred women in the room. It was standing room only. The operators were not happy. This was soon after the strike began. We had to work very hard to convince them we were on the right track. Despite our political differences early on, the nine or eleven of us on the executive always pulled together to execute the plan. We got those women to stick with the union and stay out.[14]

Financial assistance was the really big issue for members. The assistance rules required tenants to receive an eviction notice before their rent could be covered. This was due to the low amount in the strike funds. Having to strike right after the organizing campaign meant there was little in the kitty. McClelland reported that the strike fund from unions in Toronto had $2,398.92, and the national fund had $14,472.50. The average monthly rent in 1980 was $356.[15]

Just covering those in danger of eviction would deplete the fund quickly. It was too soon for operators to receive eviction notices, so there was not yet any rent or mortgage assistance. Operators who needed money found they had to pick up temporary work. Those who had not yet found jobs demanded to know what other locals were doing to help with financial assistance, and if any real financial help was forthcoming. The news was not good, but at least they knew where they stood. Those who could withstand the financial pressures and not look for other employment worked doubly hard to bolster the picket lines. The strike committee formed flying picket squads to harass the company at the craft locations and to firm up morale on the big picket lines.

On January 28, mediators met with the bargaining committees for the union and the company. The mediators imposed a media blackout. The two sides met again on February 4 and 5, but the mediators adjourned the talks on February 5 because the company refused to move on anything. The company refused to discuss the conciliation commissioner's report, or even to discuss less controversial issues such as maternity leave.

The knowledge that the strike was going to be long depressed many, and in some places there were stirrings of back-to-work movements. But the strikers generally remained defiant and committed. Janice McClelland remembers that the operators remained determined, even those that were elderly and faced physical challenges:

> I learned that it's frequently the quiet ones whom you can rely on to be solid. I remember one day on a special mission picket, with probably over a hundred operators circling a very large Bell location, and I urged the operators on the line to move faster. Subsequently I was told by a senior operator

that one of the women holding up the line could not move any faster. I instantly regretted my comment — these senior women were the backbone of the union and the strike. Bell totally underestimated their determination.[16]

By early February morale was declining. The strike was into its third full week. Winter weather and dwindling personal funds resulted in despondency for most of the union members. It was not fun anymore. The excitement of Christmas walkouts and press coverage had given way to day-to-day slogging on picket lines, with some operators searching for paid work to cover the bills. By February, however, the infrastructure was in place to support the day-to-day activities of the strike. The bargaining committee had its work to do, and established a communications strategy to get information out to the locals; and through them to the grassroots membership with phone trees, newsletters, and membership meetings.

Picket lines were in place at all the large office locations, and special pickets were happening at craft locations and regional offices two or three times a week. The national staff and local union leadership worked together to recruit picket captains and developed picket signs and forms to record picketing hours.

The Local 50 structure became more sophisticated as time went on. Meeting agendas followed a proscribed format, starting with reading of the minutes (as was the practice before photocopies were affordable and accessible) and a treasurer's report, and ending with new business.

Fundraising brought in enough to support the most at-risk members of the local. The Local 50 strike committee kept busy planning activities and soliciting support from the labour movement and the public. A weekly collection of an hour's pay from their brothers and sisters in the CWC craft locals helped those who needed financial support.

Donations came to the national strike fund from unions all over Toronto, the country, and around the world. Even with national prominence and many donations, the new union's strike fund was totally inadequate. To stretch it further and to meet the most pressing needs, the policy of giving $20 for food assistance would apply only to those in need. Ed Seymour remembers that certain individuals also provided support:

ON

PAY DAY

REMEMBER

THAT

BELL CANADA TRAFFIC AND DINING SERVICE MEMBERS

ARE ON STRIKE

CWC MEMBERS WHO ARE WORKING HAVE BEEN ASKED TO
CONTRIBUTE ONE HOUR'S PAY EACH TWO WEEKS TO THE
CWC DEFENSE FUND.

THE SUCCESSFUL RESOLUTION OF A NUMBER OF THE
ISSUES IN THIS STRIKE WILL BENEFIT ALL OF US.

THESE ISSUES INCLUDE:

* JOB POSTING RIGHTS
* BETTER DISCRIMINATION LANGUAGE
* PROTECTION AGAINST "ADMINISTRATIVE" FIRINGS
* CLEAN-OUT OF DISCIPLINARY RECORDS AFTER 12 MONTHS

AN HOUR'S PAY IS A SMALL INVESTMENT IN THE FUTURE

GIVE GENEROUSLY

Payday collection notice for craft and services members.

There was support for the operators' struggle. For instance, during the strike a craft guy in Barrie came up to me and said he wasn't married and did okay, so I was to let him know if anybody has financial problems. He would help them, but wanted to keep it between him and me. I referred a number of people to him.[17]

Stretching the strike fund was only possible because there were many young operators who lived at home with their parents; others had partners who could cover their living expenses. But many members of the bargaining unit were single mothers and sole breadwinners, usually living paycheque to paycheque. The lack of income hurt quickly.

Financial assistance was a topic that came up again and again in the strike committee meeting notes. It was heart-rending for the leadership. A wonderful chairperson of the membership assistance committee was named Barb Mercury. Calm and a solid union supporter, she was an eighth-generation Canadian woman of colour. She was a repository of local black history and told stories of famous black politicians and American jazz musicians who visited Toronto. Because she was very empathetic, she struggled with the decisions made by her committee as to who got assistance and who didn't.

Local 50 Strike Committee Meeting Minutes
for Friday, February 1, 1980

Membership Assistance Committee report:

Barb Mercury (Chair) reported that the committee received 33 applicants this morning. 8 were turned back (mainly from insufficient picketing hours) and 25 were given assistance. Barb emphasized that membership assistance is vital for the continued success of the strike.

Deputation:

Following a discussion of a new broader police powers bill for Metro Toronto, it was decided that Laurie Cumming would prepare a statement to take it to a meeting at Metro Hall.

At this meeting the committee passed a motion authorizing transportation assistance for picketing. And they authorized the purchase of one hundred TTC tokens.

These minutes show that financial assistance continued to be the most critical issue. There was finally enough money for Toronto Transit Commission tokens. Purchasing tokens would help those who could not afford them put in their picketing hours and then qualify for food assistance.

Laurie Cumming's deputation to Metropolitan Toronto Council was apparently the first political action taken by the union. Union members had gotten a taste of police power and brutality on the picket line, and were using their profile and public support to raise their concerns.

However, some of the tasks local leaders were supposed to take on were beyond grassroots organizing and could provoke anxiety. Laurie Cumming, then a very young operator, remembers being anxious and unwilling to take on some of the tasks assigned to her:

> I was completely disillusioned. I was supremely uncomfortable with some of the things I was "voluntold" I had to make an appeal at a union hall for our cause. I was uncomfortable; I think I procrastinated. I might have sent a statement in a cab [to Metro Hall.] Besides, I was seeing a new guy and he was much more interesting than public speaking.[18]

On the same day as the committee meeting, Montreal police arrested five operators and charged them with obstruction during mass picketing at 620 Belmont and Beaver Hall Hill. On February 4, an early morning blockade in Montreal at the Dorval Data Centre led to the arrest of Andre Leclair of the Quebec Federation of Labour for threatening violence. Police also arrested Claude Gobeil, an operator; and Louise Godin, a member of the bargaining committee, for assaulting police. They were all released on bail, but arrests in Montreal and increased police presence in Toronto frightened the union members, who were civic-minded workers and often provided a vital link to emergency responders.[19]

Bargaining

The union's bargaining committee settled down in Ottawa to wait for opportunities to bargain with the company. The mediator talked with both sides separately and together, but accomplished little. Fred Pomeroy recalled that bargaining styles with Bell Canada management differed between the two provinces:

Quebec Bell people were savvy or even sympathetic to our cause. Ontario managers never dealt with problems, and they just evaded them until they blew up. They were the world's worst bunch. Raymond Cyr — who was the executive vice-president at the time of the strike and later president of the company — although he was a formidable opponent, was sympathetic and you could always talk to him. Overall he was a positive force for operators.

We had fun bargaining. The breaks would go on for a long time. One day the mediation officer from the government arrived in our room. I was standing on my head in a corner. Most days we worked until midnight but sometimes finished at two-thirty in the morning. After those late nights, we would go to the Ville-Marie restaurant, and if they knew you they would give you a special coffee with cognac in it.[20]

The Daily Grind

The cold days of February were very difficult for everyone. There was little hope that the strike would be resolved soon. The most hard-pressed union members were getting jobs so they could still pay the bills. Picket lines grew weaker and scabs were still going to work. Keeping morale up was job number one, but it was not easy.

Even when dressed in snow pants and multiple layers, I was cold. I remember buying Ski-Doo boots to keep my feet warm. They were so big and bulky; it was like shuffling on the moon in those boots.

On February 5, McClelland activated the phone tree to tell the Local 50 membership that the federal mediators had called off the talks. This was very depressing news, as there were no other processes to call on to get the talks going again. All that was left to pressure the company was the strike. The phone script stated that the CWC National Executive Board was to meet the following week to develop more ways to pressure the company.

Phone Tree Call Script for February 6, 1980[21]

1. We are calling on behalf of the Communications Workers of Canada, Local 50 to keep you informed regarding bargaining and events in the local.

2. Talks between our Bargaining Committee and the company broke off yesterday, Tuesday. (February 5). The company refused to give us the Conciliation Commissioner's Report. Our Bargaining Committee presented the company with 5 items and asked them to reply to those. Those 5 items were maternity leave, benefits, union time, union security (union dues) and pay in lieu of vacation and the company refused to discuss even these items. As a result the mediators called off talks for the time being but are available to meet with us.

3. At this time it is necessary that we have maximum picketing in order to force the company back to the table. We had a special assignment today. ["Wednesday: about eighty-five operators and dining service staff participated from Manulife, Main Square, Asquith, Adelaide, and King St."]

4. We are picketing a craft location at 321 Front St. this Friday — be there at 6:45 a.m.

5. Next Tuesday is our Special Assignment Day. For this day we need maximum participation. The more operators the company sees on the picket line, the sooner they will settle.

6. Our Membership Assistance Committee will be available on Wednesday and Friday 8:00 a.m. –12 noon. If you need an appointment for financial assistance, telephone 977-9892 for an appointment first.

7. The CWC National Executive will be meeting in Ottawa early in the week to discuss new methods of putting additional pressure on the company.

8. We will be calling you to keep you informed and let you know of special picketing.

9. Can we count on your support?

Terry DiNardo, a strong supporter from 50 Eglinton, came to a strike committee meeting in February to talk about the issues there. The minutes record a motion that membership lists for DA 5, R and R (Rate and Route — an office of telephone operators that other telephone operators would connect to in order to get rates and routings that were not available to them), and TOPS at 50 Eglinton be divided among the committee for important calls to the phone tree and that they try to get more picket captains.

Another motion requested that national reps attend court on Friday, and that one person from the committee be delegated to approach Peter Klym (Ontario CWC vice-president) to arrange a meeting with the union lawyer to come to an understanding of any charges against members. Another note by Janice McClelland recorded the following: "Roberta Cole Sheila Donnelly (one egg) ??? Joan will go down to College Park to charge Zoretta Payne, Laurie Cumming was witness. Witnessed by cop #6426 (53 Division) Building Manager and Judy Roti (from Unit 6)." On another sheet of paper was contact information for Shalom Shacter from the law firm Golden Levinson. Picket line altercations were happening with increasing frequency, and the committee expected the national union to provide legal assistance.

Shenanigans

In the online Meriam-Webster dictionary, *shenanigan* is defined as a devious trick, used especially for an underhand purpose or a tricky or questionable practices or conduct. It is the right word to use in describing the mischief operators quietly undertook against the company.

In 2013, during the writing of this book, Janice McClelland happened to notice in her home a box of books. One side of the box said "My-T-Fresh, Parkinson Co-op Farm, Poultry Division, Iron Bridge, Ontario, phone 843-2181." The other side said "15 DOZEN CANADIAN EGGS, CANADA GRADE A." Seeing this reminded her of some of her favourite shenanigans. During the strike, Bell management staffed the long-distance and Directory Assistance switchboards. When she had free time, McClelland would make phone calls to keep those "management scabs" on their toes.

> One of my favourite calls was to dial 705-555-1212, which was a free call, and ask the manager who answered the call for the telephone number for the My-T-Fresh Farm.
>
> You can imagine that they had a great deal of difficulty finding the listing.
>
> "Where [is] it?" they would ask.
>
> "Well about fifty miles east of Sault Ste. Marie."
>
> "How do you spell My-T-Fresh Farm?" they would then ask.
>
> "I'm not sure, but it certainly exists and I need the telephone number...."
>
> This would consume several minutes while the manager anxiously looked for this telephone number (that they couldn't find ... because of the unusual spelling). They would usually end up giving out a "No number found" — when a number existed — which was a grave error in Bell's books at the time![22]

Managers and scabs crossing picket lines drew most of the anger and were the primary targets for shenanigans.

> We would do some crazy things. I remember someone putting nails in a big package under the wheels of a manager's car. We

got the address of one of the scabs from 50 Eglinton and went to her building, and squirted foam from the building fire extinguisher into her mailbox during the wee hours of the morning.

Someone threw bleach on a fur coat one day. I remember it was St. Paddy's Day and it happened in the evening. We then went to the Brunswick Tavern to drink green beer.

The egg marks stayed on 50 Eglinton for years after the strike.[23]

Getting into mischief relieved some of the tension and frustration of the strike. When the author interviewed the grassroots leaders for this book, these were also the most easily recalled memories. It was fun compared to walking in a circle in front of an office building day in and day out. Irene Anderson remembers an incident that got out of hand:

On a humorous note, once you've been on strike for a number of weeks, you lose your reason. One day Ann Newman, a couple of other people and I were at the corner of York Street and University Avenue. There was a technician installing phones at a business. He left his van open. He had a lot of telephone books, so we took them and started a bonfire on York Street. He was mortified. We picketed his van. It was a moment of madness. CWC told us sternly to smarten up.[24]

Family Day

When the local activated the phone tree on February 5 to tell the Local 50 membership that the federal mediators had called off the talks, the message provoked reactions of despair and disappointment. This was very depressing news to share, as there were no other processes to call on to get the talks going again. All that was left to pressure the company was the day-to-day pressure of the strike.

The news that the talks had been called off was extremely disappointing, and the membership needed morale-building events. The operators at 15 Asquith excelled at this task. Helen Middlebrooks remembers the nurturing of the older operators toward the younger:

> At Asquith most of the picketing was done by the younger women. Dot McGregor lived on Gloucester a minute-or-two–walk away. She fed a lot of people during the strike, especially for DA 1. We had pot luck once a week at her house and she would feed everyone, whether they brought something or not.[25]

After the February 6 phone tree had been completed, McClelland recorded handwritten notes from a strike committee meeting on a Wednesday (probably February 13). Her notes show that part of the meeting was devoted to bargaining news and membership reaction:

- Valhalla good response
- 15 Asquith kind of discouraging
  - How long is it going to be?
  - What are we going to do?
  - Find something for them to do
  - Boost their spirits
- Manulife disappointed, how long? Pickets' spirits low
- Main Square prepared for long strike

The notes show that the group decided they needed a bulletin to go to all members in the local. It is very likely that the idea for Family Day emerged at this meeting, even though it was to occur in only four days. Activating the phone tree was all that was needed to pull people together, and free rein was given to organizers to develop fun events.

Since the idea for Family Day had probably come from 15 Asquith folks, their picket line became the natural location for the event. Family Day took place on February 17. The goal was to help families of union members get involved in the strike, walk a picket line, meet the striker's

Invitation to Family
Day picket.

colleagues and local union leaders, and in general just have some fun. When the author looked at the photos held in private collections, almost every person interviewed had a picture taken that day. The colourful clown costumes made for great pictures. Laurie Cumming and a couple of the craft guys (the vernacular used by the strikers) dressed up in clown costumes and entertained the picketers. Most of the picketers dressed in drab winter wear on a daily basis; it was worn for warmth, not fashion or amusement, and they did not consider themselves photogenic.

Helen Middlebrooks remembered the Family Day picket fondly: "For Family Day at Asquith, Irad Munro and Owen Oiffer dressed up as clowns. We cooked hamburgers and hot dogs at Dot's. Laurie's boyfriend would go get them. Lots of people were there. Lots of kids and dogs. CUPE people might have been there, too. It was really a good day."[26]

Laurie Cumming and craft guys Irad Munro and Owen Oiffer.

Families made homemade picket signs for this event. One such sign, made on computer paper with words cut from the newspaper, said, "Thank you Operators for making last year our largest and most successful ever!" Beneath this headline was a cartoon showing a man leaving a building with a sign on it that said "Bell 1980." The man was carrying a grocery bag stuffed with money. The caption beneath the cartoon said "Gravy Train." The line at the bottom of the homemade sign said, "But don't ask about a RAISE (ho, ho)."

Family Day generated good press coverage, even though the strike was now over a month old.

Tending to Business

On February 9, another edition of the *Bell Operators & Dining Services Newsletter, Special Strike Edition* came out. Why not another CWC Local 50 bulletin? Probably because many people who respected the strike were not CWC members. Putting out an operator's newsletter made it seem like information from colleagues, not the union.

George Larter reported on bargaining and reported on progress with the new mediator, Guy de Merlis. He had told the mediator that 90 percent of the bargaining unit had rejected the company offer. The company was offering less than in the old contract on key issues like discrimination and seniority. Since the company refused to discuss even the smallest issues, the mediator had no choice but to call off the talks. George reminded the readers that they had voted to strike, and now they needed to keep up the picket lines and force the company back to the table.

In this newsletter, the local informed the members that they could come and see them for financial assistance. They might not be able to solve every problem, but they were there to help. The assistance was still minimal and hardly anyone qualified. Some people already faced the threat of losing rental housing. The timing of evictions for arrears became critical. McClelland recorded a note saying that she had talked with the Tenant Hotline and discovered that under the Landlord and Tenant Act, the Notice of Eviction was a twenty-day notice. The legislation then said that a tenant had fourteen days to pay the arrears, in which case the notice was null and void.

If the tenant failed to pay within fourteen days, on the fifteenth day the landlord could apply for an eviction notice. So the membership assistance committee adopted a policy that the committee would pay rent in arrears for those members who had received an eviction notice, but would turn down applicants who were not yet in arrears for their rent. This strategy ensured strikers did not lose their housing and minimized the drain on the committee's resources.

Along with standing items like treasurer's and secretary's reports, and membership assistance, the strike committee agendas now showed new items, including eviction notices and lawyer and court dates. The committee met during the week after Family Day, most likely February 18 or 20. According to Janice McClelland's notes, the committee discussed a strategy for augmenting picket lines the next week with flying picket squads. They decided they would visit picket lines at Asquith, Manulife, Main Square, and Crossways on Wednesday. The notes show that the

Eglinton DA units were still problematic with lots of scabs, so Terry DiNardo was going to host a coffee party on Tuesday at 7:30 p.m.

The notes also recorded a motion that the money made on the flea market be used for coffee parties to get people on the picket line. Additionally, the notes reported that on February 15, the Ottawa operators had picketed Parliament Hill to try to get the attention of the new government. Led by Joe Clark, leader of the Progressive Conservative Party, it had been elected in May of 1979. An invitation to the event was in McClelland's files, and most likely some of the Local 50 members attended.

It was at this meeting that the solidarity picket was first discussed; that gave the committee ten to twelve days to organize this major event. The committee developed a plan for the next newsletter and received the following reports:

- Report on Family Day
- Report on evictions
- CWC Local 25 Hotline

The committee also passed a motion that the union pay a supper allowance ($5 limit) to those serving on committees whose services were required from early morning to and including the evening. The operator organizers suffered financial distress too. Ann Newman remembers how she was affected by the strike: "I didn't have a home life. No clothes, no money. I gained so much weight eating fast food. It was union 24/7."[27]

Chapter 12

Outside Support
Makes the Difference

By building and demonstrating public support, the union started to win the public relations war. After all, the company was a publicly regulated company subject to political pressure: citizens and customers made lots of trouble for the monopoly company by complaining to the customer service department and on up the food chain to their MPs — who could have responded by tightening up federal regulations governing the company. The company feared this most of all because more red tape meant more costs.

Sometime in late February there was a change in focus for the strike committee. Although the issue of scabs was always on the agenda, emphasis began to move away from keeping the picket lines going and more toward building wider public support for the strike. A new tactic for this shift involved leafleting the public in subway stations. For example, undated committee notes in McClelland's files describe a special assignment day when flying picket squads converged at the following sites:

Manulife — Bay and Bloor inside subway platform 7 a.m.
Asquith — Yonge and Bloor 7 a.m. inside turnstiles northbound
Eglinton — Yonge and Eglinton 7 a.m. in front of Laura Secord's in subway

Valhalla at office at 6:40 a.m.

76 Adelaide going to King St.

Crossways — Yonge and Bloor 7 a.m. leaving at 7:20 a.m.

Main — Yonge and Bloor 7 a.m. Northbound

There was also a motion that the local purchase one hundred scab stickers.[1] Ontario locals in communities like Oshawa, Hamilton, and Belleville started holding their own solidarity pickets and Local 50 leaders were always invited. The committee passed a motion to pick up the cost of gas to drive Local 50 members to these events.

Attending partner events like the International Women's Day parade was now a priority for the local leadership, as well as building political support at all three levels of government. Union support would be achieved and demonstrated by a February 29 press conference in Ottawa and the solidarity picket in Toronto on March 1. Much of the local union support came about because of Janice's McClelland's outreach to unions. She also acted as an advocate for Local 50 members who had issues with maternity leave or other benefits like unemployment insurance.

One of McClelland's to-do lists:

1. Call UE [United Electrical Workers] re membership meeting and a plant gate collection. [McClelland would make pitches for support and the strike fund.]
2. Call Lystra [a picket captain at Manulife] re info and John Deverell [Toronto Star labour relations reporter].
3. Call CUPE re benefits of J G [unnamed member].
4. Make scab list.
5. Call re maternity leave — Labour Council president, UIC [Unemployment Insurance of Canada] help centre lawyer, UAW [United Auto Workers].

This strategy of seeking as much external support as possible made an enormous difference, and led to the union reaching a satisfactory settlement with the company. External support provided money for the strike fund and kept the union members on the picket lines. The large events and political attention garnered press coverage that won over public opinion and sent the message to the company that the women were determined to win.

Union and Public Support

The national union funded a button-and-sticker campaign to publicize the strike and gain public support, and also to raise money for the locals. The "Help Crack Bell" buttons were silver with blue text. They were very chic. Torontonians bought hundreds and wore them on their winter coats.

On February 13, Bill Howes sent the following poem to all Traffic and Dining Services contacts, asking organizers to forward it to their local papers as a letter to the editor. Written by a Kitchener telephone operator, it certainly tugs the heartstrings and reminds local communities of the central place in their lives held by telephone operators.

REMEMBER ME

I am the operator who sent the ambulance, when your mother had her heart attack.
Remember me?
I am the operator who listened, when you were despondent and needed someone to talk to.
Remember me?
I am the operator who called the fire department and saved your home.
Remember me?
I am the operator who sent the police, when a prowler was terrifying your teenage babysitter.
Remember me?
I am the operator you called to say goodbye to the world — I convinced you that it was good to be alive. Now I am not so sure.
Please remember me.
Your operator.[2]

Operators on the picket lines held up signs urging motorists to honk if they supported the strike. This encouraged a cacophony of honking horns.

> *I remember standing in front of 50 Eglinton in freezing cold temperatures day after day, and being so heartened when motorists honked and waved. It made us feel supported and not so alone.*

The national office of the CWC also printed up stickers reading "Bell Canada Is Out of Order, We Support the Strikers." Bell Canada customers were encouraged to place the stickers on their phone bills, which at the time were key punch cards. This screwed up bill-payment processing and caused major delays and frustration for the company.

Many local and national unions recognized the strike. This telegram announced support from the Canadian Union of Postal Workers:

TELEGRAM

Received February 15, 1980 11:00 a.m.

TO: PETER KLYM & FRED POMEROY   (2 telegrams)

FROM: OTTAWA

Dear Brothers,

On behalf of the 23,000 postal workers this is to inform you that we stand solidly behind you in your present struggle against your entire union employer Bell Canada.

The wages presently being paid your members in this highly inflationary period is disgraceful and must be fought against with the help of all workers.

Our members of the Canadian Union of Postal Workers are being advised of the circumstances involving your strike and are being requested to assist your members on the picket line and to offer any other assistance that you feel is necessary to bring this strike to a successful conclusion.

In fraternal solidarity

Lee Roy C. Hiltz
National Secretary-Treasurer
Canadian Union of Postal Workers

Letter to Peter Klym and Fred Pomeroy from Canadian Union of Postal Workers, February 13, 1980.

The national union decided broader public support was necessary to get the company back to the table. On February 26, 1980, Fred Pomeroy and Dennis McDermott, president of the Canadian Labour Congress, held a press conference in the National Press Club about the Bell strike.[3] McDermott put out a press release saying the CLC would intervene in the strike by coordinating a fundraising campaign among its member unions all across the country. The release stated that the strike, which had been precipitated by the actions of the company (which it called "bullying tactics"), was a threat to the following basic union rights:

- The right to belong to a union of their own choosing
- The right to a safe working environment
- The right to a living wage[4]

The CLC followed through on their pledge and the money started to roll in.

On that same day, Dan Heap, a Toronto city alderman and NDP member, sent a draft motion to Toronto City Council members asking for their support in opposing the rate increase that Bell was requesting from the Canadian Radio and Television Commission (CRTC). The motion tied the rate increase to Bell Canada's failure to bargain in good faith during both the conciliation and mediation processes. It also stated that Bell was too cheap to pay its workers what the conciliator had suggested. Heap ended his motion with a request to the federal government to place Bell Canada under public ownership. The strike was opening up conversations that the company did not want revived.[5]

Support of Craft Locals

Craft locals had been in the bargaining process and were approaching a strike during the CWC organizing campaign. Although there was not much interaction between operators and their union brothers in the craft and services units, the operators' strike really brought the two groups closer together. Picketing of craft locations was a major strategy for disrupting company operations. Although the craft guys had to cross the picket lines, they certainly were able to take their time doing so. The national union additionally instructed craft and services union members not to take acting foreman positions, as that would free up managers to scab in the operators' strike.[6]

Many craft and services union members in the CWC craft locals devoted one hour's pay per week to the CWC Defence Fund. A letter to Local 25 officers and union stewards directed them to approach every union member on every pay day for a donation, collect the money, note any reasons why the member was not donating, and send the funds to the Local 25 union office.[7]

Some Toronto CWC craft stewards also devoted many hours to walking the picket lines with the strikers.

> *Many of the craft guys picketed with us, some almost every day when they got off work. Two of them, Irad Munro (Local 25) and Owen Oiffer (Local 27), were of major support to the picket lines of my building at 50 Eglinton, where we had the highest number of scabs in the city. If there was any kind of police interaction the police would pick on them first. Romance even blossomed on the picket line, as Owen later married one of the stewards from Eglinton.*

Munro and Oiffer were members of the Toronto Liaison Committee for the Traffic and Dining Services strike, along with George Cameron from Northern Telecom Local 4 and Henry Ven Den Bosch from NT Local 9; and four members of Local 50, including George Larter, Ann Newman, Irene Anderson, and Madeline Vallieres.

This committee worked out picketing strategy, built support for mass pickets, and resolved any issues. Bill Howes recorded four meetings of this committee in his diary: February 4, 19, and 25, and March 17.

Political Support

Right from the beginning of the strike, CWC staff worked to gain the attention, support and resources, and (most importantly) the supportive voice of the Canadian labour movement and the NDP. The union developed a key message designed to resonate with the broader labour movement and the public. It was expressed succinctly in a CWC press release dated February 20, 1989. The title said it best: "Union Says Public Should Not Pay for Strike!"[8]

Along with the press release, the CWC developed a backgrounder, *Costs of the Bell Strike.* This document cited a paragraph in an article published in the *Globe and Mail* on February 14 stating that Bell was paying out the same amount to 2,300 managers and supervisors as its yearly salary budget for the striking employees. Along with $1 million a week in regular costs for its management staff, Bell was putting out $2 million a week to fund the management costs to sustain the strike.[9]

The union demanded that the CRTC force Bell to reduce subscriber phone bills to compensate for lack of service. The fact sheet claimed that customers were experiencing lengthy waits for long-distance operators, and that calls for directory assistance were going unanswered. The union sent the press release and backgrounder to all NDP members of parliament and provincial legislative assemblies. These documents provided the legislators with enough information to write letters and pressure the company and the CRTC.

Evelyn Gigantes, an Ottawa NDP minister of the Ontario provincial parliament wrote a letter dated March 4, 1979, to the company's district manager in Ottawa. Not only did she complain about the strike and the costs, she noted the women on the picket line did not look like the women in Bell Canada's advertising. Obviously, she was referring to how cold and haggard the picketers looked, not that they were unattractive.

Morale was at an all-time low after the mediation talks broke down. But the widespread support operators were starting to receive became the turning point in the strike.

During the month of March, Janice McClelland started to note tasks related to lobbying efforts. Notes from March 3 referred to obtaining MP for Davenport Charles Caccia's contact information. Other notes referred to the need for lobbying and for operators who could help lobby their MPs. Other lobbying was to be coordinated by the author with Guy Beaulieu, a consultant and former Teamsters organizer who was volunteering for the union on this project.

I have no recollection of lobbying of federal MPs, but I do remember working on a municipal lobbying campaign. I would call up city councillors, who would sometimes answer their phones or call me back. It surprised me that these public figures were so accessible. I felt even more surprised that they were very supportive and appreciated being asked to support the resolution. Everyone had contact with telephone operators, and local politicians were astounded that operators were on picket lines all over the city.

Janice McClelland drafted the following motion which became the focus for the lobbying of municipal councilors.

Resolution to the Toronto City Council By Communications Workers of Canada (CWC) Local 50

Whereas	the CWC has been negotiating with Bell Canada since August 28, 1979, on behalf of operators and dining service personnel
Whereas	Bell Canada applied for federal conciliation services on September 20, 1979, and
Whereas	on December 21, 1979, the union agreed to recommend to its members the acceptance of the Conciliation Commissioner's report as a settlement, and

Whereas	Bell Canada has continued to refuse to accept the Conciliation Commissioner's report, and
Whereas	Bell Canada's latest contract offer was rejected by 90.3% majority in a secret ballot vote, and
Whereas	over 1,400 Toronto employees of Bell Canada have been engaged in a legal strike since January 19, 1980, and
Whereas	the severe restriction of directory assistance service causes hardships for Toronto citizens and in particular those who are sick and disabled, and
Whereas	poor long distance service has an adverse effect on commercial activities in the city of Toronto
THEREFORE BE IT RESOLVED	that the Council of the City of Toronto urge Bell Canada to accept the report of the Conciliation Commissioner as a step towards resolving the dispute and restoring full telephone service to the citizens of this city.

Respectfully Submitted By

Janice McClelland
President
CWC Local 50[10]

Obtaining the support of Toronto City Council helped build support for the strikers across the city. It proved that Bell customers, and not just the union movement, supported the strikers and were siding with the operators. This put public relations pressure on the company.

Money Rolls In

Once the CLC campaign got underway, large donations began to come in to the union strike fund. Barb Mercury, chair of the membership assistance committee, announced that the local could provide funds for food, shelter, utilities, and transportation assistance. The committee set up times to meet with strikers and asked them to call ahead for appointments. Mercury emphasized that there was not enough for everyone, just for those who really had no other financial resources.

The *Bell Operators & Dining Services Newsletter* of February 27 provided excerpts from Dennis McDermott's February 26 press release announcing a $632,000 donation to the CWC Defence Fund. The CLC had taken one week to raise that amount and McDermott planned to continue raising money for the strike.[11]

In other strike committee minutes, under the membership assistance item, there was a motion to ask that two people each in the Brampton, Oakville, and Orangeville offices become membership assistance counselors, and that they bring the request forms to Toronto for approval. As funds rolled in from the union movement, it became clear that suburban locations had just as much need as central locations, and the local developed the infrastructure to make sure the money got to everyone who needed it.[12] Linda Young recalls how tough it was to serve on the membership assistance committee: "The worst part was coming down to Toronto. Marnie Veale chaired this hardship committee and I was on it along with Barb Mercury. Income support. It was a big responsibility. It was lonely for me."[13]

Deciding who got financial assistance was a difficult task. Operators who were used to earning over $150 a week and who could demonstrate need were eligible for $20 a week. Later on, when the local collected more money, strikers could apply for housing assistance. Irene Anderson remembers the tough decision-making: "I remember sitting on the assistance committee. I wanted to give money to everybody. But you couldn't. I remember there were some who wanted to take advantage, too. Hardened me up. We had a lot of single moms in dire straits."[14]

I remember a strike committee meeting where Barb Mercury was reporting on the activities and decisions of the financial assistance committee. The identities of applicants for assistance were kept confidential, but the financial assistance committee was relating intimate details of applicant's financial situations and considering some applicants more worthy than others. Committee members expressed a fear of some co-workers wasting their meagre assistance on beer or bingo. The meeting discussion focused on whether to give food vouchers or cash.

I had grown up in a working-class home and remembered the shame of getting help in one form or another, and empathized with those co-workers coming for assistance. But I was in my early twenties and not yet confident about sharing my own experience of living hand-to-mouth, so I shared what I had learned from oral histories in studying the Great Depression in university. I related to the committee the shame and stigma that are transmitted along with a food voucher as opposed to cash. They would be sending the message that the recipient can't be trusted to make good choices or to do the right thing.

The committee agreed to provide cash. Later I wished I had been braver and spoken from my own lived experience with poverty, but a blame-the-victim mentality was still prevalent at that time in Toronto.

International Support

Overseas telephone operators supported the strike, too. The Postal, Telegraph, and Telephone International (PTTI) in Europe organized a boycott of incoming and outgoing calls to and from Canada. Announcements like these really buoyed the spirits of the strikers and connected them to the international labour movement.

Help crack Bell

a newsbulletin published by the Communications Workers of Canada

Geneva, Switzerland - Accompanying their defence fund donation of $5,000, the PTTI in Geneva sent wishes for a speedy end to our strike. The letter says "We continue to make every effort to ensure that the ban of operator-assisted telephone communications with Bell Canada is effective. In making these efforts our members have been able to find out that on your side the strike is effective and the result is that as far as we know there is next to no traffic between the Provinces of Canada covered by Bell Canada and the outside world."

Dublin, Ireland - The CWC National office has received a call of support from the union representing telephone workers in Ireland. They wished us success and pledged to help win the strike in any way they can. The leprechauns are with us, too!

Toronto - February 17th was "family day" at the Asquith Ave. picket line. About 150 strikers turned out with clowns, hot dogs, pop, and prizes for the kids' best home-made picket signs. Even Ma Bell turned out in her witches' outfit!

Kingston - Picketers have been holding up mail trucks in the wee hours of the morning. Apparently the Bell managers called to the scene each time don't appreciate being hauled out of bed to deal with the picket line. Pass on the message, fellas, we'd like to see a successful conclusion to the strike, too.

Thessalon, Ont. - The town council in this municipality between Sudbury and Sault Ste. Marie has fully endorsed a resolution recommending that "the citizens of this municipality deduct 25 per cent from their telephone bills before submitting payment this month. According to a newspaper clipping, one councillor said the resolution was prompted by "The absolutely terrible service in this area.". Perhaps other municipalities should consider similar actions.

Barrie - Every picket line has its pet. In Barrie it's Bell Manager, Bob Dunlop. On Valentine's Day he urged the driver to "run over the bitch" when a picket stopped a truck. The picketers responded by handing him a Valentine's card which he refused to take. Maybe they should have waited for his day - April 1st.

Toronto - A C.O. man from Local 27 was suspended for wearing a "Help Crack Bell" button on the job. The local immediately picked up 500 buttons to sell to its members. Bell settled the grievance at Step I, and the man was paid for his lost day's pay. Thanks, Ma Bell. He'd spent the day helping striking Local 50.

Huntsville - So the public is getting service, eh? One Huntsville subscriber reported counting 249 rings before he got an answer after dialing "O" from a pay phone. And the Bell has always said they give better service to pay phone customers. After all, they might make a dime!

Toronto - One indicator of the economic impact of the strike is that the number of successfully completed outgoing toll calls in one of the two Toronto TOPS systems was down by more than 17% on February 7th compared to January 23. Customers are apparently giving up even trying to reach an operator. Calls to our office indicate that subscribers' anger with Ma Bell is reaching the boiling point.

Hamilton - From one of our secret supporters in management comes this story. One day management scabs received a number of calls from people trying to leave messages for "Joe". Finally someone called in and identified himself as "Joe" and asked if there were any messages for him. Is this a new service? We

Help Crack Bell newsletter.

Help Crack Bell was a news bulletin for the public published by the Communications Workers of Canada. Its logo was the Bell Canada bell with a crack down the front.

This story from the newsletter of how operators across the ocean were helping was especially heartwarming:

> Frankfurt, Germany
>
> The secretary of the telephone union local in Frankfurt used to work for Bell Canada as an operator. Being familiar with the way Bell treats its employees, she has taken charge of organizing her city's boycott of calls to and from Canada in support of our strike with signs and posters throughout the office. (Frankfurt is the main international exchange in West Germany.)[15]

The bulletin went on to report that on the morning of January 29, the number of calls answered was down by approximately one-third from prestrike volume. It also mentioned the donations of cash and in-kind items (like oil drums for fires) made to locals.

International support poured in from around the globe. The following text is from a telegram dated February 4, 1980, from Japanese telecommunications unions.

> Telegram received February 4, 1980, by telephone 12:15 p.m.
>
> TO: GENERAL SECRETARY, CWC
> FROM: TOKYO, JAPAN
>
> Express full solidarity with you in your industrial action for interest of your members and wish success in securing your demands.
>
> Japan Telecommunications Workers Union
> Japan Postal Workers Union
> International Telegraph & Telephone Workers Union
> The Federation of Telecommunications and Allied Workers[16]

Solidarity Picket

To bring attention to the strike and to give other trade unions and the public an opportunity to express their solidarity, the strike committee designated a solidarity picket for March 1, from noon to 2 p.m. at 55 Bloor Street West. To make this event successful, invitations had to go out through proper channels to ensure enough support. To reach the labour movement in Toronto, the union submitted a resolution to the Labour Council of Metropolitan Toronto:

Janice McClelland wrote on the document, 'Fox'[17] urges all our affiliates to the best of our abilities to vote to support the CWC financially, $1.7 million needed. Bell is an arrogant multinational company. A defeat to us is a defeat to everyone."

McClelland's handwritten organizing notes for the solidarity picket identified the following tasks:

- Irene was to get picket captains
- Ann was in charge of a petition
- Janice was to get song sheets and a drum
- And Irene was to get a banner

Irene Anderson recalls how the solidarity picket changed the course of the strike: "I think one of our biggest accomplishments was the solidarity picket at Manulife. People came from women's groups, gay and lesbian groups, and the larger labour movement. Shortly after that the strike ended. It was a defining moment. It was a long, hard slog."[18]

An invitation also went out to Montreal: "Local 50 Strike Committee invites all CWC members in Montreal to our Solidarity Picket this Saturday March 1, 12:00 noon to 2:00 p.m., 55 Bloor St. West Toronto. Social After. Join us and our brothers and sisters."

CWC secretaries Linda McCrorie and Julie Jansco helped leaflet the CUC stronghold at 50 Eglinton Avenue. Diehard CUC supporters at this location were in the habit of refusing CWC leaflets and not even reading the information. One very early morning, Linda and Julie took the initiative and went right up to the subway exits and leafleted these diehard CUC supporters when they came out, before they realized that it was a CWC leaflet and refused it.

COMMUNICATIONS WORKERS OF CANADA LOCAL 50

ASKS YOUR SUPPORT

IN A **SOLIDARITY PICKET**

Saturday March 1st , 12 noon - 2 pm

AT 55 BLOOR ST. WEST

(MANULIFE BUILDING)

AT BAY & BLOOR

HELP CRACK THE BELL! SUPPORT THE BELL TELEPHONE OPERATORS AND DINING SERVICE IN THEIR
STRUGGLE FOR JUSTICE. SEE YOU THERE!

for further information, call CWC Local 50 Strike Headquarters at 977-9892, or,
CWC National Office at 364-6678.

Solidarity picket invitation, March 1, 1980.

The political work of building support and working with the Toronto & York Region Labour Council paid off mightily. Notes from the March 3 strike committee meeting identified the supporters of the solidarity picket:

> CUPE
> Canadian Union of Public Workers (CUPW)
> UAW — 252 (Blue Cross)
> Brewery workers
> Dovercourt and Beaches NDP
> Steelworkers
> Iron workers
> Ontario Public Service Employees Union (OPSEU)
> Organized Working Women
> International Women's Day
> Christian Students York University
> United Electrical Workers
> CWC

> OFL and its President, Cliff Pilkey
> Letter carriers
> Farm workers
> Joe Grogan Humber College
> Typographers Local[19]

A handwritten note by Janice McClelland states that there were 1,500 participants, including operators from Belleville, Oshawa, Hamilton, Huntsville, Montreal, Parry Sound, and Brantford. All Ontario-based CWC staff, including secretaries, also participated. Another note in McClelland's files says that even members of the Canadian Telephone Employees Association (the last remaining company union) were donating funds to support the strike and were to send seven people to the solidarity picket.

Bell Telephone operators were now a *cause célèbre*! The solidarity picket gave everyone a big morale boost. The show of union and public support was a big win that put the union closer to a deal. Bell was losing the public relations battle.

Although I could not access any written minutes for the strike committee meeting of March 3, 1980, Janice McClelland's notes for this meeting refer to:

March 1 solidarity picket at Manulife Centre. Janice McClelland on bullhorn, Ed Seymour to the left, and Fred Pomeroy in checked hat.

- Tonight's meetings with craft
  - Prepare picket line procedure — we are asking drivers to roll down window
  - Picket line help [mentioned help of a few craft guys — Owen Oifer]
  - Minimum amount of overtime
  - Whisper campaign for a work-to-rule campaign
  - Boycott of cafeterias
- Calendar for month
- March 7 court date at 9 a.m.
- IWD, start at city hall at 11 a.m.
- Provide two parade marshals: Laurie Cummings and Ann Newman
- Irene Anderson was designated speaker on behalf of Local 50
- At 12 on there was a press conference that she would attend
- Other strategies included a dialling campaign picketing. 393 University and McClelland doing outreach to unions
- Something was to happen on March 15 and they needed a van and Owen's [Oifer] car
- Lobby of MPs; Joan Roberts will coordinate with Guy Beaulieu
- Charles Caccia contact info

The author wearing a picket sign: "Bell Canada has a childish attitude!"

Feminist Support

Sisterhood was also encouraged when Bell operators became the focus of the 1980 International Women's Day parade in Toronto. Telephone operators also joined the picket lines at Blue Cross, where women had been on strike for seven months.

The International Women's Day Parade was scheduled for March 8. The International Women's Day Committee (IWDC) at that time identified themselves as socialist feminists. As such, they were active in supporting women's economic struggles, union campaigns, and strikes with large female participation. In 1979 the IWDC organized a solidarity picket for women employees of Radio Shack, who were on strike for a first contract in Barrie, Ontario. They then became involved in building links with a number of strikes by women, including federal government clerks (Public Service Alliance of Canada), postal workers (CUPW), Ontario hospital workers (CUPE), Irwin Toy, and workers at Blue Cross.[20]

Parade organizers wanted to support the Bell operators' strike and asked CWC Local 50 to send a couple of parade marshals and a contingent of strikers to the parade. Six or seven operators showed up that day with picket signs. The organizers then wanted someone to march at the front of the parade.

Walking in the IWD parade is one of my clearest memories of the strike. Primarily because I got to walk at the front of the line wearing my picket sign: "Help Crack Bell." I was the lucky one, because everyone else was too frightened to walk with the "women's libbers." I was honoured and had called myself a feminist since I was thirteen. But to most of the working-class telephone operators, the label of being a women's libber was stigmatizing. The others stuck together for safety in the middle of the parade.

The support from union and feminist movements helped the working-class women gain a broader understanding of the world and their place in it. Laurie Cumming remembers celebrating International

Women's Day: "We had lots of fun times. I remember going to Oshawa for a rally. I remember singing 'Solidarity Forever' and keeping up the singing on some parade (IWD Day). I thought we'd been rehearsing."[21]

Some of the local leadership readily identified with the feminist agenda and others didn't. Irene Anderson, Laurie Cumming, and Janice McClelland readily admitted to their identification with the feminist movement at that time. Irene Anderson disclosed that she "was a card-carrying feminist. I had a rep as a feminist and had a subscription to *Ms.* Magazine, and was a fan of Gloria Steinem. I was aware of feminism and I definitely saw this campaign in this context."[22]

Laurie Cumming shares her memories of the time:

> I remember there were other strikes during that time. The Blue Cross strike was on. We saw through that strike that their demands were legitimate and fair, and the company was being unreasonable. It echoed our concerns and situation. How the world was unfair and we had to fight to make it fairer. That other women were there fighting the same fight.... Toward the end of high school I began to think of myself as a feminist. I had one conversation with a male friend about what he would say if his wife wants to work. He said it was okay as long as the children were taken care of. I jumped on him, accusing him of assuming that it was the wife's job to manage the kids.
>
> I did see myself as someone who was not following my mother's career path as a secretary. My parents were really proud of me and I thought of what I was doing as a feminist act.[23]

Janice McClelland recalls the unrest at the time:

> Feminism was in the air at the time. Nurses had just got themselves better unionized and made great leaps in pay. Michele Landsberg was writing daily about women's issues in the *Toronto Star*. I saw the women's movement at York. There was a lot of talk about equal pay for equal work, and

for equal pay for work of equal value and equal opportunity. I might not have used the word "feminism" at the time, but I identified with those principles.

Also, I had the experience of dealing with management at Bell, who had a very traditional view of what women could do. A very limiting view.[24]

Others in the leadership either had issues with mainstream feminism or had not really thought about it. Linda Young reflects on her thinking at the time: "I did not know anything about feminism. I am always a supporter of women. It's my natural position. I take the position of women because I read historical novels that tell you about how women are treated. I was never into the group thing. It wasn't part of my thinking."[25]

Ann Newman remembers the thinking at the time and her choices:

The company sent the message that they expected ladylike behaviour from us. A matron was on staff that would do your ironing if you were going out after work. You could have a shower. We were not allowed to wear pants. We had to wear a pantsuit. Doris Anderson interviewed us once. There were not a lot of role models for us. I had a problem with women's liberation then, as there was no place for visible minorities. I organized for better working conditions, better wages, and dignity in the workplace. I could have transferred into better jobs, but I loved the union and I cared about my members.[26]

Helen Middlebrooks recalls her opinion about feminism at that time:

I don't know if feminism was a motivator for me. I worked in a predominantly female workforce. I knew our ages were an issue. There were a lot of single moms in my office. A lot of it came afterwards when I was representing Dining Service as their steward, and I got to know immigrant women who had it really tough.[27]

So whether they identified themselves as feminists or not, they all knew that what they were doing was going to help themselves and the women they worked with.

The Dark Side: Picket Line Altercations

Although the bargaining unit was primarily women, and one might think things would be calm and ladylike, violence emerged on the picket lines — especially where colleagues were crossing the picket lines and going to work. The scabs raised high levels of emotion — including disappointment, frustration, anger, and even rage — in the picketers. After all, the primarily purpose of a picket line is to keep workers from entering the workplace. When the replacement labour crosses the picket line and walks right in the front door of the building, the picketer is likely to get very angry. The scab seems to be flaunting their warm office and regular paycheque while the striker is on a picket line in below-zero weather. The picketer takes it to mean that the company is not hurting the way they want it to hurt. It means they might be on this picket line a whole lot longer than they want to be. It's very easy to get angry.

Janice McClelland's notes throughout the strike are interspersed with references to scabs and witnesses. As the strike dragged on, scabbing was a real threat to keeping up solidarity among the strikers, and a source of irritation which led to violence. One note read: "Strike running well. Out of 1,400 members of the bargaining unit in Toronto there were less than 75 scabs." An agenda for a strike committee meeting (undated but after the solidarity picket) includes the topic of scab hunting.[28]

George Larter remembers someone who unofficially stirred the pot:

> Bell hired this guy just before the strike who worked at 50 Eglinton Avenue East. He did not follow any union protocols, but would take people out on wildcats. I would guess he was an agent for the company. He was a guy with a little moustache. Probably an agent provocateur stirring the pot.[29]

To shore up dwindling picket lines, prove broad support, make trouble for the company, and scare scabs, the strike committee began to create solidarity pickets. Operators from other Toronto locations, craft members from CWC union locals, and other union members congregated at unpublicized locations and tried to create havoc. The police were called as soon as the mass of people showed up. Having strength in numbers meant that the picketers took more aggressive action to try to stop people, cars, and trucks from entering Bell locations. 50 Eglinton was a popular location for mystery solidarity pickets, as was 393 University Avenue, the regional headquarters of Bell Canada. On February 25, 1980, the local organized a special picket at 393 University Avenue. While there were no operator offices in the building, there was a large cafeteria. Most likely there were a few scabs, but to the committee's way of thinking, it was as much a target for picketing as many of the buildings with operators in them. It was also downtown, with high visibility.

The company did not see it the same way and called the police. According to Larter:

> I remember solidarity pickets and the day a number of people were arrested. I think Irene Anderson was one. Four or five people got arrested for obstruction at 393 University, which was the head office of Bell at the time. It was in the *Globe and Mail*. I remember meeting with the police [labour relations officers]. One police officer opened his briefcase with his gun and bullets staring me in the face. I asked what that was about. He replied, "I am a police officer so I have to have a gun." They would tell us who they would arrest. They throw a few pennies up in the air and when they fall you grab a few. They admitted there was no rationale for arrests. Police officers hate the strikes. They would pretend to become our best friends while turning the screw, telling you what you can do on the picket line. And over time on the picket line, they would let you do less and less, ten-minute delays turned into five-minute delays until they would permit no delays.[30]

Janice McClelland's notes for the strike committee meeting on March 12 referred to a court date regarding assault charges pressed by the author; the officer who was a witness to the assault needed to be present. Court cases were now an ongoing theme and, along with scabs, a source of constant indignation.

Laurie Cumming remembers the tension on the large picket lines:

> There was some kind of mass picket at 393 University. Every once in a while we would do a mass picket. We knew there would be some media. We would just be slowing cars down. This was the first time I was at a picket line with police. I had been told about what had happened at Eglinton, that the pickets had their breasts touched by the police. I went there knowing there could be scuffles with the police. We knew what we had to do. We would stop cars, tell them what the strike was about, and then let them go on. The police did not like us stopping cars. People were trying to reason with police. I remember somebody being pulled. I do remember people being manhandled, being yanked out of the way. This seemed to be unreasonable to me and I might have been crying. In my mind all the police officers were male.
>
> I remember going to court. I can't remember who I was a witness for. I met with Paul Cavalluzzo before going in. He asked me a question, and when I answered, he told me I gave too much information.
>
> There was this person — someone who laid the charges. The officer flat-out denied that he had touched anyone. I knew that was the officer who had yanked someone out of the way. The officer lied under oath, and I could not believe it. I was never called to the stand and the officer was never charged. I was shocked. I still believed that we had a good police force. When I saw what happened, my world view just shifted in an instant. If police are going to lie, then what's right?[31]

Looking back over the interviews for this book, many of the leaders realized that they had often crossed the line, and regretted some of their behaviour. Laurie Cumming remembers how her feelings escalated as the strike wore on:

> Boy it was cold. Brutal. People would come out and do their time. I did not have children to manage, so I could picket when some people could not because of children. Some people took jobs. I remember people crossing the picket line, and remember doing my part to make it difficult for scabs to cross. It was like swearing at people or spitting was justified because those people weren't human anymore. Because that's how riled up I was.[32]
>
> I recall another incident. There were some scabs at Main Street office coming out at 11 p.m. My friend Heather Johnson and I went to join the mass picket. When the scabs came out to get in the company-paid taxis, I spit on one and my friend got charged, and she had to go to court. The charge stuck on Heather, and she had to sign a peace bond to stay away from the Main Street office for a year. It stuck because a police officer stated in court that he saw her spit, but he could not have — because it was me who spit. Another lie by a police officer.[33]

Irene Anderson remembers her arrest:

> The arrest came behind 393 University. We heard Cheryl Lapinta, who was on the bargaining committee for management, was coming out of the back of the building. We were pissed off with her at something she had said at the bargaining table. We decided we were not going to let her out of the parking lot, and we made some adjustments to her vehicle. The police were called. There were four of us arrested: me, Marg McColl, Dave Handley from Ottawa, and Judith Churoskie. The cops knew Marg and I were the ringleaders. Dave and Judith were not doing anything, but got pulled in, too. We were thrown into the back of the police car. Judith was wailing. While the two cops called in their report, Marg and I sang at the top of our lungs, "Solidarity Forever."

I think one of those cops tried to pick me up. He killed himself laughing. We were charged with disturbing the peace. We went to court. The CWC lawyers pushed the appearance date until after the strike. The four of us made the headline in *Bell News* the month the strike ended.[34]

The organizing campaign and strike were major events in the lives of all the people who participated. Many were already aware of their own capacity for leadership, and went on to leadership positions in the community. Looking back, violence was not something anyone was proud of. But the conditions associated with the strike — brutal cold, high levels of expectations dashed by frustration, national media attention, widespread scabbing facilitated by the company, and a heavy police presence — created a highly charged situation where violence seemed a natural response.

Police Surveillance and Telephone Taps

I remember at the solidarity pickets at both 50 Eglinton and at the Manulife Centre, I was looking up to the tops of the buildings and watching what were probably RCMP officers or Bell security filming our activities. Picketers became increasingly suspicious of this filming, and started to cover their faces and present their backs to cameras, including TV crews.

Bell Canada managed the emergency communications system of the national and provincial governments, and any threat to that system was a national security issue. However, that threat was totally overblown by the company and the authorities. Union activists, including the author, heard strange beeps on their phone lines. Suspecting the lines were being wiretapped, they acted accordingly. Craft guys confirmed that the company tapped many lines. This might have been done without any police or justice system approval, as the police needed warrants to tap phones. Once a judge gave them a warrant, the police had to ask Bell to physically tap the line. So Bell had the capability, and although it was an illegal act on their part, they didn't need to ask anyone for permission. All of these incidents just raised our awareness about the difficulty of taking on those with the most power in our society: large corporations and the government. And we were up against both.

Fred Pomeroy recalls that the RCMP was always involved in labour unrest at Bell Canada:

> The RCMP was involved in every strike at Bell. Peter Klym and I would make a decision in a secure place, and then get on the phone and share misinformation on that decision, and then wait to see how the company acted on our decision. Of course they were tapping our lines.
>
> They were not only tapping work phones. People would knock on the door once I got into bed. I got into bed one night in a hotel and there was a knock on the door. At the end of one strike, things got a little boisterous. We got a phone call asking "whether you guys need the police down there."
>
> One time in a hotel in Montreal [after this campaign], Richard Long [later the CWC Ontario VP] and I were on totally different land lines in different hotel rooms, but we could hear each other's calls. Clear as a bell. Lots of unions were hassled more. We accepted it as part of the territory.[35]

Fred also remembers RCMP monitoring of 25 Cecil Street, the Steelworkers Hall where the CWC Toronto offices were located: "We always joked about it. There were RCMP agents monitoring the Communist Party (located across the street at 24 Cecil St.) and then RCMP agents monitoring the CWC. Couldn't they have doubled up?"

Ed Seymour recalls those days:

> During the craft strike when we were on rotating strikes, we had a sophisticated way to communicate. We had some kind of code.

We would get on the phone and say we were going on rotating strike in Thunder Bay when we were targeting another location. Then all kinds of company people went to Thunder Bay.

We never got paranoid about the surveillance but we knew they were listening.[36]

Phone-Through of March 15

As things heated up on the picket lines, the bargaining committees were talking. McClelland prepared the following script for a phone-through:

- Talks are continuing in Montreal between Bell Canada, the mediators and the union. At this time the mediators are still imposing a news blackout so no info is available. As soon as the mediators lift the news blackout, we will be reporting to you.

- We continue to ask for your participation on the picket line. Strong picket lines show faith and give support to our bargaining committee. Regarding special picketing for Monday March 17th, St Patrick's Day — please contact your steward.

- If you require financial assistance, please call first and make an appointment. Those with appointments will be served first.

- CWC Local 25 Craft and Services are having a dance Saturday March 29th and local 50 can get tickets for half price for $3.00 a ticket. Tickets can be obtained at strike headquarters. (25 Cecil St.) Macedonian Community Hall on 76 Overlea Blvd. Buffet dance, door prizes, disc jockey, and bar.

- We appreciate your solidarity and support and will keep you posted on any new developments.

- PS — a few members from Local 50 stood at the gates of the General Electric Plant here in Toronto. The employees at these 2 plants members of the United Electrical Workers donated over $600 to our strike.

McClelland was also keeping a running handwritten list of donations coming in from local unions. The unions were primarily manufacturing-based, as Toronto in the seventies remained a manufacturing centre. This list of unionized workplaces is a snapshot of Toronto's industrial past. Many of these plants have now closed, thanks to the North American Free Trade Agreement.

Canada Packers
Swift Canada
Neilson's Dairy
Rothmans Pall Mall
Kimberly-Clark
Molson
Philco Ford of Canada
Rowntree
de Havilland
McDonell Douglas
Pilkington Glass
Consumers Glass
Goodyear
Inglis
Gabriel
General Motors
TTC and
Toronto Hydro

On this page alone, the donations to the strike fund totalled over $18,000.

Personal Change

The strike was gruelling, the cold seeping into the women's bodies, working to undermine their spirit and resolve. But a funny thing happened. The women — despite economic hardship — found ways to survive on little money. They built relationships to support each other emotionally, and the strike gave them a shared experience of being powerful, of being a thorn in the side of one of the country's largest corporations.

Judy Darcy and Catherine Lauzon, in their article "The Right to Strike" in Brisken and Yanz, state that going on strike was a pivotal moment in a woman's life:

> Not only is the strike a powerful weapon in the fight for women's rights, the experience of going on strike is liberating in its own right. Women's oppression is in part experienced as a sense of powerlessness and of dependence on others. And women's isolation in the home and limited experience outside their workplaces creates the feeling that politics and economics are matters beyond their grasp. But a strike gives women a sense of their own collective strength; a clear understanding of the roots of their own oppression and a broader sense of the social, economic and political relationships of the society in which they live.[37]

When looking back, the union leaders recalled how they changed and grew into their leadership roles. George Larter recalls his admiration for Helen Middlebrooks's leadership:

> I remember Helen Middlebrooks leading the women at Asquith. She did not take any nonsense. I had a problem getting angry with people. Sometimes you needed to tell people where they stood. She was like a sergeant who would tell her soldiers, "You either go over the hill or you get shot." People are fearful, so sometimes you have to push them. I was a great believer in never asking people to do what I would not do.[38]

Ann Newman remembers her own journey and that of others: "I developed more self-confidence. I owned my power and my words. Others, too, developed their voice. Not necessarily the people who should have."[39]
Irene Anderson recalls how her leadership skills developed:

> My sense of adventure inspired me. There are moments in your life when you are in a place where you should be. I always spoke up for the underdog. I was an introvert, but I was

always getting in trouble in class as a child. I got the strap quite a lot. When the teacher did something I thought was unfair, I spoke up. And I got in trouble.

It was about legitimatizing being allowed to speak out and speak up. I am allowed to say things aren't fair and to have a platform.[40]

Turning Point

In retrospect, we can see that the turning point in the strike came on February 26. Fred Pomeroy, president of the Communications Workers of Canada, held a press conference with Dennis McDermott, president of the Canada Labour Congress. McDermott announced that the CLC was throwing its full weight behind the strike by asking the entire labour movement to contribute to a national fundraising campaign in support of the strikers. To kick off the campaign, he handed over a cheque for $632,000. This support was significant because now everyone who spent time on a picket line was eligible for food assistance, and members who presented an eviction notice could get help with their rent or mortgage. This put a lot of pressure on the company because operators would be more willing to stay on strike if there was financial help. On February 29, the mediators responded to this by calling the bargaining committees back to the negotiating table. On March 4, meetings with the mediators began under a media blackout.

The company refused to change any of its positions during the first week; the union bargaining committee began to feel it was hopeless. However, they went back at it for a second week, but the company remained firm. The mediators were about to call off the talks when they asked both sides for a confidential statement of their bottom line in terms of where they would settle. The mediators then created a package of proposals as a basis for settlement. This kick-started negotiations, but union negotiators were very wary of the company, which had kept meetings going until 4:30 a.m.

The company kept up their resistance by placing conditions on the proposal. They demanded that the union bargaining committee recommend it for acceptance to the membership. If the committee refused, the company would publish the offer in the newspapers and invite operators back to work under the terms of the offer. Even though this new offer was not as beneficial as the one in the conciliation report, the union bargaining committee decided to endorse it. The members' resolve to remain on strike was weakening in the face of continued threats of back-to-work movements and increased violence on the picket lines. Fred Pomeroy related the situation at the bargaining table:

> There was a tendency on the management side to look down on the operators, thinking that they didn't know about the Cost of Living Allowance. We had hung in on a particular formula for COLA adjustments for quite a while, but in the give-and-take that goes into resolving a big package of issues, we finally agreed to the latest version that Bell had been pushing. It was an improvement, but it wasn't exactly what we wanted, but we decided we could live with it because we had other, bigger fish to fry.
>
> We were getting near the end of conciliation and there were several key items still on the go. After going back and forth for a few hours, it was about 2:00 a.m. and the company came in with revised documents for several outstanding issues. Without realizing it, they included a version of the COLA clause that we wanted, instead of their version. Lisette Sabourin, a member of the bargaining committee, and others noticed it right away. We just shut up about it without even having a caucus. We stayed at the table facing them and worked our way through all the texts that the company had responded to us on. Then we took the time to handwrite the remaining text that was needed to flesh out a full settlement based on what we had worked through. Normally, we would have agreed on what needed to be done and adjourned for Bell to prepare typed texts for us to initial off. When we adjourned for the night we had a complete offer signed off.

The conciliators were watching and realized that we had a secret. It was the only explanation for us pushing to finish the texts longhand that night without taking a break. The secret was that the company had handed out our version of the COLA text instead of the one we had decided to agree to, which was their version.

We decided on the fly to make them look like idiots because the chairman of the company bargaining committee had been such a condescending S.O.B. all through the process. Other members of their committee hadn't been very nice, either. So much so that I learned later, the conciliator told the chair of the Bell committee he wasn't up to the task.

We went for breakfast around 4:00 a.m. and the committee agreed we would eventually give the text back because we had already agreed to a different one, and our word had to count for something or we'd never be able to do business in any rational way. When I got home I unplugged the phone and slept. When I plugged it in again in the morning, the Bell vice-president called right away. We met him and exchanged texts later in the day, and made the point that they had a serious problem on their committee. That message got through, and some of the committee members were subsequently removed. It was awesome because our committee was so in tune with one another that we were able to make our decisions on the fly with the company sitting across the table. We had been working so closely together that we were able to make our thoughts known to each other with just facial expressions and the odd surreptitious note going around discreetly. I was part of bargaining with some pretty impressive bargaining committees on both the Bell and the union sides. Neither had a tendency to send weak members to the table. But that Operator Services and Dining Services bargaining committee was something special, because we could fight like hell over things at times, but in the end we always came together on how to proceed.[41]

Joan M. Roberts

LE SYNDICAT DES TRAVAILLEURS EN COMMUNICATION DU CANADA
COMMUNICATIONS WORKERS OF CANADA
CLC
25 CECIL STREET, SUITE 301, TORONTO, ONTARIO M5T 1N1 (416) 977-6678

March 20, 1980

TO: ALL TRAFFIC AND DINING SERVICE MEMBERS

On Wednesday, March 19th a tentative agreement was reached with Bell Canada on the terms for a new Collective Agreement and a Return to Work Agreement, subject to the approval of the union's members through a ratification vote. The terms of the agreement are outlined in the attached report, which outlines the changes in the company's last offer. All items not covered in the attached report would be the same as in the company's last offer prior to the strike.

The bargaining committee unanimously recommends acceptance of the proposed settlement of the dispute. We will be attending meetings across the two provinces to explain the proposed settlement and the reasons for our recommendation.

Your bargaining committee

Fred Pomeroy, Chairman
Susan Edgar
George Larter
Lisette Sabourin
Michèle Brouillette
Louise Godin
Marie Pinsonneault

opeiu 343

CWC memo to all traffic and dining service members announcing a tentative agreement, March 20, 1980.

Settlement

The union bargaining committee announced a settlement on March 19, 1980. Local 50 notified its members through the phone trees before the national union announced the news to the press the next morning.

As with any tentative union-company collective agreement, the members of the union bargaining unit had to vote to accept or reject the offer. The vote took place on March 22 and 23 in a meeting room in the Westbury Hotel. Janice McClelland recalls the special meetings that brought out most of the local:

> I remember when we won the strike vote. Our Toronto local — Local 50 — was a large local of 1,400 operators. We held the ratification vote at the Masonic Temple and there might have been 1,200 people there. George was on the bargaining committee. I chaired maybe three meetings at that place. We felt power every day. We got great publicity.[42]

Press Coverage

Media coverage was widespread and generally favourable to the strikers. The company took a beating in the press and had to resort to paying for full-page ads to get their position across to the public.

An article by Louise Brown was published on March 20 in the family section of the *Toronto Star*. It included a fabulous picture of Janice McClelland, Diane Ward, and two strikers, Lystra Lewis-Bowles and Flavia Leatham, in the Local 50 strike headquarters.

Here are some quotes from that article:

> Yet despite the hassles of being on strike — being broke, being bored, even humiliated — the strike is breeding a new sense of esteem among the women they said.

> "Backbone. That's what the strike is giving us," said Bev Bishop, 41, an operator for 14 years. "We may have been a submissive bunch of women in the past, but after this strike, we'll be a force to be reckoned with."

That backbone is evident in people like newlywed Joan Roberts, who walked an early picket line Christmas Morning, again on Boxing Day and again on New Year's Eve day, even though her relatives "went nuts" that she was out on such special occasions. She was one of three hardy souls who braved last week's blizzard to keep picket duty in front of their Bell office. "Fifteen years ago I never would have been here," she said, huddling against the gale. "But society's changed, the systems changed, women have changed — and so have I."[43]

The union counted votes on Saturday, March 29. A full 87 percent of the membership voted to accept the contract offer. The company and the union signed the new collective agreement the next day, March 30, at 10:15 p.m. In line with Bell Canada's tendency to stall, the signing of the contract occurred five hours later than planned because of disagreements about wording and interpretation over the issue of vacations.

Strike Ends

The strike was over! Quebec operators returned to work on Monday and operators and Dining Service in Ontario returned on Tuesday.

It appears that the last full strike committee meeting happened on March 26. Although there was a settlement, the votes would not be counted until the following Saturday. The local leadership seemed pretty confident that the membership would accept the agreement. The meeting agenda focused on wrapping up loose ends from the strike and building the local structure for the return to work. Also discussed were office space for Local 50 and the temporary appointment of stewards, with a note listing the number of stewards required at each of the twenty-seven locations in the local.[44]

Bell Telephone operators had changed. No longer the epitome of the feminine ideal, ladylike and passive, telephone operators had left their company union days behind them. They had taken the risks associated with a new union, voted to strike, and stayed on strike for more than ten weeks. They had beaten Ma Bell.

The Finish

by Leah Harrison, Local 40

Our picket days are over
Our striking days are done
We voted to go back to work
Here endeth all our fun.

We had our fresh air daily
And our exercise as well
But none of it was wasted
Cause we cracked Old Mother Bell.

Chapter 13

After the Strike

Operators were happy with their new contract. Wages for the highest-paid operators would increase to $291.40 a week by September 1981. The drastic disparity between operators working in different regions would be eliminated the month after.[1] The company paid everyone retroactive back pay of 15.9 percent on wages earned from November 2, 1978, to November 25, 1979; and 12.2 percent for the time period after November 25, 1978. On November 2, 1980, wages were to increase by a further 9.0 percent with a COLA provision for inflation beyond 8 percent on November 1, 1981. The new contract expired on November 24, 1981.

The agreement included provisions that the company would have to use just cause in terminations or demotions, protect persons from layoffs for two years when their job changed due to tech change, and remove any record of disciplinary action after two years.

Fred Pomeroy wrote to Dennis McDermott sharing the good news about the contract improvements and ended with:

> The victory could not have been possible without the overwhelming support of the rest of the labour movement.

> On behalf of CWC and the members who were on strike, I want to thank the Congress, the Federations of Labour, Labour Councils and affiliates for all the support we received. We will always remember that together we helped crack Bell.[2]

On April 11, McDermott wrote to all the federations of labour, labour councils, and affiliates; attaching Pomeroy's letter thanking them all for their support, and emphasized:

> There is no doubt that the unprecedented massive support provided by the Canadian Labour movement made the difference between victory and defeat in this battle between the trade union David and the corporate Goliath. This is a good beginning example of the worth and potential of planned coordinated collective action. It should provide an effective object lesson to other employers who share the same prestrike Bell Canada mentality.[3]

If the labour movement had not come through with money, many strikers would have had to return to work. Labour and public support put immense pressure on Bell to settle, and damaged its reputation for years to come. Michael Cassidy, leader of the Ontario NDP, wrote a lovely letter congratulating Fred Pomeroy on the success. He reported visiting many picket lines across the province: "… and know as you do, just how cold and discouraging it's been for the operators as the strike dragged on, particularly when so many were discovering for the first time what a union is about."[4]

Return to Work

When operators walked out the door in Toronto, the top pay for an operator was $194.29 a week; when they walked back in on April 1, 1980, the new negotiated top pay for an operator in Toronto was $255.10 a week. This was a very significant raise in salary, and many other rights were gained in this first collective agreement.

Operators returned to work to face those they knew who had scabbed, and others they did not know about, but soon found out about. At the same time, they had to deal with managers who were frightened of an office with what they considered a militant union. And even a good, solid contract was only as good as the stewards and members who applied it. That meant union stewards had to confront management on day-to-day working conditions. As one might surmise, there was a good deal of tension in the workplace.

An incident mentioned in the arbitration hearing with respect to the author's suspension gives a taste of what relations were like between strikers and scabs:

> The second incident raised by the union to support its claim of discrimination took place in May of 1980, over six weeks after the strike had ended. It occurred, however, because of antagonisms that had developed during the strike. Ms[.] Barbara Harrington, an employee in the bargaining unit at 50 Eglinton Ave East, testified that on the day in question she temporarily moved her work station to a different location for better lighting. She stated that as she was leaving that location at the conclusion of her shift, another employee, Ms. Christine Page, got up, grabbed her waist-length hair from behind and threatened that she would like to cut her hair off with a knife. After Ms. Page let go of Ms. Harrington, Ms. Harrington contacted their manager who called them into the conference room. At this meeting Ms. Page admitted to what had happened, called union supporters "the scum of the earth" and further stated that she would still like to send someone after Ms. Harrington with a knife to cut her hair off.[5]

There were no repercussions or discipline from the company for Page.

The union had lots of follow-up work to do as well. The second clause of the return-to-work agreement addressed the discipline imposed on strikers by the company during the strike period. The clause permitted the union members to grieve the disciplinary action and get it sent to arbitration if necessary. Attachment A of the new collective agreement was a list of all the people disciplined by the company for the period November 14, 1979, to March 19, 1980. The national office of the CWC coordinated the fight against this disciplinary action with local stewards.[6]

The return-to-work agreement dated March 19, 1980, reduced my original suspension from four weeks to two weeks for the egg incident. So I did not return to work until the two weeks were over. The union grieved the suspension, and on June 5 a Step 4 grievance hearing was held. The company refused to budge, so the grievance went to arbitration on December 9, 1980. Because the company had no evidence that I was the one who hit the scab on the neck, the Board of Arbitration reduced the suspension to three days.

Bell also tried to extend the discipline periods of those who had been disciplined before the strike. On June 23 the CWC threatened to file a complaint of unfair labour practices to the CRTC against the company. In response, Bill Howes asked stewards to fill in complaint forms about such cases and send them along to him.[7]

Time for Fun and Learning

As soon as the vote was over, the celebrations began. Irene Anderson remembers the celebrations and the organizing required for the big events:

We did a lot of stuff that was not done before. Marg McColl was big on feeding people. We'd have a hot dog day or a picnic, and Marg would get stuff for free. She called other unions. We had a great leadership team. It helped to establish camaraderie and a sense of family to keep it together.

Marg organized a lot of parties. One might have been the solidarity dance two weeks after the strike ended. [Local 25 dance held on March 29, 1981.] She and her roommate cooked twenty or thirty turkeys for the event. It was a beautiful meal. She was good at pulling people in to help. She had volunteer bartenders and pulled it off on a shoestring. It was a great party. Local 50 had a reputation for organizing lots of great parties.[8]

Local 50 returned to having monthly meetings, and on May 3 hosted an all-day Local 50 stewards' meeting. Capacity-building and developing the local administration became the top priorities. The local continued to have regular stewards' meetings along with monthly meetings of a grievance committee.

The local put together a special *Bell Operators & Dining Services Newsletter — Local 50* on April 13, 1980, with the list of scabs on the front page. Life was not going back to normal, and it was now public knowledge just which of their colleagues had scabbed.

Ann Newman wrote an article as a grievance coordinator urging local members to read their new contract, and informed them, "It's up to each member and each steward in their respective offices to make sure that management abides by this new collective agreement."

George Larter wrote an article with the amusing title, "I'm Going … to the Washroom." He detailed what was happening in the offices when operators just got up and went to the washroom when they needed to. Some managers tried to intimidate operators into falling back in line with the card-posting system of one operator in the washroom at a time. Larter informed them that they no longer needed a short card, and they were to just go. He went on to say that if the company disciplined anyone, the union would grieve it and take it to arbitration. He urged the readers to imagine the arbitrator's face when the operator said, " I was suspended because I had to go for a pee."

The old ways were dying out fast.

Marg McColl ended the newsletter with a short article called "PARTY." The local was hosting a solidarity party at the St. Lawrence Market on May 30. The local invited craft and services members and the entire labour movement in Toronto. There was a lot to celebrate![9] The mood got even better on May 14, when everybody received their retroactive pay.

By May, Bill Howes's diary was filled with training courses and regular union events such as the CWC convention at the Sutton Place Hotel, held

June 11–14, 1980. Life for CWC staff and local union leadership began to reach a new normal. It was not as eventful as the organizing campaign and strike, but the leadership assumed new projects and causes, and continued to make a difference in the workplace at Bell Canada.

Just What Was Accomplished by the Strike?

More than anything else, the strike changed the patriarchal relationship between the company and operators forever. The company knew the operators had toughened up on those picket lines. Meek and mild compliance was now a thing of the past.

Janice McClelland looks back and reflects on the change the strike brought to labour-management relations:

> The company learned that its employees would not accept the paternalistic style of management it had used since its inception. Labour relations became formalized, with workplace issues resolved through the grievance procedure and not the old consultative process. Afterwards there was a quality of work life initiative by the company.[10]

The strike had brought a good raise and raised consciousness of the power of a union. McClelland outlined additional benefits:

> There were both short- and long-term benefits for organizing the operators. We improved our wages and benefits after that first contract. Pay equity, however, took many years to settle, but when it came, it made a difference to their pensions.
>
> Because of the significant numbers of women joining the CWC, other women could feel confident about joining. For instance, a few years later, Expertech associates from the CTEA joined the CWC and eventually all CTEA members merged into the CWC.[11]

Ann Newman thinks that the strike brought tangible benefits to the union members: "I have a lot of good memories from the strike. The contract we got was good. The pay hike was good. We had no increase for four years and when we came back we had a 15 percent increase."[12]

*   *   *

All the media coverage generated by the mass pickets, as well as the support of the Canadian Labour Congress and provincial labour federations, heightened the profile of telephone operators within the labour movement and the broader community. Suddenly, it was cool to be a telephone operator. Strangers told them they admired their guts and courage.

The strike developed class-consciousness among the new union members. Operators who had previously thought of themselves as middle-class began to identify as working-class and as staunch union members. The benevolent workplace where matrons ironed telephone operators' evening clothes was now a thing of the past.

What Were the Costs to the Organizers?

Maintaining a reservoir of guts and courage through two organizing campaigns and a strike took its toll on the primary organizers. They did whatever it took to make sure that their efforts succeeded. Despite the support of family and friends, working a regular job and then volunteering every waking moment for over two years strained their relationships and affected their personal and family lives.

Ann Newman recalls that the gains from the strike were offset with some losses to seniority and personal health: "There were negative effects, too. People lost seniority from the strike. I lost about eight months over my career. I picketed early in the morning to late at night. Operators would get $20 a week picket pay. The toilet at 25 Cecil Street would overflow and we ended cleaning up the shit."[13]

Janice McClelland remembers the toll the campaigns and strike took on her life:

> My home life was virtually nonexistent. At the time, I lived in a fully attached house. I had very few visits back to the Sault. But I was engrossed. I believed I was doing a great thing. I

remember I would make pancakes with corn syrup in order to walk outside for four hours. I would not remember phone calls that I took at night as I was so tired.[14]

George Larter remembers his devotion to the union cause and his leadership challenges:

Well, there was no work-life balance. It was 100 percent union, all day, every day. This was not a challenge to me. All my projects are all-consuming. I'm extremely competitive. I bit and I stuck. Keeping people going in the right direction could be problematic. We had to counter anti-CWC leaflets. I think you get isolated in leadership. You then become what people want you to be. I tried to keep it real. People trusted what I had to say. I can sell, not because of technique but because I am sincere. I am an emotional person. That takes a lot of energy. That was also the fun part. It was a struggle and felt like a struggle. The weather was cold, really cold. I remember we did not have any money. My parents helped me survive. And when it was over, we were all depressed. It felt like we had to go back to jail.[15]

Linda Young remembers the impact of the campaigns and strikes on her personal life:

My marriage broke up a couple of years later. When you go through something like that, there is no going back. I was given an ultimatum; I had to choose between the union and my marriage. I made my choice, and you have to choose. I paid a price for it with my children; it was the beginning of a slippery slope.[16]

What Happened to the Leaders?

The organizing drive and strike provided a personal development opportunity for the grassroots leadership. The skill sets and experience they gained became a springboard for many of them to launch careers in the labour movement or the nonprofit sector.

Janice McClelland became the first president of Local 50 after the organizing campaign. In September 1980, soon after the strike, she became a national representative for the CWC. She talks about her journey after the strike:

> Encouraged by my operator colleagues, I became a national rep for the CWC. I negotiated employment equity while I was national rep. I came up with the idea of employment equity moves [lateral transfers]. At the time there was pressure on Bell to look at employment equity and the female-dominated job ghettos. There was no career path for operators except for management. Transfers between bargaining units were unheard of, as there were separate collective agreements. I came up with the idea of piloting some employment equity projects. By allowing exceptions to the seniority list, a few operators moved into jobs in the technician units. Many of them became active in the union. A few years later, Bell downsized drastically and things stalled. However, the language still exists in the contract and could be reactivated.[17]

Thirty-one years later, in April 2011, Janice McClelland retired from the merged successor union — the Communications, Energy and Paperworkers Union of Canada (CEP).[18]

Once McClelland joined the staff of the CWC, George Larter became the president of Local 50. George brought an international focus to the work of Local 50 with a campaign against apartheid in South Africa.

> This union campaign and my international anti-apartheid movement work were the highlights of my life. Later on we organized a boycott. Operators would not take calls from South Africa.
>
> I was a telephone operator for eleven years. I had to forgo a lot of income. I graduated from university when I was

twenty-six. But money was never important to me. I don't enjoy the work while I am doing it, but if at the end of the day I feel good, then I know it was worthwhile.[19]

Larter left Bell Canada in the mid-1980s and became involved in the co-operative housing sector. He and the author worked for a co-op housing developer called the Labour Council Development Foundation developing affordable housing in Toronto. Larter subsequently founded his own development and property management companies, Community First Developments, Inc. and ComField Property Management.

Ann Newman became the third president of Local 50. As a woman of colour, she pioneered new roles for both women and people of colour in the labour movement. She says:

I became president of the local after George. I was president until 1999 — must have been over ten years. VDT breaks, and health and safety committees came out of the work of our local.

I was on the policy committee at Labour Notes and founded the Coalition of Black Trade Unionists. I am proud of the workplace health and safety committees I started. Fred once told me, "You are just ahead of other people." It was an experience. I enjoyed it and it made me a better person. I accept people for what they are. I used to be more judgmental that they don't think the way I think. By the time I retired, however, I was so stressed I ended up in St. Mike's with a heart attack, and now I wear a pacemaker.[20]

Linda Young remained an operator for a time, got divorced, and moved to Toronto. She recalls her next moves: "I had some opportunities open up to me from my doing human rights training and activism with the unions. I got a job at Metro Labour Education Centre [MLEC] and ended up developing the first literacy program for non-English speakers in the country."[21]

Young later married George Larter and worked with Helen Middlebrooks at MLEC.

Soon after the strike, Helen Middlebrooks became chief steward of all Asquith and all of Dining Services:

> While with Bell and active in the CWC, I taught ESL in the workplace and did anti-racism training. We went to the CLC human rights course. Linda and I went to race-relations training. I co-facilitated an anti-racism training weekend for Steelworkers District 6 and also for the Sudbury Labour Council. When I left Bell, I joined the Ontario Workers Health Services Centre [that Stan Gray founded] and then I got a job at Metro Labour Education Centre where I was for twenty-one years until I got laid off.[22]

Helen passed away during the writing of this book, but was a great help and support to the author up to the end.

Irene Anderson remained at Bell until 2008, when she was laid off for the fifth and final time. Having created her "exit strategy," she realized her dream of being self-employed as a personality-type expert and facilitator, and as a career coach. Anderson continues her volunteer activity and is the president of the Ontario Association for the Application of Personality Type and has recently opened a chapter of the Canadian Association for Retired Persons in her community. She lives and works in Oshawa, Ontario.

Laurie Cumming remained an operator for a short time and started to get involved in union leadership. She did some volunteer work with the United Farm Workers and started consumer boycotts by going to stores and asking shoppers whether they knew where that lettuce or those grapes had come from. She later became a teacher with the Toronto District School Board. She looks back on the strike:

> There were people I made great friends with. I was there for five years. I tried to keep up a few relationships. It played a big role in how I viewed myself as an adult. When I went to Ryerson, I did a paper on the strike for a history course. But it was how I self-identified that motivated me to become involved in

organized labour and fight for what was right and just. I continued to fight. I am in an elementary school union. I still think about those days and how they tried to break our union. Now when I see those same tactics employed by management at the school board, I draw on the resilience I developed during those days at Bell. I compare my situation with what is said in the media — that it costs too much and that if we keep our good wages we will lose our jobs overseas. I think how it must feel for people who are struggling now, and how they blame unions instead of looking to unions to protect what we have won. We'd look at films like the *Triangle Fire*[23] or working conditions in the past. Even though we might hear that our conditions are better now than in the past, the reality is that we did need a union. We had to fight to keep those hard-won benefits.[24]

The author left Bell a few months after the strike. She had two children, became active in community organizations, and then joined George Larter at the Labour Council Development Foundation developing nonprofit housing. She was the founder of an anti-corruption campaign in the late eighties that put a couple of municipal politicians and a developer in jail. She was then elected to the municipal council for the City of York. Once the City of York was amalgamated into the megacity of Toronto in 1998, Roberts began her own consulting and training business. She considered her organizing and union work at Bell Canada to be a key formative experience, and decided to honour all those she learned so much from by writing this book.

Ed Seymour continued to do education work and started the union newspaper *CWC News* in 1980. Elected Ontario region vice-president in 1985 by the union membership, he replaced Pete Klym. He soon realized it was a bad fit, so he resigned and later served as national rep. Seymour left the CWC in 1986 and went to Edmonton, Alberta, in June 1986 to do the PR for the United Food and Commercial Workers during the Gainers strike. After the strike ended, working for his own company, Solidarity Consulting, he was an employee nominee for the Grievance Settlement Board until the Bob Rae government got rid of nominees. He has written two books, including a history of the International Brotherhood of Electrical Workers Local 353, and a book on the Carpenters Union of Canada. Not yet fully retired, he spends his spare time tracking the genealogy of his Newfoundland family and spending time with his ten grandchildren.

Following the operators' strike, Bill Howes serviced local unions throughout Ontario for several years. However, his main interest was in organizing, and the union assigned him to coordinate the campaigns for office, technical, and operator units in Newfoundland, New Brunswick, Ontario, Manitoba, Alberta, and British Columbia. He wrote articles and leaflets and taught seminars on organizing. In 1989, he left the Communications, Energy and Paperworkers Union of Canada to serve as executive assistant to the president of the Toronto & York Region Labour Council. There he served as Toronto labour's link to social justice movements. In 1995 and 1996 he helped coordinate labour and social justice group days of action throughout Ontario against the labour-despised government of Mike Harris. He was one of two coordinators of Metro Days of Action — three days of political action which culminated in the first-ever one-day general strike in Toronto, which included the largest political demonstration and march in the history of Toronto. He retired from the Labour Council in 2000 and established Organizing Resources, offering consulting to unions for organizing campaigns. He finally fully retired from paid work in 2002 and was a co-founder of Not Just Tourists, which collected many tons of surplus medicine and medical supplies and sent them with tourists to Cuba and other developing countries — ten kilograms at a time. This project ended after five years, and Howes went to work on behalf of feral cats in the Greater Toronto area, coordinating the building of more than one thousand winter shelters. He continues to devote much of his time to this cause. He and his wife, Fikret, spend six months a year living in Istanbul.

Fred Pomeroy continued as president of the Communications Workers of Canada. He piloted the union through a merger with the International Electrical Workers Union in 1984, when the official name changed to the Communications and Electrical Workers of Canada. He continued as president until the union merged in 1992 into the Communications, Energy and Paperworkers Union of Canada.[25]

In 1992, the forty thousand members of the CWC joined the sixty-nine thousand members of the Canadian Paperworkers Union and the thirty-five thousand members of the Energy and Chemical Workers Union to form a new union: the Communications, Energy and Paperworkers Union of Canada. The position of president in the new union went to a paperworker, but by July 1995 the new union elected Pomeroy as president of one of Canada's largest unions. He served as president until July 2000, while bringing in new locals of communications employees from the Maritimes and Newfoundland. He retired on June 30, 2000, and stays busy as a retired labour activist.

Many operators went on to craft jobs and many remained as operators until the company completely phased out the job of telephone operator.

What Was the Importance of This Strike to the CWC and the Broader Labour Movement?

Organizing the operators was important to the CWC because the union moved toward its vision of becoming the national telecommunications union. Once the craft and services unit and operators unit of the largest telecommunications company in Canada were welcomed into the fold, it was only a matter of time until Bell's clerical unit would join as well.

In a conversation with me, Ed Seymour explained the value of the telephone operators bargaining unit to the CWC:

> Fred Pomeroy had an incredible sense of where he wanted to go and come to be. Fred wanted a sea-to-sea communications union. And he would do it through merger or raid (he called it "liberating"). Fred called the process moving the line forward toward one big telecommunications union across the country. The clerical unit under CTEA was important to bring into the tent too. Everyone understood if we only have the craft we are weak. The operators group strengthened the union's power base because the women had the balls.[26]

Organizing telephone operators into a legitimate union was part of the trend toward increased female participation in the workforce during the 1960s and 1970s. More female participation eventually led to more female membership in unions, which led to the demand that unions become more responsive to the needs of women and other vulnerable groups. Over the last thirty years it is women like the women in this book who have changed unions and forced them to become more receptive to the diverse needs of union membership and the unorganized.

Jan Kainer, in her article "Gendering Union Renewal: Women's Contributions to Labour Movement Revitalization," argues that women's involvement in the labour movement changed the very nature of organizing:

> Women's labour organizing contributed significantly to building and sustaining rank-and-file participation, developing new democratic structures such as women's caucuses, organizing the unorganized, and forging political alliances with non-labour groups. That the past organizing work of women has been, and continues to be, important to the life of labour movements is evident in the many references made in the union renewal literature to strategies that actually originated from the organizing work of labour women over the past twenty to thirty years. For instance, in many discussions of renewal strategies, the common themes identified include, "organizing the unorganized," "community-based organizing," "coalition building," "diversifying leadership," "democratizing unions," and "devising alternative visions for social change."[27]

Achievements of Local 50 and the CWC

In addition to regular improvements in wages and benefits and mitigating the impact of technological change, improving the working conditions of operators and dining service members also included adopting broader feminist imperatives like improved maternity leave and pay equity.

However, these victories came only after years of protracted negotiations and extremely expensive legal struggles. In practice, the legal struggle for pay equity has only benefitted women working for large employers, mainly where a union has been prepared to actively press the case.[28]

Maternity Leave

The idea that a woman could keep her job while off to have a child did not take hold in the public consciousness until the 1960s. Until then, pregnant women had to quit their jobs as soon as they started to show. The federal government convened the Royal Commission on the Status of Women in 1967 in response to a campaign mounted by a coalition of thirty-two women's groups. Women across the country started to question the logic that kept women out of the workforce once they became mothers and instead presented a different perspective: that child-bearing was a social benefit, and that pregnant women were entitled to receive benefits while on maternity leave — and to return to their jobs after having a child.

In 1971 the federal government amended the Unemployment Insurance Act to allow mothers with at least twenty weeks of insurable earnings to claim up to fifteen weeks of benefits through the Unemployment Insurance system. The labour movement saw maternity leave as a benefit that could be improved through collective bargaining beyond what unemployment insurance provided.

In the summer of 1981, the Canadian Union of Postal Workers (CUPW) went on strike over the issue of maternity leave benefits. The women's movement was fully onside with the union, as success here would be a wedge for further gains. The union achieved seventeen weeks of fully paid maternity leave for its members. The Public Service Alliance of Canada followed CUPW's lead and forced their employer, the government, to pay benefits to cover the two-week waiting period expectant mothers had to undergo when applying for maternity leave covered by unemployment insurance benefits.

Once the public sector achieved these historic gains, the CWC decided that Bell Canada would be the first private-sector company targeted for maternity leave enhancements. Before the 1980s, telephone companies in Canada had paid no added benefits beyond what unemployment insurance provided. In 1982 the CWC successfully bargained for a 75 percent top-up to unemployment insurance maternity benefits. Bell Canada became the first private-sector employer to provide supplemental benefits for maternity leave. These achievements paved the way for improved employment insurance and maternity leave provisions introduced by the federal government in the mid-1980s, and laid the groundwork for unions to bargain for additional leave and expanded benefits; including paternity leave, compassionate leave, and adoption leave, as well as extending these benefits to same-sex partners.[29]

Pay Equity

Pay equity is a concept that demands equal pay for work of equal value. It was a very popular demand in the eighties and nineties by the women's and labour movements in the struggle to improve the wage gap that stubbornly persists between male and female workers. The struggle for pay equity at Bell Canada emerged as the new union members compared the value of the work done by male and female telephone company workers. Men generally worked in plant and installation, while women worked as operators and clerical workers. Because of the formalized job descriptions in use for all jobs, the work could easily be described and analyzed in terms of whether one form of work called for higher wages than another. Women workers were then able to make the case for better wages as they compared levels of stress and customer contact as well as other job functions among the different occupations.

In 1992, the union, now the Communication, Energy and Paperworkers Union (CEP), filed a pay equity complaint under the federal Human Rights Act with the Canadian Human Rights Commission. A company-union study completed in November 1992 identified wage disparities of up to 20 percent between operators and similar male-dominated jobs.[30] Brenda Simmons recalls that Bell operators and their union also used direct action at times, taking their protests to the streets, as well as golf tournaments, to pressure the company:

> One time at the Bell Open in Markham [Ontario], we had twenty-three busloads of protestors from as far away as Montreal and Thunder Bay. Bell got an injunction that kept us one mile away from the golf course. It was very discouraging. There was no press. No one bothered to come to see us other than *Toronto Star* columnist Michelle Landsberg, who marched with us.[31]

Over the years, the case meandered through a preliminary investigation, mediation, and many legal challenges to the Federal Court, the Federal Court of Appeal, and to the Supreme Court of Canada. By the winter of 2004, with only three hundred telephone operators left at the company, the federal pay equity tribunal convened a hearing. The commission urged the company and union to work out a deal through mediation. On May 15, 2006, the union announced it had reached a pay equity settlement. The union then held twenty-five ratification meetings during May and June across Ontario and Quebec. The settlement provided an operator working at Bell Canada who had worked the full period covered by the settlement (1993 to 1999) a $16,500 settlement payment: $6,000 in pain and suffering (tax exempt), and a maximum of additional pensionable earnings of $13,530.[32] "This result brings an end to one of the longest battles for pay equity in the private sector," said CEP president Brian Payne. "This victory by telephone workers is a victory of the Canadian labour movement."[33]

Other Major Achievements

In addition to improved collective agreements, the union gained major rights and concessions through the arbitration process. In 1981, soon after the first strike, the union took a grievance concerning call-in pay to arbitration. The company had called the grievor to report at about 11:15 a.m. She reported for work at 2:00 p.m. and worked until 10:00 p.m. She was not paid from 11:15 a.m. to 2:00 p.m. The arbitration board ruled that the employee was to be paid between the time the company called her to work and the time she reported.[34] Although the union won this grievance, the company resisted and the union had to file another grievance. A third operator with the same issue was convinced by management not to file a grievance because they said there was no way the union could win. She did not get the $50,000 awarded to the grievors. This was a major success for the union, and the monetary cost to call in operators from home would act as a deterrent to that bad practice.

One arbitration hearing held on March 8, 1984, resulted from a grievance filed by two telephone operators in Hamilton. The company reassigned these two operators to another office when technological change forced their PBX switchboard office to close. They were both eligible to retire under the contract for a termination allowance of $50,000. The company disagreed, but the board of arbitration directed the company to give the termination allowances to the operators.[35]

The increased benefits and substantial pay increases that resulted from collective bargaining, arbitration awards, and pay equity resulted in increased severance packages and pensions. Because of the union campaigns, telephone operators were able to retire with livable pensions. This mattered even more when the company decided it no longer needed the voice with the smile, and outsourced the occupation.

The End of the Telephone Operator at Bell Canada

Less than twenty years after the historic organizing campaign and strike, Bell Canada decided that the job of telephone operator was no longer needed as part of the in-house workforce. Jenish D'Arcy, in a *Maclean's* article entitled "A Shock Down the Line: Bell's Plan to Quit the Operator Service Puts 2,400 Jobs On Hold. (Bell Canada Outsources Operator Operations)," reported the Bell Canada announcement that operators would be phased out:

Eunice Gill, a steward in local 42, presenting a cheque to operators Doris Biggs and Lois Anderson.

Chris King expected to spend the afternoon talking wages and benefits when she sat down for a union-management bargaining session at a downtown Montreal hotel on Jan. 11. King, a Bell Canada operator from Windsor, Ont., was part of a 15-member team negotiating a new contract for 2,400 unionized operators employed by the Montreal-based telecommunications giant. Bargaining began last October and continued until Dec. 18, when the two sides broke for Christmas. According to King, Bell negotiators told the union team that they would have an offer on wages and benefits ready when negotiations resumed in the New Year. Instead, they returned with a bombshell announcement: Bell intends to sell its operator-assistance division to Tempe, Ariz.–based Excell Global Services, which provides local and long-distance information, among other things, to telephone companies in five countries. "It was sort of like a bad dream," recalls King, a Bell employee for 22 years. "It's hard to explain how I felt."

Others registered their emotions immediately. Many members of the largely female workforce, who handle 411 and 0 calls, wept openly as Bell managers at 55 offices throughout Ontario and Quebec broke the news to them. While company spokesmen insisted the jobs would remain in Canada, they later acknowledged that some offices will be closed and that pay will be cut. Union members say wages, which currently average $19.50 per hour, could be reduced by as much as 40 percent, and claim they may be stripped of seniority and benefits. The deal may also jeopardize a potential equity settlement that the workers have been attempting to negotiate with Bell. Labour leaders were furious. Canadian Labour Congress President Bob White described Bell as "outrageous, irresponsible and just plain greedy," particularly since its profit was $829 million in the first nine months of 1998, compared with $852 million for all of 1997.

But Bell president John MacDonald insists there are valid business reasons for selling the operator service. He told *Maclean's* it is a high-cost and money-losing operation, although the company has not released specific figures. The decision to sell is part of a larger corporate transition that began in 1992, when the federal government ended Bell's decades-old monopoly on long-distance services.[36]

Although the plan was to outsource the job function by March 2000, the turnover did not actually happen until early 2001. Telephone operators used to making $19 an hour at Bell Canada were now offered jobs with Excell Global Services at rates under $12 an hour. Bell still had 2,400 operators on its payroll, but operators were no longer at the core of the telephone business. Even though their numbers had declined dramatically, Bell defended the decision, saying the old style of operator assistance was too expensive.

What Happened to the CWC?

As mentioned earlier, the CWC joined with the Canadian Paperworkers Union and the Energy and Chemical Workers Union in 1992 to form the Communications, Energy and Paperworkers Union of Canada. Although it has been one of Canada's biggest private-sector unions over the last two decades,[37] the trends of globalization and the loss of Canadian manufacturing forced the CEP to explore consolidating its membership with another private-sector union, the Canadian Auto Workers.

The unions' memberships ratified the proposal to merge and the new union's founding convention was held August 30 to September 1, 2013, in Toronto. UNIFOR is the name of the new union. By adapting to the changing realities of the economy and increased need for grassroots organizing, this new union will be able to organize new workplaces.

Chapter 14

Wrapping Up and Thinking about the Future

What Was the Context of the Organizing Campaign and Strike?

For any organizing to take root, conditions needed to be ripe for change. The primary condition at Bell Canada was that the company had fallen behind on its tradition of keeping its wage rates competitive with other telephone companies and local employers. Added to that, "the times they were a-changin'" as Bob Dylan so aptly wrote. The sixties and seventies were characterized by widespread questioning of authority, and the workplace at Bell Canada was no exception.

Traditional female-dominated workplaces across Canada, including hospitals and government offices, were organizing into powerful unions. Women were joining the workforce in greater numbers every year. And although many women were eager for career fulfillment, many others needed to work, as they were primary or supplemental breadwinners. All of these factors culminated in dissatisfaction among Bell telephone operators and dining service staff.

Women, in particular, were inventing a new story about themselves. That story was that women are strong, they are leaders, too — and that when women are no longer happy with things as they are, they will fight for their rights. This new story about women and the example of Bell crafts-men organizing into a legitimate mainstream union gave Bell Canada staff a new vision of their workplace and their relationship with their employer. The possibility of change at the large system level came about because the CWC wanted to expand its membership in Bell Canada and was willing to invest in an organizing campaign; and because there was enough grass-roots leadership with the energy and passion to take the first steps. But that systemic change could happen only if potential members underwent their own change process, experiencing personal dissatisfaction and buy-ing into a new story for their workplace and themselves. Workers then invested their own time, energy, and money into securing a new reality. The strength of their decision to fight back was severely tested: they had to fight not only during the first campaign, but also a second. They had to consolidate their successful organizational change by engaging in a gruel-ling three-month strike in the dead of winter.

Why Was This Campaign and Strike Significant?

The Bell operators' strike really was no more significant than many other campaigns and strikes that occurred around the same time. Increasing num-bers of women were organizing into nurses and teachers unions. The 150 women who went on strike at the Fleck manufacturing plant in Centralia, Ontario, in 1978 faced more intense harassment, intimidation, and violence than anything CWC members faced in Toronto. But in the strike at Bell, it was significant that it was non-professional women who organized in a pri-marily a white-collar workplace. At a time when working-class conscious-ness was waning, these were women from working-class and middle-class backgrounds who had believed they were not really working-class, but had moved up the social ladder by working for the Bell! By the end of the strike, they wore their working-class label with pride.

Women's history and labour history are still ignored. A strike by over 1,500 workers in one city is a big deal when it is happening. Think of the personal connections of each of those workers. If just ten relationships are identified for each operator, then that strike affected fifteen thousand people. The shops and services they supported would be impacted. More broadly, imagine the impact on the public due to the gap in service when telephone operators removed their labour. Computerization had just been introduced to long-distance calling and had not yet extended to directory assistance, so the public still received service from live, local telephone operators. The experience of calling telephone operators who knew the streets of the city of Toronto — who took pride in knowing where all the area codes in North America were geographically situated, who could tell you the time in all cities in the world, and who could name the neighbourhood of a local telephone number — was still fresh in the memory of the public.

Many Torontonians, especially those in unions, remember the strike and retain memories of driving past the strikers and honking their horns in support. It was very unusual to see strikers on downtown streets and main thoroughfares, and the fact that they were female was novel as well.

While those involved in the strike now look back on it with fondness, it was a huge challenge, and some think the strike may not have been necessary. According to Fred Pomeroy:

> The operators' campaign was one of the most fulfilling cam-
> paigns of my life. The operators came a long way and gained
> a big difference in pay and respect. The operators' strike was
> a message to the clerical unit that they would be on strike if
> they joined the CWC. There was no reason for the strike.[1]

Despite the demise of the occupation and the merger of the union into larger organizations, one thing deserves to be celebrated. Bill Howes gives a lot of credit to the CWC for taking on the challenge of organizing both craft and services and telephone operators:

> A small union — some five thousand members strong — had
> the guts to take on a major Canadian corporation and a bar-
> gaining unit that was three times its existing membership.
> Credit for the decision to do that must go to Fred Pomeroy,
> who had the vision and the chutzpah to tackle the challenge.
> Had that not happened and been successful, the operators bar-
> gaining unit would not have had the resources to organize.[2]

Why Did the Strike Become a *Cause Célèbre*?

Not many organizing campaigns and strikes garner the attention of the provincial and national labour movements. But both the Ontario Federation of Labour and the Canadian Labour Congress denied membership and therefore any legitimacy to the CUC; supported both CWC campaigns through endorsements, motions of support, and direction to member unions to help in any way possible; and came through with money and fundraising campaigns during the strike. Feminists also considered it important, and said so by putting Bell strikers at the front of the International Women's Day March in Toronto in 1980. The New Democratic Party took up the cause in the legislature, and the Toronto City Council also passed a motion of support.

It was very important to Toronto's history too; the city's population was so supportive of the strike that the company had to take out full-page ads in local newspapers defending their position. It was reminiscent of a time when Toronto was a union town, and most importantly, it was significant and life-changing to all those who participated. Throughout every interview with the organizers, both CWC staff and grassroots leaders shared how the experience was transformative and meaningful in their life.

Was This a Feminist Struggle?

Although Local 50 union women may have had mixed feelings about the women's movement, and the CWC had mainly male organizers working in Toronto, the organizing campaign and strike laid the foundation for an ongoing relationship with the NDP and the International Women's Day Committee.

In the early days, union leaders might not have identified the struggle to organize Bell's operators and dining service workers into a legitimate union as a feminist issue, but over time and through many battles, feminist issues became *their* issues. Bread-and-butter issues remained a high priority, but feminist struggles gained traction. By 1984, the cover of the newly renamed *Operator Services and Dining Services Newsletter,* which proudly displayed the CWC logo and the Local 50 tagline, featured a picture of two Local 50 delegates wearing sandwich boards in support of a pro-choice rally at the Ontario Federation of Labour convention. Inside the newsletter, a section entitled "No Women Need Apply" discussed the action taken by the local's Affirmative Action Committee about problems faced by operators when attempting to transfer into traditionally male jobs in the craft and services unit.

Equity and social justice issues were close to the organizers' hearts. Ann Newman went on to co-found the Coalition of Black Trade Unionists. Bill Howes and Ed Seymour supported the grape and lettuce boycotts led by Cesar Chavez and the United Farmworkers of America. George Larter got involved in the anti-apartheid struggle in South Africa.

> In spite of many years of feminist dialogue on women's organizing as a model for transforming unions and labour movements, there is limited recognition of the history of women's organizing efforts that have contributed to developments such as coalition building, rank-and-file activism, or devising alternative labour agendas to reflect new identities and new work forms.
>
> Central to women's labour activism is an equity strategy to achieve greater fairness for women and minority members within unions — a strategy that has evolved to bring about greater internal union democracy, and one which supports a social movement model of unionism promoting social and economic justice.[3]

How Did the Organizers Grow into Leaders from This Campaign?

If the grassroots leaders did not see themselves as leaders at the start of the campaign, they recognized it afterwards. They learned leadership from experienced CWC organizers and other labour organizers. They learned from each other in meetings and in formal training events, and they learned from their experiences organizing and on the picket line.

Irene Anderson reflects on what she learned as a grassroots organizer:

I learned how to persuade people. Being exposed to labour movement folks taught me a lot. I learned some stuff about marketing. The flyers and newsletters taught me about getting a message across. The labour movement was good at getting people's attention. The literature has to be compelling enough to get them to read.

A lot of meetings at Cecil Street were teaching and learning moments. Even down to what to put on picket signs. We learned how to regulate ourselves. In the situation where Carol Wooten threw down our material, we kept our cool. We were taught not to react but to keep our cool. I can hear Bill Howes saying, "Keep your cool, keep your cool."

The only thing is that there were pretty key people who will never come forward and share about how important their contribution was. Ann Newman, for instance. She was selfless and had such a dedication to the campaign, and never had a hidden agenda. She never had aspirations to do anything but advocate for anyone but the operators. I remember Janice asked me to ask them to tone down the risks we took (we being Ann, Marg, and myself). Without them the strike would not have been as successful as it was.

I was telling a family member that I was going to be interviewed. She asked why I would do that. Because, I said, it was a defining moment for the labour movement and for women's rights.[4]

Helen Middlebrooks recalls how her life changed as a result of the campaigns and strike:

People came together. I would not have had any reason to talk to dining services staff. The campaign and strike created new kinds of bonds in the work environment. There were some people still soured from the experience. And who knows the pressures at home people experienced. I was a little more understanding.

My life changed in a positive way. The strike was the first step in my personal development. I learned that I had leadership skills and became clear on my social justice principles. The experience gave me greater tolerance for different people and diversity. When we went back after the strike, the company started putting pressure on an operator with narcolepsy. She was not meeting the performance standards. By fighting that case, when Mechanized Directory Assistance Records came in we got the company to recognize that older operators might not be able to make the average work times in the same manner as younger operators.

The strike made a difference for hundreds and hundreds of operators. The raise we got was big. Something like $196–$225.[5]

The investment of time and energy along with learning paid off in many ways for the organizers. In the short term, they and their colleagues improved their wages and benefits, and gained rights and dignity in the workplace. In the long term, the learning that they gained from the experience was transferable to many other situations.

What Was the Impact on My Life?

This experience led me to devote my life to social change. Soon after the strike, I took my back pay, quit the company, and took a two-month trip to Europe. As much as I had grown throughout the campaign, the work of being an operator was monotonous for me.

However, knowing that I did (along with a group) take on a big system and win gave me confidence to acknowledge to myself that I was a leader who could make things happen. Soon after my second child was born, I took on City Hall to get my kid's playground cleaned up and new playground equipment installed. That first park revitalization led to another one; neighbours wanted my help to stop their basements from flooding; the local NDP needed volunteers; corrupt politicians threatened to sell the community pool; and one thing led to another until I ran for municipal council. Once my political career ended, I developed a consulting practice, working primarily with the non-profit sector. My time as an organizer with the CWC campaign taught me about how to influence people, gave me the organizing skills to run any kind of campaign, and the confidence to say what I thought and to stand up and advocate for others.

Offers of Management

As much as the organizers were a thorn in the company's side, the display of courage and leadership by grassroots organizers did not go unnoticed. Bell always had an in-house management training program, and getting into that program was considered a benefit of going to work for the company, especially for university graduates of generalist programs who had limited job prospects.

To the amazement of some of the organizers, despite a bitter strike with the company and disciplinary action in some individuals' personnel files, the company realized that they had failed to recognize the potential of the grassroots leaders and offered management positions to some of them. No one jumped on the offers at that point, but later some talented union leaders would make the leap to management.

George Larter remembers how he reacted to the company's offer of management:

"When they offered me management I told them I would not take any less than district manager. The manager making the offer said you have to work your way up to that level. I replied I was there already."[6]

After the strike I spent three weeks on suspension, and upon my return had to deal with the move of my office to a downtown building because the company had found asbestos in the ceilings and walls of 50 Eglinton Avenue. I had planned on quitting as soon as we received our retroactive pay, and one day in June went to see my manager to give notice. To my surprise, she wanted to recruit me into management. My immediate response, not verbalized, was that if they wanted someone like me, who had just returned from a three-week suspension and had major disciplinary actions in her file, they were desperate for talent.

What Can This Story Teach Us about Leadership?

Individuals have to feel powerful enough to step up and help make change. Many of the grassroots leaders already had a sense of purpose and personal power developed earlier in their lives. Leadership is not only what we traditionally associate with those in positions of authority; it could also be expressed by sharing opinions, advocating for change, and doing whatever it takes to survive.

Irene Anderson analyzes her leadership style at the time of the campaign and strike: "I did have a sense of myself as being a leader from a young age. I take it for granted since I have been in leadership all my life. Leadership is learned, and I guess I learned a lot of those skills growing up. At that time I was an accidental leader — an informal leader."[7]

Ann Newman shares her learning gleaned from her participation:

> People believed we had rights, that we could be heard and be treated with equality. We experienced a sense of freedom walking the picket line. I learned that movements start with a small group of people. One or two people and it's a beginning. You build it and they will come. Working-class people are practical. They only fight when their back is against the wall.[8]

Fred Pomeroy recalls how he observed the leaders developed:

> Leaders came to the forefront early. You could see how some
> people would come to a meeting and get into the most in-
> tense conversation. I would watch to see who other people
> gravitate to. Who is the opinion leader? I think most of the
> leaders had it in their personality and then developed it; with
> experience, success reinforces taking on more risks. The edu-
> cation provided by the union helped people learn by doing.
>
> The most amazing thing, management considered oper-
> ators as just women working for pin money, but lots of
> operators were the main breadwinner. They ran a family, raised
> their family, and had a very practical approach to things.[9]

Individual leaders often had already developed a sense of social justice. Many of them came from working-class families with family members who were union members, and had experiences of fighting grievances or being on strike. In their worldview, it was not difficult to see the
failings of the company union and name the reasons for change. Linda
Young remembers her thought process behind her decision to get involved and her emotions once engaged in the campaigns and strike:

> I asked, "Why me?" Look at the opportunity I had. For a while
> I was able to be useful. We made a difference in a lot of people's
> lives. I felt good about that when people were treated unjustly,
> when those women faced management and found their voice
> and spoke up for themselves. I was always scared. But I had cour-
> age. I just did it. I would have hated myself if I hadn't done it.[10]

George Larter identifies some of the characteristics necessary for a
successful team working together for economic justice including shared
values, discipline and a belief in human potential:

> We were able to develop a disciplined group of leaders, who
> learned during the campaign and the strike to trust each

other, and believed in the democracy and where things were going in the union movement. People believed they had a right to have raised expectations, and they were more complete human beings; in fact that they were political entities able to make a difference.[11]

Learning was much of the work in organizing and leadership. Grassroots leaders also saw the learning they gained as a benefit and payoff for their investment of time and energy. The regimented and highly monitored job of telephone operator did not leave much room for creativity and learning. For the grassroots leaders, just the opportunity to meet new people was exciting. And taking on big bad Ma Bell was an opportunity to shake their lives up.

Irene Anderson identifies while that the financial benefits of leadership in the union movement were nonexistent, the intangible benefits made up for it:

> Benefits of being a leader.... Well, there are no monetary perks, but lots of internal benefits, including being exposed to leaders in the labour movement — stuff we learned about the labour movement. There were opportunities to move ahead in the labour movement, although we didn't know it then. It became a badge of honour to have participated in the campaign and strike. Everyone knew me. I stood out in other people's minds.[12]

Janice McClelland analyzes her experience of leading the campaigns and strike:

> Leadership gave me lots of experience to talk with hundreds, even thousands, of people. I learned what people were thinking. In confronting the company and company union I often saw people who were quite afraid. I learned to be in tune with our membership.
>
> I had to think tactically and strategically. You might have goals, but you also have to deal with reality. I had to get others

involved. I remember talking to Ann Newman at the beginning and she was very resistant to getting involved. She replied to my request with, "I don't want to get burned again." I had to learn to tailor my approach. Ann, George, and I realized we needed a leadership platform got ourselves elected as CUC reps, so we could have a leadership position from which to organize for the CWC.

Leadership came to me gradually. I paid my dues by putting my time and my skills into the cause. People saw that I was willing to give my all, and they could see I was honest and wanted to work, and I was doing it for the good of the group. The end product was a real union. I fit the circumstances, then demonstrated my leadership skills with action.[13]

Ed Seymour observes:

With any new group the same dynamic exists; with both craft and operators the first task is to get people to believe in themselves to be effective. I am talking about the steward or local officer. If they don't lead, then how can they expect their members to?

You see the hesitancy at the beginning. Once they win their first grievance, the leader sees that they have some power.[14]

Leadership required personal growth for everyone. Union and grassroots leaders had to move out of their comfort zone to meet day-to-day challenges. Personal attacks came with the territory.

Laurie Cumming recalls what she learned from the experience:

I hadn't considered myself as a leader. I felt a whole lot stronger after that experience. People got really mad at me, would cross the picket line, and my relationships were impacted, but the world didn't end. I made wonderful friendships and got to see the opportunities within the union. I saw how many women were incredibly comfortable with being assertive, and I could see how it looks to be standing by your convictions and not backing away from them if people didn't like you anymore. I was pleased that people would come to me. I was only twenty and they had me help them talk to a boss.[15]

Janice McClelland exuded leadership. Even the police respected her as a leader. She recalled, "The Labour Relations Squad of the Toronto Police Service would call me wanting to know the location of our next mystery picket." When they were not told, one of those cops remarked to another, "She's got more balls than most men I know."

For some the personal challenges were related not just to the organizing campaign and strike, but also to widespread racism. Ann Newman never stopped having to face the racism prevalent in the company and city at that time. She recalls the additional challenges she faced as woman of colour and taking on a leadership role:

> You have no idea what it was like for me to speak out on issues. I was a woman of colour in a sea of white faces. I had an American accent. A lot of members were really nice, but sometimes I faced occasional racial slurs.
>
> At the beginning, in 1966, I wanted to go to DA. I was told to come back when I got my immigration papers and they promised to make me a manager. I went back and wanted to be an operator, and they then promised me a promotion within six months. Come on, they never offered me one. Black people did not get promotions at Bell.[16]

Each person went through a unique change process to meet the demands of a leadership or supporter role. That change process involved learning — especially acquiring new skills to communicate more effectively; the ability to research, analyze, and solve problems; confidence that grew from doing things never done before; and managing the risks presented by confronting management and the withdrawal of labour.

George Larter recalls how his upbringing as a working-class child did not prepare him to take the risks involved in advocating for labour justice: "You get raised as a working-class kid to respect the boss, so we would be fearful, too. The capitalist system is pretty powerful. We had to get over our aversion to risk. I learned, though the more calculated risks you take, the more rewarding life can be."[17]

Helen Middlebrooks recalls how the strike changed her: "During the strike I was picket captain and became really involved. I used to be really shy and really quiet. I would not have done this interview. My communications skills improved, I built confidence. I got to be aware of social justice."[18]

Middlebrooks watched how the membership in a legitimate union changed the members who worked in Dining Service:

> Dining Service people were really timid during the strike, but the operators developed wonderful solidarity. They finally had a voice to complain about the working conditions, which were stressful because of tediousness, abuse from customers, constant monitoring, and the stupidity of company policies around absenteeism and lates.
>
> The responsible relationship clause in the collective agreement was helpful. It put a boundary around management so they could not do what they wanted as easily as before.[19]

Irene Anderson reported a change to the way others saw her: "I was labelled as a gutsy broad, but the experience gave me a way to express myself and a foundation to focus on human rights and women's issues. Those issues that have shaped who I am."[20]

Linda Young observes how the women she worked with changed, too, and provided support to her:

> I wasn't surprised at myself, but the three or four women who came to be leaders during the strike in Orangeville surprised me. They surrounded me and encouraged me. They were gentle, respectful, unimposing women on the job, but then after we went on strike they stepped up to the plate and made sure everything got done. The mouthy ones disappeared.[21]

Cynthia Tenute, an operator in Hamilton, recalled how having a real union changed the nature of the relationship with management: "Back in the workplace once the union was in place, we had a tremendous feeling of security. We could object to management practices, and argue, and call in support during those conflicts with management. We didn't have to take all their crap anymore. I was really sorry about the merger into CEP."[22]

The organizers formed intense bonds from their experiences that have endured over the years. The idea for this book was sparked at a sixtieth birthday party for George Larter. Cynthia Tenute recalled the additional benefit of lifelong friendships: "My life changed a lot. My best friends came out of that ordeal. We have remained friends all of these years. We achieved some control over our situation. We gained a voice and some power."[23]

Why Do Women Still Need to Look to Unions as the Solution to Many of Their Problems?

Canadian women have joined the workforce in record numbers since the 1960s and 1970s.

In Chaykowski, and Powell's article "Women and the Labour Market: Recent Trends and Policy Issues" they present the statistics showing the increase in women's participation in the Canadian workforce at the time period examined in this book:

> Overall female LFP [labour force participation] rates have increased steadily since the turn of the century — rising slowly from a level of around 18 percent just after World War I, but then doubling to roughly 50 percent in the period extending from the end of World War II to the beginning of the 1980s. In 1998, the LFP rate among Canadian women 15 years and older stood at 58.1 percent, up substantially from 48.5 percent in 1978. The male LFP rate in 1998 was 72.4 percent.[24]

In 2006, 73.5 percent of women aged fifteen to sixty-four were participating in the paid workforce, either working or actively seeking work. This compares to an Organization for Economic Co-operation and

Development (OECD) average of just 60.8 percent.[25] For women aged fifty-five to fifty-nine, the participation rate has jumped from just under half in the mid-1990s to 62.3 percent in 2006. Almost half of women aged sixty to sixty-five are now still in the paid workforce, up from just one-third a decade or so ago.[26]

Although many women joined the workforce to fulfill their needs for accomplishment and purpose, there were growing numbers of women who were sole breadwinners, and many other women needed to join the labour force to keep up family income levels due to the decline in the real wages of men. The ability to buy a home, enjoy an annual vacation, and put children through post-secondary education depended upon women joining the workforce and contributing to household income. Almost all women have to work. No ifs, ands, or buts.

The wage gap persists.

The gender wage gap is the difference between wages earned by men and women. It's caused by many factors: women often leave and re-enter the workforce to have and raise children, or to serve as caregivers to family members; they often work in "pink-collar ghettos," such as childcare and clerical work (telephone operators were certainly a pink-collar ghetto); female workers show lower rates of unionization and a higher incidence of discrimination in hiring and promotion. Statisticians estimate that as much as 10 percent to 15 percent of the gender wage gap is due to discrimination.[27]

Table 3 – Average Hourly Wage, Workers Aged 25–54 (Current dollars)		Males	Females	Ratio
Total employees	All employees	25.91	22.00	0.849
	Employees with union coverage	26.96	25.28	0.937
	Employees without union coverage	25.42	20.18	0.794

Permanent employees	All employees	26.38	22.24	0.843
	Employees with union coverage	27.17	25.53	0.926
	Employees without union coverage	26.00	20.46	0.786
Temporary employees	All employees	21.01	19.75	0.940
	Employees with union coverage	24.85	23.29	0.939
	Employees without union coverage	18.94	17.26	0.911

Average hourly wage, workers by gender, aged 25 to 54[28]
Source: Table prepared by the author using data obtained from Statistics Canada, "Labour force survey estimates (LFS), wages of employees by job permanence, union coverage, sex and age group, annual (current dollars)," Table 282 0074, CANSIM (database), Using E-STAT (distributor), 10 September 2010.

You can see from this table that the hourly wage gap is larger in non-unionized jobs (in which women earn 79 percent as much as their male counterparts) than in unionized jobs (in which they earn about 94 percent as much).[29]

Faced with the double burden of being lower earners and being out of the workforce for extended periods, women also receive lower pensions when they retire. Of course, many women retire with no pensions and are doomed to lives of poverty. The low income rate of single elderly women significantly exceeds that of men (8.4 percent compared to 3.2 percent in 2005).[30]

Unionization has improved wages and benefits for many working women, especially lower-paid women. However, unionization rates for women in the private sector are low.[31]

Unionization brings major benefits.

- There is no doubt that workers earn higher wages when unionized. Workers under a collective agreement usually earn 10 percent to 25 percent more than non-unionized workers, while women workers covered by a union contract receive higher pay and wages more nearly equal with men than non-unionized women.

- The Canadian Labour Congress at their 2012 convention put a dollar figure on the union "advantage" that higher wages give the economy: "On average, Canada's 4.5 million organized workers earn $5.11 more per hour than non-union workers, it said, adding up to about $793 million per week to the economy. All of this, insists the CLC, goes right back into the Canadian economy. In Toronto, that translates to $4.59 per hour more for unionized workers, about $91 million more per week."[32]

- Union collective agreements include grievance procedures that provide workers with protection from arbitrary decisions made by managers and unjust terminations. If a grievance is not settled between the union and the company, the union has the right to take it to third-party arbitration, where an independent arbitrator or arbitration panel can assess the dispute and make a decision which is binding on both parties.

- Collective agreements are legally binding agreements backed by government legislation. The legislation has legal penalties which the government can impose on companies that fail to bargain in good faith or violate the collective agreement.

- Health and safety is a top priority for unionized workers, and this area receives close attention from union stewards and health and safety committee members.

- Unions are one of the most democratic organizations in our society, much more so than our governments. Union members get to vote for their local representatives, union stewards, and local officers; and often vote directly for national officers or vote through a form of grassroots representation and participation at union conventions. As well, union members can suggest proposals to improve workplace conditions for collective bargaining.

- It is only through unionization that unskilled workers such as cleaners and hospitality service workers can make a living wage.

- Unions are also taking up women's issues. They are moving forward on issues like maternity leave and pay equity.

- Unions are reaching out to community partners with common causes to work on issues like precarious work and redevelopment of industrial land.

Despite the benefits of unionization, workers are finding it difficult to organize and maintain their unions. As overall rates of unionization have declined, all unionized workers have suffered lower wage rates, increased corporate union-busting activities, and a reduced share of the economic pie.

The significant drop in the rates of unionization has placed individual workers at a disadvantage in negotiating wage rates with employers. "In 1981, 38 percent of Canadian workers belonged to a union; by 2010 that figure had dropped to 29.6 percent."[33]

A Few Final Words

In the 1970s and 1980s, women were successfully unionizing in the public sector, but the CWC campaign to organize Bell operators and dining service staff was a breakthrough for women in white-collar and pink-collar jobs in the private sector. There were drives to organize banks and large retailers in the 1980s, but they failed and did not live up to the promise of transforming the private sector. The success at Bell stood out.

The story begins with conditions for change, including how the occupation of telephone operator evolved, and how the company transformed the workplace through computerization. The narrative takes place within the context of widespread societal rejection of authoritarian and paternalistic attitudes, and the day-to-day work of organizing workers into a legitimate trade union. Even if the story had ended without a fight for a first contract, it would still have been a great achievement. But the story played out further with a gruelling strike over the winter of 1980. And more challenges did not stop the momentum. These workers were determined to obtain dignity in their workplace and achieve a more equitable share in the wealth of society.

Irene Anderson observes, "Young women don't know the legacy we created. This new generation needs to claim its voice. We might have been afraid, but we did it anyway. We knew we were changing the world."[34]

The collective action by the labour movement sent a strong message to corporate Canada, but the labour movement was not able to sustain the momentum toward collective action and organizing the unorganized. Working people are now more marginalized than ever. By documenting this story of collective action and the courage of ordinary workers in confronting workplace injustice, the author hopes that a new generation will claim their right to organize their workplaces.

Image Credits

Page	Caption	Ownership/Permission
24	Bell on the telephone in New York.	Library and Archives Canada: C-014483.
30	Telephone operator in 1910.	Library and Archives Canada: PA-069041.
34	Circular letter of Civil Service Commission of Canada.	Carolyn Bett.
80	*Points to Ponder* leaflet by concerned union members.	Janice McClelland files.
114	The toll office in the sixties and seventies.	Library and Archives Canada: PA-144837.
140	Ann Newman (black coat with placard) and Marg McColl (white coat) [distributing leaflets] at Bell Canada's regional headquarters at 393 University Avenue, Toronto.	Photographer unknown, Ed Seymour Archives, McMaster University.

161	CUC flyer attacking Ann Newman.	Janice McClelland files.
162	CUC *Invite to a Rally*.	Janice McClelland files.
166	CWC applies for a vote.	Janice McClelland files.
178	TOPS office.	*Toronto Star*. Used by permission.
190	March 9 Toronto campaign summary report, p.1.	Ed Seymour archives, McMaster University.
191	CUC flyer: *Do You Really Think They Are YOUR Meal Ticket?*	Janice McClelland files.
194	Ann Newman, Connie Graham, George Larter, and Irene Anderson sitting at an information table at 15 Asquith Avenue.	Author.
201	March 16 campaign report.	Ed Seymour Archives, McMaster University.
204	CWC bulletin announcing the signing of 3,750 cards.	Janice McClelland files.
211	CUC flyer: *Paper Tiger in Action*.	Janice McClelland files.
218	Bill Howes with vote results.	Author.
229	Local 50 flyer for the public.	Janice McClelland files.
232	Leaflet: *'Twas the Night before Christmas*.	Janice McClelland files.
237	Notice to Local 50 membership regarding upcoming strike votes.	Janice McClelland files.
245	"Help Crack Bell" button.	Ann Newman.
252	Eglinton Avenue picket line.	Author.
257	Payday collection notice for craft and services members.	Janice McClelland files.
266	Invitation to Family Day picket.	Ed Seymour Archives, McMaster University.

267	Clowns: Laurie Cumming and craft guys Irad Munro and Owen Oiffer.	Helen Middlebrooks.
273	Letter to Peter Klym and Fred Pomeroy from Canadian Union of Postal Workers, February 13, 1980.	Ed Seymour Archives, McMaster University.
281	*Help Crack Bell* newsletter.	Janice McClelland files.
284	Solidarity picket invitation, March 1, 1980.	Janice McClelland files.
285	Janice McClelland on bullhorn, Ed Seymour to the left, and Fred Pomeroy in checked hat at March 1, 1980, solidarity picket at Manulife Centre.	Frank Rooney. Used with permission.
286	The author wearing a picket sign, "Bell Canada has a childish attitude!"	Helen Middlebrooks.
302	CWC memo to all traffic and dining service members announcing a tentative agreement, March 20, 1980.	Janice McClelland files.
324	Eunice Gill presenting a cheque.	Ed Seymour Archives, McMaster University.

Notes

Introduction

1. Betty Friedan, *The Feminine Mystique* (New York: W.W. Norton and Co., 1963)
2. Ontario Federation of Labour, *1900–2000 A Century Of Women And Work,* Ontario Federation of Labour, 10.
3. Ibid., 28.
4. Ibid., 37.
5. Balkan, Donna, "Practicing What We Preach : Women Unions And Affirmative Action," *Canadian Woman Studies/ Iles Cahiers De La Femme,* 6, no. 4 (1985), 49.

Chapter 1

1. David Massey, Telephone Tribute, accessed January 31, 2011, www. telephonetribute.com/telephonetrivia.html.
2. Parliament of Canada, *Hansard of the Government of Canada,* 37th Parliament, 1st Session, no. 211, June 21, 2002, p.1620/ cumulative p.13006, time mark: 12:05, accessed January 9, 2012, www.parl.gc.ca/HousePublications/Publication. aspx?Pub=Hansard&Mee=211&Language=e&Parl=37&Ses=1.
3. "Reference for Business: Company History Index (2011): BCE Inc. —

Company Profile, Information, Business Description, History, Background Information on BCE Inc.," accessed November 22, 2011, http://www. referenceforbusiness.com/history2/87/BCE-Inc.html.

4. Michele Martin, *Hello Central? Gender Technology and Culture in the Formation of Telephone Systems* (Kingston: McGill-Queen's University Press, 1991), 30.

5. Laurence B. Mussio, *Becoming Bell; The Remarkable Story of a Canadian Enterprise* (Montreal: Bell Canada, 2005), 15.

6. Martin, 29

7. Ibid.

8. *Gale Directory of Company Histories* (n.d.), Bell Canada, accessed December 15, 2011, www.answers.com/topic/bell-canada.

9. Wikipedia, "Bell Canada," accessed December 11, 2011, http:// en.wikipedia.org/wiki/Bell_Canada.

10. "Bell Canada History," accessed December 13, 2011, www. fundinguniverse.com/company-histories/BELL-CANADA-Company-History.html.

11. *Gale Directory of Company Histories*, "Bell Canada."

12. Ibid.

13. Martin, *Hello Central?*, 42

14. Mussio, *Becoming Bell*, 19

15. Ibid., 23.

16. Ibid., 37.

17. Ibid., 43.

18. Ibid., 49.

19. Ibid., 50.

20. Ibid., 57.

21. Ibid., 61.

22. CBC Digital Archives, accessed January 9, 2012, http://archives.cbc.ca/ science_technology/technology/topics/1139-6257/.

23. Mussio, *Becoming Bell*, 69.

24. *Canadian Register of Commerce & Industry*, "The Bell Telephone Company of Canada," held in the Western Libraries at the University of Western Ontario, c. 1959, accessed January 5, 2012, www.lib.uwo.ca/programs/ companyinformationcanada/cr-bell.htm.

25. Mussio, *Becoming Bell*, 71.

26. Ibid., 76.

27. Mike Filey, "Toronto Was Experimenting With 'Cell' Phones 60 Years Ago," *Canoe News*, December 23, 2007, accessed August 21, 2010, http://cnews. canoe.ca/CNEWS/WeirdNews/2007/12/23/4738356-sun.html.

28. Mussio, *Becoming Bell*, 76.

29. Ibid.

29. Ibid., 82.

30. Ibid.

Chapter 2

1. Jean-Guy Rens, *The Invisible Empire. A History of the Telecommunications Industry in Canada, 1846-1956*, translated by Käthe Roth (Montreal: McGill-Queen's University Press, 2001), 71–72.

2. Martin, *Hello Central?*, 56.

3. Joan Kuyek, *The Phone Book: Working at the Bell* (Toronto: Between the Lines, 1979), 16.

4. Martin, *Hello Central?*, 57.

5. Ibid., 60.

6. Joan Sangster, "The 1907 Bell Telephone Strike: Organizing Women Workers," in *Rethinking Canada: The Promise of Women's History*, 2nd Ed. (Toronto: Copp Clark Pitman, 1991), 110.

7. International Association of Electrical and Electronic Engineers, *Global History Network*, "Telephone Operators," accessed January 13, 2012, www. ieeeghn.org/wiki/index.php/Telephone_Operators.

8. Clayton, "The Telephone," accessed June 6, 2011, http://library.thinkquest. org/04oct/00451/telephone.htm.

9. Martin, *Hello Central?*, 65.

10. The ideas of efficiency and scientific management, developed by Frederick Winslow Taylor, were put into practice in the workplace, with Henry Ford developing the assembly line, allowing the development of the Model T car — an affordable vehicle built for the masses — or at least the middle class. For further information read, *The One Best Way: Frederick Winslow Taylor and The Enigma Of Efficiency* by Robert Kanigel.

11. Martin, *Hello Central?*, 66. BCA d24096 is a numerical reference in the Bell Canada Archives located in Montreal.

12. Ibid., 68.

13. Ibid., 70.

14. Ibid., 73.

15. Ibid., 72.
16. Ibid., 72.
17. Ibid., 75.
18. Ibid., 76.
19. Toronto had 14,900 subscribers in 1907. *Report of the Royal Commission on a Dispute Respecting Terms of Employment between Bell Telephone Company of Canada and Operators at Toronto*, Ottawa: 1907, accessed June 11, 2011, http://archive.org/stream/reportofroyalcomcanarich/reportofroyalco0canarich_djvu.txt.
20. Ibid.
21. Sangster, "The 1907 Bell Telephone Strike," 121.
22. Martin, *Hello Central?*, 80.
23. "Historical Timeline of Canadian Telecommunications Achievements," (n.d.), accessed March 12, 2013, www.itu.int/newsarchive/wtsa2000/english/media/timeline.pdf.
24. Martin, *Hello Central?*, 99.
25. Ibid., 100.
26. Ibid., 107.

Chapter 3

1. Sangster, "The 1907 Bell Telephone Strike," 109.
2. "We Stand on the Shoulders of Giants: A Biography of Julia O'Connor," accessed June 12, 2012, www.union1.org/Giants/indexW.htm.
3. Communications Workers of America, "History of the CWA, Local 7032," (n.d.), accessed June 23, 2012, www.cwalocal7032.org/history/history.htm.
4. Sangster, "The 1907 Bell Telephone Strike," 125.
5. Kuyek, *The Phone Book*, 40.
6. April Middeljans, "Weavers of Speech: Telephone Operators as Defiant Domestics in American Literature and Culture," *Journal of Modern Literature* 33, no. 3 (Spring 2010): 38(26), accessmylibrary: www.accessmylibrary.com/article-1G1-231610127/weavers-speech-telephone-operators.html.
7. Ibid., 7.
8. Government of Canada, *Labour Gazette*, March, 1936, accessed March 12, 2012, https://archive.org/details/labourgazette1936cana_djvu.txt.
9. Vorster, Menno G., *A Study in Corporate Unionism: The Canadian Telephone Employees' Association*, unpublished paper for York University, 1972, 2.

10. Mussio, *Becoming Bell,* 50.
11. Jean Roddy, personal interview with author, Toronto, 1982. Roddy was a Bell telephone operator during the 1950s and '60s.
12. Communications Union of Canada, "Never Underestimate," (n.d.) Toronto: CUC, 24.
13. Roddy, personal interview.
14. Vorster, *A Study in Corporate Unionism,* 16.
15. Traffic Employees Association, "Articles on the Function, Methods and Responsibilities of Unions," (Toronto: Traffic Employees Association, January 1960), 1.
16. Ibid., 1.
17. Ibid, 11.
18. Pat Connelly, *Last Hired, First Fired* (Toronto: The Women's Press, 1978), 18.
19. Ibid., 24.

Chapter 4

1. Linda Young, personal interview with author, Toronto, July 14, 2011. Young, then Linda Wilton, was a telephone operator and union organizer in Orangeville, Ontario.
2. Janice McClelland, undated private notes, personal files of Janice McClelland, Acton, Ontario.
3. Marc Zwelling, "They Treat Us Like Kids at Bell," *The Telegram,* March 5, 1970.
4. McClelland, private notes.
5. Ministry of Labour, Government of Canada, "Report of Douglas Fisher, November 2 1971," contained in a report of a Conciliation Board chaired by Thomas O'Connor, November 1, 1971, 8.
6. Ibid., 9.
7. Ibid., 8.
8. Ibid., 8.
9. Wilfred List, "$20 Weekly Pay Raise in New Bell Contract," *Globe and Mail* November 25, 1971.
10. Telephone Employees Association, *Belle Femme,* Spring 1970, 4.
11. Communications Union of Canada, "Never Underestimate,"
12. *Belle Femme,* Spring 1974, 3.
13. Helen Middlebrooks, personal interview with author, Toronto, July 19,

2011. Middlebrooks was a telephone operator and grassroots organizer in Toronto.

14. Mary M. Lennox, "Women Need Night Taxis Bell Union President Says," *Toronto Star*, March 28, 1974, B5.

15. Fred Pomeroy, personal interview with author, Ottawa, January 28, 2012. Pomeroy was president of the Communications Workers of Canada.

16. The timing of this is circa 1973.

17. Pomeroy, personal interview.

18. Fred Pomeroy was the president of the CWC at the time of the craft and operator organizing campaigns. Quoted in the webpage "Building the Communications and Electrical Workers of Canada," accessed July 31, 2012, 7, http://cep649.ca/cmsupload/fckeditor/beginning-e.pdf.

19. Communications Union of Canada, *Communiqué*, May/June 1976, 1.

20. CUC, *Communiqué*, January 1976, 2.

21. Pomeroy, personal interview.

22. Pomeroy, personal interview and email correspondence dated July 4, 2013.

23. Michelle Dust, (1999), "Day of Protest October 14, 1976, An Expression of Solidarity," winning Norm Quan Bursary essay, Toronto: CUPE, 1999, www.cupe1975.ca/bursary/burs399.html.

24. CUC, *Communiqué*, January 1976, 3.

25. Communications Union of Canada, "General Council Report" (Toronto): CUC, 1976, 6.

26. "National Day of Protest against Wage Controls," undated, personal files of Janice McClelland, Acton, Ontario.

27. "Promises, Promises," personal files of Janice McClelland.

28. George Larter, personal interview with author, Toronto, July 5, 2011. Larter was an operator in Toronto and one of the grassroots leaders.

29. Ann Newman, personal interview with author, Toronto, July 19, 2011. Newman was an operator in Toronto one of the grassroots leaders.

30. Newman, personal interview.

31. Communications Union of Canada, "Administration Report," 76th General Council meeting, June 21, 1977, 3, Ed Seymour Archives, McMaster University.

32. Ibid.

33. Ibid.

34. Personal files of Janice McClelland, Acton, Ontario.

35. Newman, personal interview.

36. Fred Pomeroy, letter to Ray Van Eenooghe, April 24, 1975, personal files of Janice McClelland.

37. McClelland, personal interview. McClelland was de facto grassroots leader of the Toronto campaign.

38. Marion Pollock, "Under Attack: Women, Unions and Microtechnology," in *Union Sisters: Women in the Labour Movement* (Toronto: The Women's Press, 1983).

39. Bell Canada, *TOPS and You* (Toronto: Bell Canada, 1977), 18.

40. Bell Canada, *TOPS: More about TOPS and You* (Toronto: Bell Canada, 1977).

41. Pollock, Under Attack," 104.

42. Ibid., 104.

43. Traffic Employees Assoc., *TEA's 25th Anniversary*, Spring 1970, 5.

44. Janice McClelland, "Technological Change in the Operator Services-Dining Services Group at Bell Canada, 1957–1986," in *Working People and Hard Times* (Toronto: Garamond Press, 1987).

45. Most likely this refers to the CUC General Council meeting held on November 29, 1977, at Bond Place Hotel in Toronto.

46. Pomeroy, personal interview.

47. *Bell Operators Newsletter #1*, February 3, 1978.

48. Mary Lennox, to Fred Pomeroy, December 1, 1977, Ed Seymour Archives.

49. Fred Pomeroy, letter to Mary Lennox, March 9, 1978, Ed Seymour Archives.

50. Joan Roberts, "Co-optation and Resistance: A Case Study, Telephone Operators at Bell Canada," unpublished paper, 1981.

51. Boris Mather, phone message to Janice McClelland, June 6, 1979. Mather was a staff person for the Canadian Federation of Communications Workers (an umbrella organization that included the CWC and the TWU in British Columbia). The message said that an article appeared in the *Financial Post* on January 18, 1958, stating the TEA had eleven thousand members. The 1960s had brought a decline in TEA membership, likely due to the move to direct dialling.

Chapter 5

1. CUC submission to the Anti-Inflation Board, "A Request for Reconsideration," 3, personal files of Janice McClelland, Acton, Ontario.

2. Bill Howes, personal interview with author, Toronto, March 21, 2011. Howes was a national representative with the CWC and Ontario campaign coordinator.

3. Newman, personal interview.
4. Janice McClelland, email correspondence with author, July 23, 2013.
5. Howes, personal interview.
6. McClelland, personal interview.
7. Larter, personal interview.
8. Training for grassroots organizers from the ranks of the CUC. The CWC had offices at 25 Cecil Street in the United Steelworkers building.
9. Bill Howes, daily diary entries, 1978. CUC referred to the grassroots organizers from the CUC now working on a possible CWC campaign.
10. Mary Lennox, letter to Diane MacDonald, Quebec vice-president of the CUC, May 16, 1978, Ed Seymour Archives.
11. A written note by Janice McClelland says it was issued May 1978, personal files of Janice McClelland.
12. Newman, personal interview.
13. Jen Francis, *Switchboard Operator*, June 1978, 16. This was a feminist paper published in Toronto in the 1970s.
14. Fred Pomeroy, note to all craft locals re the resolution passed at the CWC convention, February 28, 1980 Ed Seymour Archives.

Chapter 6

1. Pomeroy, personal interview.
2. Ibid.
3. McClelland, personal interview.
4. Newman, personal interview.
5. Ed Seymour, personal interview with author, Hamilton, May 2, 2012.
6. Seymour, personal interview.
7. Seymour, personal interview.
8. Terry Meagher, secretary treasurer of the Ontario Federation of Labour, notice to affiliates, labour councils, and staff associations, June 1978, Ed Seymour Archives.
9. McClelland, personal interview.
10. Ibid.
11. Howes, personal interview.
12. McClelland, personal interview.
13. Irene Anderson, telephone interview with author, Toronto, August 9, 2011. Anderson was a telephone operator and grassroots organizer.
14. Laurie Cumming, personal interview with author, Toronto, March 1, 2012.

Cummings was a telephone operator and grassroots organizer in Toronto.

15. Linda Young, personal interview with author, Toronto, July 14, 2011.
16. Young, personal interview with author.
17. Anderson, phone interview. Cesar Chavez was a co-founder of the United Farm Workers Union. At that time he was organizing a grape boycott across North America.
18. Young, personal interview.
19. Newman, personal interview.
20. McClelland, personal interview.
21. Pomeroy, personal interview.
22. Anderson, phone interview.
23. Larter, personal interview.
24. Cumming, personal interview.
25. Ibid.
26. Pomeroy, personal interview.
27. Seymour, personal interview. Seymour was a national representative and education officer for the CWC.
28. Young, personal interview.
29. Janice McClelland, email to author, July 23, 2013.
30. *Bell Operators Newsletter*, September 5, 1978.
31. Anderson, telephone interview.
32. Seymour, personal interview.
33. Ibid.
34. McClelland, personal interview.
35. Undated document, personal files of Janice McClelland.

Chapter 7

1. Middlebrooks, personal interview.
2. "Population," personal files of Janice McClelland.
3. Anderson, telephone interview.
4. According to the November 30, 1978, balance sheet, the CUC had investments of $399,074 in 1977. This amount decreased to $233,581 in 1978; Barbara Morgan, letter to Fred Pomeroy, finance director, CUC, November 12, 1979, Ed Seymour Archives.
5. Handwritten note on the letter stated it was not sent because Cheryl Hamilton was a CUC staffer, not an operator.
6. Middlebrooks, personal interview.

7. Young, personal interview.
8. Newman, personal interview.
9. This organization was a branch of the International Labour Organization.
10. Seymour, personal interview.
11. This was the top wage rate a Bell operator could earn.
12. Shirley Nicholson, letter to Fred Pomeroy , September 1, 1978.
13. Pomeroy, personal interview.

Chapter 8

1. Having been exposed at the August debate at the King Edward Hotel, Cheryl Hamilton was free to go public. Untitled and undated CUC flyer, Ed Seymour Archives.
2. Mary Lennox, letter to General Council, CUC, October 3, 1978, Ed Seymour Archives.
3. OPEIU 343 was the Office and Professional Employees International Union local of the CWC clerical staff; "Opeiu 343" was added at the end of all the work they produced to indicate a unionized employee did the typing.
4. Dennis McDermott, letter to Fred Pomeroy, January 8, 1979, Ed Seymour Archives.
5. Janice McClelland to CWC, list of Ontario contacts and members, February, 18, 1979, Ed Seymour Archives.
6. Shirley Nicholson, vice-president of CUC, undated press release, Ed Seymour Archives.
7. Ed Seymour asserted that the CWC had the numbers needed to win in the first campaign; this is repeated in the history of the CWC by James McCrostie, *Just the Beginning: The Communications, Energy and Paperworkers Union of Canada* (Ottawa: Communications and Paperworkers Union of Canada, 1996), 20, accessed May 14, 2013, www.cep.ca/sites/cep.ca/files/docs/en/beginning-e.pdf.
8. Letter to CUC representatives entitled "CUC WINS CLRB REJECTS CWC APPLICATION," February 28, 1979, personal files of Janice McClelland.
9. Young, personal interview.

Chapter 9

1. McClelland, personal interview.
2. Newman, personal interview.

3. Seymour, personal interview.
4. Ibid.
5. Howes, personal interview.
6. Note in Ed Seymour Archives.
7. "CUC and Bell Canada Return to Bargaining Table," CUC newsletter, March 8, 1979, Ed Seymour Archives.
8. Document on CUC letterhead, n.d., Ed Seymour Archives.
9. Ibid.
10. CUC press release, n.d., Ed Seymour Archives.
11. Anderson, telephone interview.
12. Handwritten letter on CUC letterhead, March 24, 1979, Ed Seymour Archives.
13. Donald Montgomery, letter to CUC acting president Shirley Nicholson, March 21, 1977, Ed Seymour Archives.
14. CUC press release re: CLC rejection, April 2, 1979, Ed Seymour Archives.
15. Document on CUC letterhead, n.d., Ed Seymour's Archives.
16. Shirley Nicolson, letter to CUC representatives, April 5, 1977, Ed Seymour Archives.
17. The official number was 4,027 cards.
18. CWC press release, April 2, 1979, Ed Seymour Archives.
19. The CWC craft and services contract provided increases of 10, 11, and 12 percent over three years. The total amount paid back to the company came to $250,000 and represented a total of $10.00 from each member.
20. Document with CUC logo but not titled as a bulletin.
21. Press release on CWC letterhead, April 25, 1979, Ed Seymour Archives.
22. "Bell Workers in Wildcat Walkout," *Ottawa Citizen*, April 21, 1979, 15.
23. CNCP Telecommunications, telegram to William Howes, Communications Workers of Canada, June 11, 8:31 a.m. (Original font all capitals.)
24. CUC bulletin, July 1979, Ed Seymour Archives.
25. www.gov.mb.ca/labour/labbrd/index.html 08/2008, June 2012. The Labour Code and the way of counting votes have remained virtually the same since the period covered in this book.
26. Newman, personal interview.
27. Anderson, telephone interview.
28. Fred Pomeroy, letter to Bell Canada, August 3, 1979.
29. Deverell, John, "Ma Bell's Paternalism under Fire," *Toronto Star*, August 4, 1979, B-6.

30. Ibid
31. Anderson, phone interview.
32. CUC, minutes of 3rd Special Council Meeting, August 2, 1979, Ed Seymour Archives.
33. Paul Cavalluzzo, Letter to Bill Howes, August 10, 1979, Ed Seymour Archives.

Chapter 10

1. Capacity-building is a term that refers to the processes that enhance the ability of an individual or organization to achieve goals. It includes building infrastructure, tools and policies, learning and decision-making processes.
2. Larter, personal interview.
3. Pomeroy, personal interview.
4. Young, personal interview.
5. Ibid.
6. Howes, personal interview.
7. Cumming, personal interview.
8. Newman, personal interview.
9. Howes, personal interview.
10. McClelland, personal interview.
11. Memo dated January 10 (says 1979 but the year was a mistake) to all CWC Ontario staff from Peter Klym, Ed Seymour Archives.
12. Cumming, personal interview.
13. Personal files of Janice McClelland.

Chapter 11

1. Handwritten notes, personal files of Janice McClelland.
2. Lincoln Alexander, telegram to Doug Lewis, MP, January 30, 1980, Ed Seymour Archives.
3. *Bell Operators and Dining Services Newsletter*, Strike Edition, February 9, 1980.
4. Personal files of Janice McClelland.
5. Middlebrooks, personal interview.
6. Two well-known CUC officers and scabs working in Directory Assistance Office # 3, 50 Eglinton Avenue.
7. Middlebrooks, personal interview.
8. Anderson, phone interview.

9. Middlebrooks, personal interview.

10. Minutes of Arbitration Hearing held on December 9, 1980, Bell Canada and Communications Workers of Canada in the matter of a grievance regarding Joan Roberts. The arbitration board reduced the suspension from three weeks to three days, finding there was no evidence that the author struck the scab in the neck.

11. Ibid., 8.

12. Howes, personal interview.

13. This must have been referring to a 50 Eglinton special picket.

14. Anderson, telephone interview.

15. City of Toronto, *Perspectives on Housing Affordability*, July 2006, accessed December 14, 2011, www.toronto.ca/planning/pdf/housing_afford.pdf.

16. McClelland, personal interview.

17. Seymour, personal interview.

18. Cumming, personal interview.

19. Personal files of Janice McClelland.

20. Pomeroy, personal interview.

21. Personal files of Janice McClelland.

22. Janice McClelland, email to the author, January 8, 2013.

23. Middlebrooks, personal interview.

24. Anderson, telephone interview.

25. Middlebrooks, personal interview.

26. Ibid.

27. Newman, personal interview.

Chapter 12

1. Undated Strike Committee notes, personal files of Janice McClelland.

2. Author unknown, reproduced in memo dated February 13, 1980, from Bill Howes to Traffic and Dining Services contacts, Ed Seymour Archives.

3. Notice of news conference, Public Relations Department of CLC, Ed Seymour Archives.

4. CLC press release, February 26, 1980, Ed Seymour Archives.

5. Notice of motion to Toronto City Council, February 26, 1980, Ed Seymour Archives.

6. Peter Klym, letter to presidents of Locals 25–49, February 25, 1980, Ed Seymour Archives.

7. Local 25, letter to all union officers and stewards, February 9, 1980, Ed

Seymour archives.

8. "Union Says Public Should Not Pay for Bell Strike," CWC press release, February 20, 1980, Ed Seymour Archives.

9. "Cost of Bell Strike," Ed Seymour Archives.

10. Motion submitted to Toronto City Council by Local 50, personal files of Janice McClelland.

11. "Membership Assistance," n.d., Ed Seymour Archives.

12. Strike Committee minutes, March 12, personal files of Janice McClelland.

13. Young, personal interview.

14. Anderson, phone interview.

15. "Help Crack Bell", n.d., CWC news bulletin, personal files of Janice McClelland.

16. One of two telegrams expressing support from Japanese telecommunications unions, February 4, 1980, Ed Seymour Archives.

17. "Fox" was most likely a reference to Sam Fox, the president of the Amalgamated Clothing and Textile Workers Union and president of the Toronto and York Region Labour Council at the time. He was a wonderful supporter.

18. Anderson, phone interview.

19. This union was missing from the meeting minutes but included in a handwritten note, personal files of Janice McClelland.

20. Carolyn Egan and Linda Yanz, "The Right to Strike," in Brisken and Yanz, 369. Carolyn is a member and local president of the United Steelworkers Union and a driving force in both the labour and feminist movements in Toronto.

21. Cumming, personal interview.

22. Anderson, phone interview.

23. Cumming, personal interview.

24. McClelland, personal interview.

25. Young, personal interview.

26. Newman, personal interview.

27. Middlebrooks, personal interview.

28. Agenda, Local 50 Strike Committee, n.d., personal files of Janice McClelland.

29. Larter, personal interview.

30. Ibid.

31. Cumming, personal interview.

32. Ibid.

33. Ibid.

34. Anderson, phone interview.

35. Pomeroy, personal interview.

36. Seymour, personal interview.

37. Judy Darcy and Catherine Lauzon, "The Right to Strike," in Brisken and Yanz, 179.

38. Larter, personal interview.

39. Newman, personal interview.

40. Anderson, telephone interview.

41. Pomeroy, personal interview.

42. McClelland, personal interview.

43. Louise Brown, "Picket Line Transforms Women," *Toronto Star*, March 20, 1980.

44. Local 50 Strike Committee, Minutes, March 26, 1980, personal files of Janice McClelland.

Chapter 13

1. Appendix C, Operator weekly rates in Montreal and Toronto, Return to Work Agreement between Bell Canada and CWC, March 19, 1980, Ed Seymour Archives, McMaster University.

2. Fred Pomeroy, letter to Dennis McDermott, president of the Canadian Labour Congress, April 8, 1980, Ed Seymour Archives.

3. Dennis McDermott, letter to all the federations of labour, labour councils, and affiliates, April 11, 1980, Ed Seymour Archives.

4. Michael Cassidy, letter to Fred Pomeroy, April 16, 1980, Ed Seymour Archives.

5. Minutes of the Arbitration Hearing held on December 9, 1980, Bell Canada and Communications Workers of Canada, p. 10.

6. Return to Work Agreement between Bell Canada and CWC, March 19, 1980, Ed Seymour Archives.

7. Bill Howes, memo to all local presidents and vice-presidents, June 23, 1980, Ed Seymour Archives.

8. Anderson, phone interview.

9. *Bell Operators & Dining Services Newsletter*, April 13, 1980.

10. McClelland, personal interview.

11. Ibid.

12. Newman, personal interview.

13. Ibid.

14. McClelland, personal interview.
15. Larter, personal interview.
16. Young, personal interview.
17. McClelland, personal interview.
18. The CEP has amalgamated with the Canadian Autoworkers Union. The new union is called UNIFOR.
19. Larter, personal interview.
20. Newman, personal interview.
21. Young, personal interview.
22. Middlebrooks, personal interview.
23. "The Triangle Fire" refers to the Triangle Shirtwaist Factory Fire of March 25, 1911, in New York City. It was one of the worst industrial accidents in U.S. history. The fire caused the death of 146 garment workers. Given the 2013 building collapse of Rana Plaza in Bangladesh that caused the death of over one thousand garment workers, it is clear that not much has changed.
24. Cumming, personal interview.
25. James McCrostie,, "Just the Beginning: The Communications, Energy and Paperworkers Union of Canada," 1996, accessed May 14, 2013, www.cep.ca/sites/cep.ca/files/doca/en/beginning-e.pdf.
26. Seymour, personal interview.
27. Jan Kainer, "Gendering Union Renewal: Women's Contributions to Labour Movement Revitalization," in *Unions, Equity, and the Path to Renewal* (Vancouver: UBC Press, 2009), 9.
28. Canadian Labour Congress, *Women in the Workforce: Still a Long Way from Equality*, (Toronto: Canadian Labour Congress, 2008), 15, www.canadianlabour.ca.
29. *A Struggle to Remember: Fighting for our Families.* Directed by Aaron Floresco. Winnipeg: Past Perfect Productions, 2012.
30. Jenish D'Arcy, "A Shock Down the Line: Bell's Plan to Quit the Operator Service Puts 2,400 Jobs on Hold", *Maclean's*, January 25, 1999, accessed May 10, 2013.
31. Jane Stinson, "Show Us Our Money: A Pay Equity Cross-Country Check-Up," *Our Times Magazine*, February–March 2004, accessed from BNET Business Network, 9-20-2008.
32. "Bell Canada Operators Accept Pay Equity Deal," *Canadian HR Reporter*, June 20, 2006, accessed May 9, 2013, employmentlawtoday.com.
33. "Bell Canada, Union Agree to $100M Pay Equity Settlement," CBC

News, May 15, 2006, accessed May 9, 2013, www.cbc.ca/news/business/story/2006/05/15/bellcanada-payequity.html.

34. Bell Canada OS/DS, Arbitration Hearing Betty Stewart, May 5, 1981, and Margaret Irvine, Grievance T40-80-2B2, Arbitration hearing held October 28, 1981.

35. Bell Canada OS/DS, Grievances T42-83-34 & 35, D. Biggs & L. Anderson. Arbitration hearing held on March 8, 1984.

36. D'Arcy, "A Shock Down the Line."

37. CEP was the largest private-sector union in Canada and the eighth-largest union in the Canadian Labour Congress.

Chapter 14

1. Pomeroy, personal interview.

2. Bill Howes, email to author, November 16, 2013.

3. Kainer, "Gendering Union Renewal."

4. Anderson, telephone interview.

5. Middlebrooks, personal interview.

6. Larter, personal interview.

7. Anderson, personal interview.

8. Newman, personal interview.

9. Pomeroy, personal interview.

10. Young, personal interview.

11. Larter, personal interview.

12. Anderson, personal interview.

13. McClelland, personal interview.

14. Seymour, personal interview.

15. Cumming, personal interview.

16. Newman, personal interview.

17. Larter, personal interview.

18. Middlebrooks, personal interview.

19. Ibid.

20. Anderson, telephone interview.

21. Young, personal interview.

22. Cynthia Tenute, personal interview with author, Hamilton, May 2, 2012.

23. Ibid.

24. Richard P. Chaykowski, and Lisa M. Powell, *Women and the Labour Market: Recent Trends and Policy Issues* (Kingston: McGill-Queen's

University Press, 1999), S-4, http://qed.econ.queensu.ca/pub/cpp/
womenwork1999/Chayk.pdf.

25. Canadian Labour Congress, *Women in the Workforce*, 4.

26. Ibid., 3.

27. Pay Equity Commission, Government of Ontario, "The Gender Wage
Gap (Toronto: Pay Equity Commission, Government of Ontario, 2012),
accessed June 13, 2013. www.payequity.gov.on.ca/en/about/pubs/
genderwage/wagegap.php.

28. Julie Cool, "Wage Gap Between Women and Men," *Report of the
Social Affairs Division, Parliament of Canada* (Ottawa: Parliament of
Canada, 2010), accessed June 19, 2013, 1, www.parl.gc.ca/content/lop/
researchpublications/2010-30-e.htm.

29. Ibid., 1.

30. Canadian Labour Congress, *Women in the Workforce*, 7.

31. Ibid., 4.

32. Antonia Zerbisias, "Can Unions Save the Middle Class?", *Toronto Star*,
September 1, 2012, IN1.

33. Tom Sizys, *Working Better: Creating a High-Performing Labour Market in
Ontario* (Toronto: Metcalf Foundation, 2011).

34. Anderson, telephone interview.

Bibliography

A Struggle to Remember: Fighting for our Families. Directed by Aaron Floresco. Winnipeg: Past Perfect Productions, 2012.

Backhouse, Constance. "The Fleck Strike: A Case Study in the Need for First Contract Arbitration," *Osgoode Hall Law Journal* 18, no. 4 (December 1980). Accessed May 24, 2013.

Balkan, Donna. "Practicing What We Preach: Women Unions and Affirmative Action," *Canadian Woman Studies/Iles Cahiers De La Femme* 6, no 4 (1985).

Bell Canada OS/DS. *Arbitration Hearing Betty Stewart, May 5, 1981 and Margaret Irvine, Grievance T40-80-2B2.* Arbitration hearing held October 28, 1981.

Bell Canada OS/DS. *Arbitration Hearing Joan Roberts January 28, 1980, Grievance 50-3.* Arbitration hearing held December 9, 1980.

Bell Canada OS/DS. *Grievances T42-83-34 & 35, D. Biggs & L. Anderson.* Arbitration hearing held on March 8, 1984.

Bell Canada. *TOPS and You.* Toronto: Bell Canada, 1977.

Bell Canada. *TOPS: More about TOPS and You.* Toronto: Bell Canada, 1977.

"Bell Canada and the Communications Workers of Canada, Collective Agreement, Traffic and Dining Services Employees". Ottawa, 1980.

Bibliography

"Bell Canada Operators Accept Pay Equity Deal". *Canadian HR Reporter.* June 20, 2006. Accessed May 9, 2013.

"Bell Canada, Union Agree to $100M Pay Equity Settlement." *CBC News.* May 15, 2006. Accessed May 9, 2013.

Bell Operators and Dining Services Newsletters. February 1977–May 1980.

Bett, Carolyn. Personal files. Toronto.

Briskin, Linda, and Linda Yanz, eds. *Union Sisters: Women in the Labour Movement.* Toronto: The Women's Press, 1983.

Canadian Labour Congress. *Women in the Workforce: Still a Long Way from Equality.* Canadian Labour Congress, 2008. www.canadianlabour.ca.

CAW/TCA Canada. *Where Did Our Rights Come from: The Rand Formula and the Struggle for Union Security.* Toronto: CAW/TCA (now Unifor), (2013). Accessed July 15, 2013.

Chaykowski, Richard P., and Lisa M. Powell. *Women and the Labour Market: Recent Trends and Policy Issues.* Kingston: McGill-Queen's University Press, 1999. http://qed.econ.queensu.ca/pub/cpp/womenwork1999/Chayk.pdf

City of Toronto. *Perspectives on Housing Affordability.* Toronto: July 2006, 8. Accessed December 14, 2011. www.toronto.ca/planning/pdf/housing_afford.pdf.

Clayton. "The Telephone." Accessed June 6, 2011. http://library.thinkquest.org/04oct/00451/telephone.htm.

Communications Union of Canada. *Communiqué,* Toronto: CUC, January 1976.

Communications Union of Canada. *Communiqué,* Toronto: CUC, May/June 1976.

Communications Union of Canada. "General Council Report," Toronto: CUC, 1976

Communications Union of Canada. "Never Underestimate." Toronto: CUC, n.d.

Communications Workers of Canada. *CWC Bulletins,* Toronto: CWC, July 1978.

Communications Workers of America. "History of the CWA, Local 7032 (n.d.)." Accessed June 23, 2012. www.cwalocal7032.org/history/history.htm.

Connelly, Pat. *Last Hired, First Fired.* Toronto: The Women's Press, 1982.

Cool, Julie. "Wage Gap Between Women and Men." *Report of Social Affairs Division, Parliament of Canada.* Ottawa: Parliament of Canada, 2010. Accessed June 19, 2013.

Darcy, Judy, and Catherine Lauzon. "The Right to Strike." In *Union Sisters: Women in the Labour Movement.* Toronto: The Women's Press, 1983: 171–181.

Di Tecco, D., G.Witco, A. Arsenault, and M. André. "Operator Stress and Monitoring Practices." *Applied Ergonomics* 23, no. 1 (1992): 29–34.

Dust, Michelle. "Day of Protest October 14, 1976. An Expression of Solidarity." Winning Norm Quan Bursary essay. Toronto: CUPE, 1999, www.cupe1975.ca/bursary/burs399.html.

Ed Seymour Archives. William Ready Archives and Research Division. Libraries, McMaster University.

Filey, Mike. "Toronto Was Experimenting With 'Cell' Phones 60 Years Ago." *Canoe News.* December 23, 2007. Accessed August 21, 2010. http://cnews.canoe.ca/CNEWS/WeirdNews/2007/12/23/4738356-sun.html.

Francis, Jen. *Switchboard Operator.* 1978.

Franzway, Suzanne. "Sisters and Sisters? Labour Movements and Women's Movements in (English) Canada and Australia." *Hecate* 26, no.2 (2006):31-46.

Friedan, Betty. *The Feminine Mystique.* New York: W.W. Norton and Co., 1963.

Gerachty, Isabel. "Telephone Historical Collection." *Archivaria* 7, (Winter 1978): 118–124.

Government of Canada. *Labour Gazette.* March, 1936. Accessed March 12, 2012.

Howes, Bill. 1978–1981 Daytimers, Toronto.

International Association of Electrical and Electronic Engineers. Telephone Operators. www.ieeeghn.org/wiki/index.php/Telephone_Operators. Accessed January 13, 2012.

Kainer, Jan. "Gendering Union Renewal: Women's Contributions to Labour Movement Revitalization." In *Unions, Equity, and the Path to Renewal.* Vancouver: UBC Press, 2009. www.ubcpress.ca/books/pdf/chapters/2009/UnionsEquityAndThePathToRenewal.pdf.

Kanigel, Robert. *The One Best Way: Frederick Winslow Taylor and the Enigma of Efficiency.* Cambridge, MA: MIT Press, 2005.

King, Mackenzie. *Industry and Humanity: A Study in the Principles Underlying Industrial Reconstruction.* Boston: Houghton Mifflin, 1918. Accessed July 24, 2012. https://Archive.Org/Details/Industryhumanit00king.

Kuyek, Joan. *The Phone Book: Working at the Bell.* Toronto: Between the Lines, 1979.

Bibliography

Martin, Michele. "Capitalizing on the 'Feminine' Voice." *Canadian Journal of Communication* 14, no. 3: 42–62. Accessed June 14, 2011.

———. *Hello Central? Gender, Technology and Culture in the Formation of Telephone Systems.* Kingston: McGill-Queen's University Press, 1991.

McClelland, Janice. "Technological Change in the Operator Services–Dining Services Group at Bell Canada, 1957–1986." in *Working People and Hard Times.* Toronto: Garamond Press, 1987.

McClelland, Janice. Personal files. Acton, Ontario.

McCrostie, James. *Just the Beginning: The Communications, Energy and Paperworkers Union of Canada.* Ottawa: Communications and Paperworkers Union of Canada, 1996. Accessed May 14, 2013.

Middeljans, April. "Weavers of Speech: Telephone Operators as Defiant Domestics in American Literature and Culture." *Journal of Modern Literature* 33, no.3 (Spring 2010): 38. www.accessmylibrary.com/article-1G1-231610127/weavers-speech-telephone-operators.html.

Mussio, Laurence B. *Becoming Bell: The Remarkable Story of a Canadian Enterprise.* Montreal: Bell Canada, 2005.

Ontario Federation of Labour. *1900–2000: A Century of Women and Work.* Toronto: Ontario Federation of Labour, 2007.

Parliament of Canada. "*Hansard of the Government of Canada,*" 37th Parliament, 1st Session. Accessed January 9, 2012. www.parl.gc.ca/HousePublications/Publication. aspx?Pub=Hansard&Mee=211&Language=e&Parl=37&Ses=1.

Pay Equity Commission, Government of Ontario. *The Gender Wage Gap.* 2012. Accessed June 13, 2013. http://www.payequity.gov.on.ca/en/about/pubs/genderwage/wagegap.php.

Pollock, Marion. "Under Attack: Women, Unions and Microtechnology." In *Union Sisters: Women in the Labour Movement.* Toronto: The Women's Press, 1983.

Rebick, Judy. *Ten Thousand Roses: The Making of a Feminist Revolution.* Toronto: Penguin, 2005.

Rens, Jean-Guy. *The Invisible Empire. A History of the Telecommunications Industry in Canada, 1846–1956.* Translated by Käthe Roth. Kingston: McGill-Queen's University Press, 2001.

Ministry of Labour, Government of Canada. "Report of Douglas Fisher, November 2 1971." In Thomas O'Connor. *Key Elements in Successful Conciliation*. Ottawa: Queen's Printer, 1971.

Report of the Royal Commission on a Dispute Respecting Terms of Employment Between Bell Telephone Company of Canada and Operators at Toronto. Accessed June 11, 2011. http://archive.org/stream/ reportofroyalcomcanarich/reportofroyalco0canarich_djvu.txt.

Roberts, Joan. "Co-optation and Resistance: A Case Study, Telephone Operators at Bell Canada." Unpublished paper, 1981.

Sangster, Joan. "The 1907 Bell Telephone Strike: Organizing Women Workers." In *Rethinking Canada: The Promise of Women's History*. Third edition. Toronto: Copp Clark Pitman, 1991: 249–268.

Sizys, Tom. *Working Better: Creating a High-Performing Labour Market in Ontario*. Toronto: Metcalf Foundation, 2011.

Stinson, Jane. "Show Us Our Money: A Pay Equity Cross-Country Check-Up," *Our Times Magazine*, February–March 2004, Accessed from BNET Business Network, September 20, 2008.

———. "Why Privatization is a Women's Issue," *Canadian Woman Studies/Les Cahiers De La Femme* 23, Nos. 3–4 (Spring/Summer 2004): 18–22.

"Telephones Become a Necessity, Not a Luxury." Canadian Broadcasting Corporation radio archives. April 20, 1945 (posted Jan 27, 2012). Accessed December 11, 2011, www.cbc.ca/archives/categories/science-technology/ technology/canada-says-hello-the-first-century-of-the-telephone/ telephones-become-a-necessity-not-a-luxury.html.

Traffic Employees Association. "Articles on the Function, Methods and Responsibilities of Unions." Toronto: Traffic Employees Association, January 1960.

———. *Belle Femme*. Toronto: Traffic Employees Association, Spring 1970.

———. *TEA's 25th Anniversary*. Toronto: Traffic Employees Association, Spring 1970.

Uppal, Sharanjit. "Diverging Trends in Unionization, 1981–2004, Unionization 2010." In "Perspectives on Labour and Income." *The Daily* (Statistics Canada) XI, no. 10 (2010): 18.

Vorster, Menno G. *A Study in Corporate Unionism: The Canadian Telephone*

Employees' Association. Unpublished paper, York University, Toronto, 1972.

"We Stand on the Shoulders of Giants: Biography of Julia O'Connor." Accessed June 12, 2012. www.union1.org/Giants/indexW.htm.

White, Julie. *Sisters and Solidarity: Women and Unions in Canada*. Toronto: Thompson Educational Publishing, 1993.

Interviews

Anderson, Irene. Interview by author. Telephone interview. Toronto, August 9, 2011.

Cumming, Laurie. Interview by author. Personal interview. Toronto, March 1, 2012.

Howes, Bill. Interview by author. Personal interview. Toronto, March 21, 2011.

Larter, George. Interview by author. Personal interview. Toronto, July 5, 2011.

McClelland, Janice. Interview by author. Personal interview. Acton, June 30, 2011.

Middlebrooks, Helen. Interview by author. Personal interview. Toronto, July 19, 2011.

Newman, Ann. Interview by author. Personal interview. Toronto, July 19, 2011.

Pomeroy, Fred. Interview by author. Personal interview. Ottawa, January 28, 2012.

Seymour, Ed. Interview by author. Personal interview. Hamilton, May 2, 2012.

Tenute, Cynthia. Interview by author. Personal interview. Hamilton, May 2, 2012.

Young, Linda. Interview by author. Personal interview. Toronto, July 14, 2011.

Index

Index